P9-EAI-514

DATE DUE

DE 30 '94	NO 18 02		
MY 26 '95	JE 10 03		
DE 15 '95	NO 11 03		
AP 19 '96	DE 9 04		
AG 1 '96	AG 5 04		
NO 18 '97			
AP 9 '98			
AP 9 '98			
MY 21 '98			
DE 12 '98			
DE 6 '99			
DE 18 '99			
NO 8 '00			
DE 17 '01			
MY 29 '02			

DEMCO 38-296

Television and America's Children

Communication and Society, edited by
George Gerbner and Marsha Seifert

IMAGE ETHICS
The Moral Rights of Subjects
in Photographs, Film, and Television
Edited by Larry Gross, John Stuart Katz,
and Jay Ruby

CENSORSHIP
The Knot That Binds Power and Knowledge
By Sue Curry Jansen

THE GLOBAL VILLAGE
Transformations in World Life and Media in
the 21st Century
By Marshall McLuhan and Bruce R. Powers

SPLIT SIGNALS
Television and Politics in the Soviet Union
By Ellen Mickiewicz

TARGET: PRIME TIME
Advocacy Groups and the
Struggle over Entertainment Television
By Kathryn C. Montgomery

TELEVISION AND AMERICA'S CHILDREN
A Crisis of Neglect
By Edward L. Palmer

PLAYING DOCTOR
Television, Storytelling, and Medical Power
By Joseph Turow

Television
&
America's Children

A CRISIS OF NEGLECT

Edward L. Palmer

OXFORD UNIVERSITY PRESS
New York • Oxford Riverside Community College
Library
4800 Magnolia Avenue
AUG '94 Riverside, California 92506

Oxford University Press

Oxford   New York   Toronto
Delhi   Bombay   Calcutta   Madras   Karachi
Petaling Jaya   Singapore   Hong Kong   Tokyo
Nairobi   Dar es Salaam   Cape Town
Melbourne   Auckland

and associated companies in
Berlin   Ibadan

Copyright © 1988 by Edward L. Palmer

First published in 1988 by Oxford University Press, Inc.,
200 Madison Avenue, New York, New York 10016

First issued as an Oxford University Press paperback, 1990

Oxford is a registered trademark of Oxford University Press

All rights reserved. No part of this publication may be reproduced,
stored in a retrieval system, or transmitted, in any form or by any means,
electronic, mechanical, photocopying, recording, or otherwise,
without the prior permission of Oxford University Press, Inc.

Library of Congress Cataloging-in-Publication Data
Palmer, Edward L.
Television and America's children: a crisis of neglect / Edward L. Palmer.
p.   cm.   Bibliography: p.   Includes index.
1. Television programs for children—United States—History.
2. Public television—United States
3. Children's Television Workshop. I. Title.
PN1992.8.C46P36 1988
791.45′088054—dc19   88–4223   CIP
ISBN 0-19-505540-3
ISBN 0-19-506321-X (Pbk)

2 4 6 8 10 9 7 5 3 1

Printed in the United States of America

For Meredith and Her Generation

Preface

The first time I saw television, just after graduating high school in 1951, my instant reaction was skepticism that the stations could possibly fill the great amount of time available on several different channels operating day in and day out year after year. I was impressed with the technological feat of capturing a broadcast signal to create coherent moving pictures in a box, and by the fact that television would be viewed by people right in their homes. But in my mind as I turned to walk away from the furniture-store window that day was a promise to myself that I would watch to see how well the people who ran television could satisfy its enormous appetite for programming. The question lay largely dormant until 1968 when Joan Ganz Cooney asked that I join with her and others in starting Children's Television Workshop and *Sesame Street*.

I am grateful to Joan for time to begin my work on this book before I left the Children's Television Workshop in the mid 1980s. If my exuberance for the Workshop shows in this volume, it reflects the sixteen years I spent there, going back to the beginnings of *Sesame Street*, as the company's first vice president for research. I am grateful also to the Andrew W. Mellon Foundation for funding that helped to support research and travel and a special international conference in New York as background. The views and conclusions expressed in the book are entirely my own, and do not necessarily reflect those of the Children's Television Workshop, the Andrew W. Mellon Foundation, or persons who were consulted in its preparation. Encouragement by Mr. Lloyd Morrisett, president of the John and Mary R. Markle Foundation, was crucial at the time of the book's genesis, and I have him to thank for suggesting its strong international focus.

The international conference brought expert foreign advisors from Japan, Sweden, and Britain into contact with diversely specialized U.S. advisors, presenters, and observers. Foreign advisors included Dr. Tsune Shirai from Japan, Mrs. Kerstin Stjarne of Sweden, and Mrs. Joy Whitby from Britain. U.S. advisors were Mr. Erik Barnouw, Mrs. Marion Wright Edelman, Dr. Gerald S. Lesser, Mr. Lloyd Morrisett, and Dr. Ithiel de Sola Pool. Represented among them were academics specializing in communications and education, a children's television producer, advocates broadly concerned with matters affecting children, especially children from low-income and minority backgrounds, one foundation head, a board member of a national public broadcasting entity, and the author of a major history of U.S. broadcasting. Their exchanges contributed useful insights into the roles of institutional structures and traditions, and different national visions and values, as forces that shape each country's television offering for children.

Additional presenters at the conference shared generously, each drawing upon significant experience in or significantly related to the field of U.S. children's television. They are Mr. Tyrone Brown, former member of the Federal Communications Commission; Mrs. Peggy Charren, founder and head of Action for Children's Television; Mr. Lewis Freedman, then head of the program fund at the Corporation for Public Broadcasting; Mr. Kenneth Mason, former Quaker Oats president; Dr. Robert Pepper, academic expert on cable TV; Mr. Squire Rushnell, representing ABC-TV; and Mr. George Tressel, of the National Science Foundation.

Fact-finding visits to Britain, Japan, the Federal Republic of Germany, and Australia afforded invaluable opportunities to illuminate the status of U.S. children's television through comparisons with counterpart institutions and practices abroad. These visits were made to pinpoint the many respects in which other countries surpass us in their television offerings for children and to better understand the factors underlying their ability to forge and sustain specific advantages. The aim in part was to return with useful lessons, but never with the thought that particular practices in other countries could, or should, be reproduced exactly. The goal, precisely and more realistically, was to press us by their example to seek remedies and reforms in our own unique national terms. What I found, in fact, is that while different national circumstances and practices vary widely, we nevertheless share crucial concerns with thoughtful individuals in different countries whose only aim is to realize the best for children through television. Examples of our common concerns are to maximize each year the amount of fresh, new, age-appropriate program fare for children's out-of-school viewing, to achieve a sensible balance between purely entertaining programs and ones that are informational and educational, to schedule the children's offering at the most convenient and appropriate hours for child viewing, to regulate or somehow adequately counter-balance the excessive candy-store diet of cartoon animations offered on the commercial stations, and to find ways to reach and serve the real needs of children in a time when their tastes in television are shaped through constant exposure to the sophisticated visual effects used in commercial programs.

For their generous hospitality, and the help of their insights, I am grateful to many individuals. In Japan, my special gratitude goes to my hosts at the Japan Center for International Exchange, Mr. Tadashi Yamamoto and Mrs. Sachiko Matsumoto, for helping to organize my itinerary of meetings, for translation (both linguistic and cultural) when needed, and for innumerable kindnesses. Especially helpful at NHK (the Japan Broadcasting Corporation) were Mr. Yasuhiro Kondo, Chief Producer, School Broadcasting Division; Mr. Koichi Sato, Chief Director of Preschool Children's Programs; Mr. Sumio Gotoda, Chief Director, School Education Division; Mr. Akira Kojima, Chief Director, Correspondence School Education Programming Group; and Mrs. Sachiko Imaizumi Kodaira, NHK Radio and TV Culture Research Institute. For their insights from the academic point of view, I wish to thank Dr. Takashi Sakamoto of the Tokyo Institute of Technology and Dr. Sumiko Iwao of Keio University. I am grateful also to Hiroji Minoura, General Secretary, The Japan Prize Contest, and to Mrs. Midori Suzuki, Leader, Forum for Children's Television. I especially appreciate the many opportunities for extended conversations on Japanese children's television with Mr. Nobuyuki Ueda while he was a student at Harvard University and a consultant to NHK. To another longtime acquaintance, Mr. Tadashi Yoshita, consultant to the founder of the Sony Corporation, formerly of NHK, my thanks for helping me to grasp better the profound commitment of the Japanese to the intense, early intellectual stimulation of children, beginning at or even before their birth. Finally, my thanks to Mr. Koichiro Noda, children's TV producer, for insights into Japanese commercial children's television.

In Britain, I thank Ms. Monica Sims and Mr. Edward Barnes, both former heads of the BBC Children's Programmes Department, and Mr. David Hargreaves, Deputy Head of the BBC Children's Programmes Department. I am grateful to Mr. Kim Taylor, the Independent Broadcasting Authority's Head of Educational Programme Services, and to Deputy Head Christopher Jones, for organizing a special meeting for my benefit, and to those who attended: Dr. Mallory Wober, IBA Deputy Head of Research; Mr. Peter Scroggs, Executive Producer (Schools), at Thames TV; Mr. Lewis Rudd, Assistant Programme Controller, Southern TV; Mr. Gerald Dawson, Assistant Education Officer, HTV-Bristol; and Mr. Peter Murphy, Senior Producer, Children's Programmes, Yorkshire TV.

Also in Britain, my thanks to journalists Stuart McClure and Caroline O'Grady of the *Times Educational Supplement*, and Rick Rogers of *New Statesman Magazine*. Rounding out my meetings in Britain were much appreciated discussions with Dr. Anthony Bates of the Open University and Dr. Ray Brown of the University of Leeds Center for Television Research.

For helpful insights and access to the archives of the Prix Jeunesse Foundation in Munich, Federal Republic of Germany, I thank the Director, Mr. Ernst Emerich, and the Associate Director, Ms. Ursula von Zalinger. My gratitude also, for generously sharing her views, to Dr. Hertha Sturm, professor at the University of Munich and Scientific Director of the Internationales Zentralinstitut für das Jugend- und Bildungs-Fernsehen, and to her colleagues, Dr. Marianne Greve-Partsch and Dr. Manfred Meyer.

In Australia, my appreciation for advice and many gracious courtesies to Dr. Patricia Edgar, Chairman and Executive Director of the Australian Children's Television Foundation, and, for information and assistance, to Ms. Henrietta Clark, Head, Children's and Education TV, Australian Broadcasting Corporation. And to my longtime friend and colleague, Dr. Samuel Ball, professor at the University of Sydney, for hospitality and advice, my special thanks.

To my collaborator of twenty years, Professor Gerald S. Lesser of Harvard University, my special gratitude for generous assistance in the form of his travel to Sweden to glean background for the book from that country's approach to children's television. Lesser formed his assessment of the Swedish situation through meetings with Ms.

Ingrid Edstrom, Head of Regional Television, Malmo; Lasse Haglund, Executive Producer, TV2; Ms. Britt Lidne, Children's Programme Acquisitions, TV1; and in Audience and Programme Research, Ms. Leni Filipson, Ms. Ingegard Rydin, and Ms. Ingela Schyller. Finally, he met also at the time with Ms. Ada Haug, Controller of Children's Programmes, Norway. What he found at that time in the early 1980s was a system in transition which was jeopardizing Sweden's history of high-quality programs for children. A new policy of decentralization, democratic in intent, was stretching its production talent too thin; a policy of life-long employment was creating a sense of stagnation. Recent modifications of these policies have re-established Sweden's fine record of television services to children.

Sweden is not alone; heads of children's program departments all around the world must constantly spend time and energy fighting to avert forces of decline. These forces vary from country to country. They include decentralization and the stultifying effect of a life-long employment policy in one country. In another, it is the emergence of commercial television under a policy which allows it to grow and compete largely head-on with the prior daily children's schedule on public TV, thus creating inefficiencies for both sides. The pattern seen again and again is deterioration of children's TV offerings not because of any flaw in a country's established program offering but because changes driven by forces that have essentially nothing to do with children and their best interests—but nevertheless are deleterious in their effects on children's television—are instituted and, worse, once instituted are tolerated.

The text of the book itself gives little attention to problems in other countries' TV offerings for children. That is because the book is first and foremost, as the title suggests, about children's TV in the U.S. Its approach reflects my belief that the U.S. public needs to be shocked, and that one way to shock them is to contrast other countries' strengths with our own weaknesses.

My debt to CTW's executive vice president, David Britt, is considerable. David could not have been more generous with his time and insights. Also Pauline Brooks at CTW gave a most helpful reading of the near-final manuscript. Comments by former CTW colleague Robert Hatch were helpful at an earlier stage.

Definitely on the short-list of persons most helpful in the book's preparation is Paul Mareth. Impressed by his background and fine writings on communications, I asked him to transform early drafts of selected sections into a style I could strive to emulate. He agreed, and I have incorporated many extended passages he penned.

Professor George Gerbner, retiring Dean of the Annenberg School of Communications, University of Pennsylvania, and his associate, Ms. Marsha Siefert, provided frequent and invaluable editorial advice as the book neared completion, in their capacity as brokers between Oxford University Press and myself.

I come finally to thank my wife, Vera, from whose high spirit flows unsurpassed patience and loving support.

Philadelphia   Edward L. Palmer, Ph.D.
January 1988

Contents

Introduction

Television institutions around the world emerged and operate according to fundamentally different patterns in different countries. Their program offerings for children, as a result, vary strikingly. Our own children, compared with their counterparts in some other modern countries, are poorly served. They are underserved too in absolute terms. For many and complex reasons, the commercial and noncommercial institutions of television in this country fail them. Corrections are urgently needed.

America's children deserve equitable treatment from commercial television, but U.S. commercial television is recalcitrantly opposed to bestowing it. Not a single regularly scheduled weekday children's series appears on any of the nation's three major commercial television networks. The network position has been to go all out for the extra profits to be realized in adult programming and advertising. Their stance and actions over the past two decades are increasingly open in opposition to public advocacy and occasional threats of regulation by the Federal Communications Commission or the U.S. Congress.

Children deserve better treatment from U.S. public television, but public television overall is drastically underfunded. PTV is growing, but hasn't nearly the resources to effect the improvement that is needed. The public television systems in some other modern countries surpass U.S. public television in annual output of fresh, new programs for children by a factor of four to five times. The prospects for substantial near-term improvement are impeded because public television cannot or will not on its own single out the children's program area to advance it freely and apart from the slow and uncertain economic growth of public television overall.

Parents would help, but no mechanism exists by which to collect and channel dedicated parental contributions to a funding pool exclusively for children's productions. Nor is there anything remotely approaching an adequate children's program offering through cable or cassette. These two sources inevitably will remain limited both in wide enough availability and in volume of fresh informational and educational content until far into the twenty-first century at the earliest.

Children in the U.S. therefore deserve all the more to be treated as an exceptional case for purposes of regulation, but the U.S. Federal Communications Commission (FCC) is currently under sway of single-minded deregulators. They recently ruled against a petition of fourteen years' standing that sought just an hour of commercial television time each weekday for school-age children, and half an hour for preschoolers.

Congress can't get a bill out of committee to override the FCC, and scarcely looked at a draft bill that would have separated out children's public TV, to free it from the yoke of fiscal impoverishment and the uncertain growth prospects of public television. This was an unsuccessful proposal to create a national endowment for children's television.

If television's potential to enrich the lives of children were minimal or were by this time in television's development still unclear, none of this would matter. But thanks to the efforts of thoughtful producers around the world in the forty-five years during which household television has existed, a great deal now is known about the ways in which the medium can respond to children's diverse real needs. Parents in this country have almost no chance to see the full spectrum of possibilities.

We in the U.S. see fine children's programs from time to time, but not nearly often enough. Consequently, our vision of what constitutes fine quality is limited and in other ways distorted. Most of us know a really good program when we see one, although we might not all agree. But few stop to consider that to provide just an hour of fresh, new programming per weekday for a year requires 260 hours of production. Also, we pay little attention to the balance of informational and educational compared with purely entertainment programs. We almost never ask how many of the best programs are new or how many are tarnished from endless repeats.

These are not the only concerns. Out-of-school programs which educate or inform (for instance, drama, history, science, current events) must be age-appropriate, in the same way graded textbooks have to be. Also valuable are television's largely hidden qualities as teacher and nurturer. By these I mean its tendency to be patient and nonpunitive, accessible to nonliterates and to children experiencing reading difficulty (who need the extra help most), vivid and therefore memorable, capable of giving a broad overview but equally capable of zooming in on and dramatizing human interest or other detail, and able to communicate nonverbally by artful juxtaposition of images. And—not to be forgotten—TV can couch messages for the head or the heart or the social self in engaging, popular entertainment forms.

The substantial and equitable funding support for children's public television which other countries take for granted, we can only look upon with envy. Some of them describe their offerings for children as microcosms of the program types that interest thoughtful adults. They encompass news, light entertainment, sports, how-to, music and drama, nature, public affairs, documentaries and historical re-enactments, among other categories.

The underlying factors that make a difference in the quality of U.S. children's television are numerous. They include founding statutes, institutional aims and incentives, sources and amounts of program funding support, approach to regulation (accountability), established industry traditions, precedence on air of the commercial versus publicly supported system, protections against censorship and other forms of outside influence, and the value we place on children and education.

Partly because we lack a national policy and regular funding in the U.S., most of the children's out-of-school programs seen on public television link to the nation's education agenda. They are funded individually, each on an ad hoc basis, in response to acknowledged nationwide education deficiencies. The several series produced by the Children's Television Workshop are prototypic of this genre. Yet after twenty years during which the Workshop has demonstrated again and again the special niche in education of its invention, the home-and-school program hybrid, the government has taken no steps to establish permanent funding for children's out-of-school programs, either of this type or any other.

We are stalled in a proving phase. It is well past the time when we should take stock of the accomplishments so far, worldwide, so we might forge national policies to allow comprehensive children's offerings to emerge on both commercial and noncommercial television. A part of the stake is the individual well-being of the 42 million U.S. children who range in age from two through thirteen years—a group about as large in number as the total population of the average European country. Another is the national stake in children's well-being, which on the one hand translates to the compelling need to provide appropriate alternatives to much of what they now view, and, on the other, would take sensible advantage of the most cost-efficient—but still the most neglected—form of engaging and ubiquitous educational technology ever invented.

There should be no mistake that this is a national-level problem and concern. The states cannot afford to create television programs which can compete in quality with the commercial fare children are accustomed to seeing. The "new federalism" of the 1980s cannot apply, because the great cost-efficiencies possible with television come directly as a result of audience size, and the larger the better. Many urgent informational and educational needs exist nationwide for these programs to address—for instance, in reading and literature, science and technology, history and geography, mathematics, career choice, health and fitness, social and emotional adjustment, world affairs, consumerism, and the choice of futures for the planet. The schools need help in all these areas, and that need is ubiquitous.

We in the U.S. pay substantially less per capita for public television than do people in Britain, Japan, or Sweden. But in any case, the required expenditure is negligible and should not be a factor. For less than a penny a day per child, we could afford for our young people a markedly improved and stable program offering. Government's failure to take advantage of broadcast television's educational cost-efficiency is sheer economic folly.

But there are barriers. Try to tell the commercial stations what to program in any portion of the daily schedule on our (the public's) airwaves, and they threaten lawsuits on grounds of censorship and run to lobby Congress about the "unfair" negative impact on their profits. Or try to separate out for preferential treatment any audience or program category served by public television, and many in that community will protest that all viewer groups are worthy, not just children. Yet children have special needs and enjoy nothing comparable to the range and number of viewing choices available to adults.

I personally believe that the clinching point by which to overcome such barriers—to justify both regulation on the commercial side and a legislated special government appropriation on the noncommercial side—is somehow to clearly enough establish that the remedial actions taken are not precedents for all audiences and program categories, but onetime exceptions made for the sake of children as a special class of persons, unempowered as a lobby, unfranchised, unemployable, and therefore uniquely incapable of exacting from our broadcasting institutions, as they now operate, their fair share of programs and benefits.

A new advocacy push is needed, a major ad hoc forum to seek and widely publicize the search for solutions. Renewed vigor in advocacy is called for in both the commercial and noncommercial spheres. Because children cannot lobby, they will need surrogates— friends in high places. Congress and the industry must be told clearly and resoundingly that this crisis will not go away or be resolved by neglect, but that, on the contrary, the urgency of the situation will only continue to mount. This forum should not supplant the activities of the long-standing advocacy organizations. Every reasonable new approach should be debated; previously rejected suggestions should be considered.

How else shall it be done? A precedent already exists for establishing centers of programming excellence in U.S. public television through external funding allocations, including dedicated government funding for science and the arts, and for minority children through the Emergency School Assistance Act of the 1970s. I believe, in conclusion, that Government must come through with substantial, new, dedicated funding support on the non-commercial side.

In Britain, the quasi-governmental agency that actively manages commercial broadcasting reserves periods of time in each day's schedule for children's and in-school programs on each of the two channels which otherwise serve as commercial advertising vehicles. By contrast, we license out the entire channel day. From the children's and the general public's points of view the British alternative represents a superior "contract" arrangement. Britain started commercial television some fifteen years after we did, and they credit their advantage to the chance they had to learn from our mistakes.

Perhaps it is that in our own start-up years we failed to anticipate television's public service benefits to children. Or maybe we couldn't imagine at the time that the commercial stations would be—or could get away with being—so penurious. Either way, there is urgent cause to continue to work for a remedy. Importantly, it should be a remedy that includes informational and educational fare. The alternative is to deny children their due just because they don't purchase many expensive advertised products.

From the time *Sesame Street* went on the air until the conclusion of its twentieth consecutive season, it will have been viewed regularly—at least once a week, and typically, three times—by an average of six million two- to five-year-old children a year. That translates to 120 million child years of time spent viewing television that teaches while it entertains. Yet parents will search in vain for as much as an hour each week of new informational and educational out-of-school PTV programming for either six- to nine- or ten- to thirteen-year-olds. This great disparity is a measure of our lapse and of our children's and our nation's loss.

Foreword

Ernest L. Boyer
President, Carnegie Foundation for the Advancement of Teaching and former U.S. Commissioner of Education

In the summer of 1938, the great essayist and novelist E.B. White sat in a darkened room and watched transfixed as a big electronic box began projecting eerie, shimmering images into the world. It was his first introduction to something called television. His comment at the time was, "I believe television is going to be the test of the modern world, and that in this new opportunity to see beyond the range of our vision we shall discover either a new and unbearable disturbance of the general peace, or a soaring radiance in the sky."

Fifty years have passed and television has, to a remarkable degree, fulfilled both of White's predictions. It is at once a "soaring radiance" and, particularly as far as children's needs are concerned, an "unbearable disturbance." The technology that allows Americans to "see beyond the range of our vision" also squanders time and seems to distract our children, rather than educate or inspire.

In the print-dominated culture of the past, ideas were built and assimilated slowly, often at great effort. Perhaps because of that effort, ideas were more important and enduring. In the present video culture, with its emphasis on speed and ease, ideas have, it seems, become more fleeting and less valued. We are drawn toward those images that pack a bigger punch, provoke a more visceral reflex, or capture more cunningly our mercurial attentiveness. We have become the age of the flash and the zap, the hour-long epic, the thirty-minute encyclopedia, the five-minute explanation, the one-minute sell, the ten-second teaser. The temporal restrictions of the technology have imposed their limitations on us as human beings.

When I was young there was no television in our home. I was twelve years old before we purchased our first radio. We did receive a daily newspaper and the *National Geographic*, which I eagerly devoured as soon as it arrived. Our Model A took us on short excursions from our Ohio home, rarely more than 100 miles or so. School was *the* central learning place and the teacher was the key source of knowledge.

For students coming to our schools today, that world I knew is ancient history, and the glimpses of the outside world I found in the *National Geographic* have broadened into expansive vistas available at the flick of a switch. An avalanche of publications, audio and visual recordings, and opportunities for travel compete on equal footing with the teacher and the textbook. Today, for better or worse, Archie Bunker is better known than Silas Marner, Fellini is more influential than Faulkner, and the six o'clock news is more compelling than the history text. Through dramas and comedies, children see images of themselves and form their stereotypes of the good life. Through advertising, their wants are transformed into needs.

The potential of our new electronic teachers is awesome. Television can take students to the moon and to the bottom of the sea. Calculators can solve problems faster than the human brain. Computers can instantly retrieve millions of information bits. Word processors take away countless hours of drudgery from writing and editing. The classroom of the future can be a place where the New York Philharmonic comes live from Lincoln Center.

Further, technology can free teachers from the rigidity of the syllabus and tap the imaginations of students to an extent never before possible. Many teachers and school librarians have access to audio and visual recordings that add extra spark and dimension to student interest. Instructional television in the classroom and videocassettes now replace the filmstrips and single-reel films of the previous generation. Today, self-study can be more enjoyable and materials more accessible, and learning can proceed at a far more rapid pace.

Educators would be naïve to ignore these influences, which have become, in effect, a new curriculum. We must acknowledge these stimuli and work to close the gap between the school and the reality of children's lives, using what they have learned at home, formally or informally, as the starting point for further learning.

Clearly, if America is to achieve excellence in education, the nation's formal and informal teachers must become partners in the process. But the potential of technology has been largely unfulfilled. Dr. Edward Palmer, in this timely and important book, records the especially disappointing relationship of America's television industry to children. His convincing arguments lead persuasively to the conclusion that American children are victims of a multi-billion-dollar trade-off that amounts to a tragic tale of child neglect.

Some observers go so far as to blame TV for the drop in school performance. On the other side, Jack Valenti, president of the Motion Picture Association of America, tells us that the solution to good education is not less television, but "discipline in the classroom, no mucking around with excellence, and a stern commitment to the basics of learning. That is the province of schools and teachers, and no amount of scolding or TV will erase the logic."

Still, Palmer reminds us that the classroom and TV should not be in competition with each other. The job of educators is to recognize that the world has changed, to rejoice in the marvel of expanding knowledge, and to find ways to relate the classroom more closely to the networks of information outside the school.

The accomplishments of Children's Television Workshop which Palmer outlines in this book are outstanding examples of how television can serve children's education needs. Joan Cooney and Lloyd Morrisett, who conceived the brilliant, creative *Sesame Street* and found $8 million in grants to launch its first season in 1968, recognized in their original proposals that many children, especially those from disadvantaged families, arrive at school ill-equipped to handle formal learning. Their ambitious proposal was designed in part to address the inequities of education.

The record of Children's Television Workshop is enormously impressive. *The Electric Company*, *3-2-1 Contact*, and *Square One TV* joined *Sesame Street* as the richest educational programming our country has developed, a creative mix of entertainment and instruction. Public Television has also advanced the educational needs of students with inspirational series such as *The Adams Chronicles*, *The Ascent of Man*, and *Masterpiece Theatre*, which have been linked successfully to courses and special texts.

As *Television and America's Children* documents, however, the educational potential of the electronic teacher remains appallingly untapped. Industry leaders have, in fact, turned their backs on children. With rare exceptions, the three major commercial television networks have failed to offer regularly scheduled quality programs for children. The Federal Communications Commission of the 1980s has shrugged off attempts to protect children's interests on the airwaves. Congressmen repeatedly have buried the issue in committees. Public television, meanwhile, is chronically underfunded. The success of Children's Television Workshop, a model for the nation, should have been replicated many times over in the past twenty years. Instead it is virtually the *only* example of good children's programming this country has to offer.

It is no longer enough simply to read and write. Students must also become literate in the use and understanding of visual images as well. Our children must learn how to spot a stereotype, isolate a social cliché, and distinguish facts from propaganda, analysis from banter, and important news from "coverage." In a world where students are deluged with messages from every side, we must help them become more sophisticated as message senders *and* receivers.

Whether the new electronic teachers become a constructive force in education or remain an "unbearable disturbance" will depend on whether the industry can be challenged to pursue larger goals and admit their obligation to children. The challenge is not to view technology as the enemy, or to convert the school into a video game factory, competing with the local shopping center. Rather, the challenge is to build a partnership between traditional and non-traditional education, letting each do what it can do best.

Palmer proposes a number of excellent solutions to the current crisis, focusing in turn on the role of government, commercial television, and public television. His international comparisons highlight our nation's impotence, but also let us know that good television for children is possible at minimal expense. This call for a comprehensive solution to the crisis of children's television should be welcomed by every child advocate and parent.

Palmer further reminds us in compelling ways that television, with its pervasive reach, is an equal opportunity classroom. If in our urgent search for excellence in the school, we do not take advantage of the electronic teacher in the home, we will have denied opportunities to those who have been poorly served by our educational system.

Parents and other children's advocates must support high-quality television fare for children. They must lobby for more reliable funding mechanisms for public television. Networks, in turn, must join the crusade for excellence in education. By becoming full partners in the educational and social development of our children, television may yet emerge as a "soaring radiance in the sky."

Television and America's Children

1 | Our Crisis in Children's Television, Our Deficiencies in Children's Education

> This instrument can teach, it can illuminate; yes, and it can even inspire. But it can do so only to the extent that humans are determined to use it to those ends. Otherwise, it is merely wires and lights in a box. There is a great, perhaps decisive battle to be fought, against ignorance, intolerance and indifference. This weapon of television can be useful.
>
> —EDWARD R. MURROW

> ...the first people who understood television, at least in the United States, were the advertising community. They grasped its significance immediately. The second group in the United States who figured it out were the politicians, because they saw the consequence the television would have in campaigning, in reaching the electorate. The last group which is finally awakening from its slumber are the educators, the teachers. They finally are beginning to realize that television is a monumental change in the way people think, in the way people spend their time.
>
> —NEWTON MINOW

Everything we see on television for children is a reflection of somebody's vision. Programs do not just "happen"; they are a product of policy—even if that policy is one of indifference and neglect.

What is our vision? How do we, as Americans, collectively decide (or fail to decide) how this vital medium affects our children? What are the forces that shape our vision? And how do they compare with the forces that shape other countries' visions of children's TV?

Somebody's vision—good or bad, actively sought or passively accepted—becomes our children's television reality. In speaking of "vision," I mean not only the subjective issue of program content and quality but, equally important, the objective quantifiable considerations on which the entire superstructure of programming rests. Are children's programs conveniently available at suitable viewing times, and well distributed throughout the week and year? What total

3

amount of new programming is available each year? What is the ratio of new to repeat programs? Are shows geared to narrow bands of age in keeping with growing children's rapidly changing needs, interests, and understandings?

Two different TV systems in the U.S. have the capacity to reach and serve our total child population. They are commercial broadcasting and public broadcasting, both with penetration levels that exceed 95 percent of all households.[1] Cablecasting and videocassette recordings are a distant but emerging third force, although within this century neither will reach more than perhaps three-quarters of all children in the country, at most.

For the near term, we can look only to our commercial and PTV broadcast systems to serve all our children abundantly and well, with high-quality, age-appropriate programs, rich and varied in horizon-expanding subject matter. Yet, by any measure we may care to use, both of these systems are woefully deficient in their children's offerings.

Our Best, Our Worst, and Our Crisis of Neglect

The extent of our deficiency will probably surprise most Americans. After all, do we not export programming all over the world? And do we not boast of a fine weekday children's offering on public TV? What of programs like *Sesame Street* and *Mister Rogers' Neighborhood* for preschoolers, and the *3-2-1 Contact* science series for children aged 8 to 12? It is true that these series and *The Electric Company*, the now retired reading series for 7- to 10-year-olds, served for many years as the four traditional cornerstones of the PTV children's out-of-school program block.

All have been well received by parents and children, and by their backers in an assortment of foundations and government agencies, corporations, and PTV organizations. In addition, so well regarded is *Sesame Street* worldwide, and its unique model of planned education presented through television's most engaging entertainment forms, that eleven different countries have solicited cooperation from CTW in creating their own *Sesame Street* adaptations, featuring their own languages, cultural symbols, educational goals, and characters. Moreover, our traditional PTV children's favorites have been joined in the early 1980s by a lively new series called *Reading Rainbow*, which promotes books and reading, and by a new weekly series of hour-long family cultural dramas presented under the umbrella title of "WonderWorks" and scheduled for play in the early evening, to encourage shared viewing by children and their parents. *Square One TV*, a major new math series for children 8 to 12 years old, by CTW, had its premiere in 1987.

So what can be so far awry? In fact, the status of children's TV is bleak in both commercial and public television.

On the commercial side, the abysmal fact is that *not one of our three major networks supports a regular weekday program schedule for children*. With the exception of occasional late afternoon specials, commercial children's programming is geared mainly to entertainment and confined to Saturday morning. Commercial TV's neglect of children on weekdays is especially regrettable when we consider that 90 percent of all child viewing takes place on weekdays.[2]

It is true, particularly in the largest U.S. commercial TV markets, containing the greatest numbers of channels, that the independent (i.e., non-network) stations frequently schedule children's programs before or after school; however, with rare exceptions, these programs are reruns of already heavily exposed Saturday morning network cartoons.

The strong swing toward deregulation in the 1980s has only worsened the situation and is directly responsible for a decline in children's informational and educational features on commercial television.[3] The advocacy group Action for Children's Television had appeared before the Federal Communications Commission (FCC) in 1970 asking for regulated reforms that included daily programming for children.[4] After long delays that involved an on-again, off-again series of hearings, inquiries, proposed rule-makings, reports, policy statements, petitions, complaints, and other regulatory red tape, while we waited for improvements through industry self-regulation that were never to come, an FCC decision of December 1983 finally ruled against the ACT petition.[5]

An earlier FCC of a different mood, in 1979, had issued a task force report which concluded that the industry leaves children "dramatically underserved."[6] This view was soon to be set aside, however, with hardly a moment's blush, by an administration intent upon dismantling as much as possible of the federal regulatory function. One of the first casualties to result from the massive move toward deregulation of the 1980s was the long-running and well regarded *Captain Kangaroo* children's TV series, which CBS promptly dropped from its weekday schedule.

Meanwhile, repeat programming in the PTV children's schedule hovers just short of 90 percent for all children, and is even higher for children above preschool age. Public television aired 1200-plus hours of children's programs in 1982–83, according to the FCC's landmark 1983 Report and Order on children's television.[7] Yet, for children 6–13 years old, public television in a typical recent year offered, on a year-round average, an ungenerous amount of less than ten minutes of new programming each weekday. In the 1984–85 PTV broadcast season, only 41 new program hours in total were produced for 6- to 13-year-olds, counting *3-2-1 Contact*, 10 hours; *Reading Rainbow*, 2.5 hours; *Voyage of the Mimi*, 6.5 hours; and *Wonder-Works*, 22 hours.

So underfunded is children's public television in the U.S. that it has never yet had the need or occasion to ask what form a well-conceived and managed, comprehensive children's program schedule might take. We know, however, from other countries such as Japan and Britain, and from our own more limited experience, that for the most part the program needs of 6- to 9-year-olds are distinct from those of 10- to 13-year-olds, especially when the programs are informational or educational.

To offer each of these two age groups one program hour each weekday, 260 days per year, would require 520 schedule hours per year. PTV's 41-hour offering for 6- to 13-year-olds in the 1984–85 broadcast season would constitute a program renewal rate of less than 8 percent in this modest 520-hour-per-year schedule.

Television emerged scarcely more than forty years ago, rapidly to become ubiquitous in the lives of America's children. Since that time, we have seen a wide variety of program forms emerge with qualities which enrich children's lives. Many parents who grew up in the first "television generation" will remember with nostalgia some of the old favorites they loved and learned from. I am thinking of titles like Leonard Bernstein's *Young People's Concerts*, the venerable *Captain Kangaroo* series, going all the way back to the mid-fifties, and *Mr. Wizard*, whose primitive production values were more than offset by its host's earnest fascination with things of science. Or who in this generation does not remember *Kukla, Fran and Ollie* or the perils of *Lassie*?

Then came television's "wasteland" years of the 1960s, as they were characterized at the time by FCC Chairman Newton Minow. Violence in the children's schedule became so great a concern that the Surgeon General undertook a major study to examine the effects on children's attitudes and behaviors.[8] It was at this time, too, in the late 1960s, that Action for Children's Television was formed.

A third milestone event in children's television came at around the same time, in 1966, when *Sesame Street*'s co-conceivers, Joan Cooney and Lloyd Morrisett, sat over dinner to first discuss not just a new production idea but how television for children's at-home viewing could be tied to the national education agenda. What made this event even more significant is that they shared an extraordinarily ambitious vision. In an era when PTV children's shows were all local productions, done on shoestring budgets, and commercial cartoons were being turned out like so many sausage-factory look-alikes, Cooney and Morrisett asked for—and received—the funding to transform all of the most expensive of television's artistically and technically sophisticated forms into vehicles for teaching. To do this, they started a new organization, independent of public broadcasting: Children's Television Workshop.

Their dream was to showcase the best of what this promising but underdeveloped invention could achieve. They were pioneers. And they succeeded.

Their shared vision, realized, establishes beyond any reasonable question that television can be taken seriously as a cost-efficient educational tool. Independent research and testing have demonstrated that programs in the style of those produced by the Workshop can garner an impressively large following of voluntary child viewers and at the same time bring about measured educational outcomes.[9] The Workshop's heavy investment in pre-broadcast planning and in child testing to help guide program design had proved its worth.[10] A few professional reports and articles and then hundreds appeared to document the Workshop's program-design strategies, to prove measurable effects, to question and probe—and, in general, to create a body of knowledge and experience which might serve as shoulders for future practitioners to stand on.[11]

A wonderful kind of yin/yang balance pervades in the Workshop's productions and approach. For example, the programs both educate and entertain, and to bring this about, they are created by collaborating academics and television artists. The goals are idealistic, and they are promoted by public relations professionals. These program series focus on the special and otherwise unmet needs of children from low-income households, and they are wholly embraced by the middle-class parents as a source of valuable educational experiences for their children.[12] The Workshop itself is chartered as a non-profit educational corporation, but it has developed tax-paying, profit-making subsidiaries to help keep vintage series in production and develop new ones.[13]

Since *Sesame Street*'s initial appearance in 1969 as a means to prepare young children for school, the Workshop has produced, in addition, three other major home-and-school educational TV series. One is *The Electric Company*, an aid to children experiencing reading difficulty. Another is *3-2-1 Contact*, which encourages career preparation in science and technology by documenting and explaining the activities of the people who work in the field. And the most recent is the mathematics series, *Square One TV*, to strengthen children's skills, understandings, and interest in this important field. The latter two are intended primarily to serve the 8 to 12 age group.

On the international front, CTW recently completed an entirely original, major TV production titled *Al Manaahil* designed to help teach reading of Arabic to Arab children. The series consists of 65 half-hour programs modeled partly on *The Electric Company* and produced in Jordan.

The work in production design at CTW may be looked upon as a deliberate attempt to appropriate or adapt for educational use every suitable form known in television. A great deal has been made of the fact that *Sesame Street* copies the short, punchy format of the television commercial. As a result, it succeeds at encouraging preschool children to go away from the TV humming the alphabet or singing a jingle about cooperation or geometric forms. What is often overlooked is that the series' producers also incorporate many other forms by commissioning some of the best documentary filmmakers, cartoonists, music writers, puppeteers, and performing artists. As a result, television artistry, in all its manifestations, has become one of the most powerful allies of parents and educators. Building on the tradition of Sophocles and Horace, DeFoe and Twain, Aesop and the *Laugh In* TV series, CTW set out with *Sesame Street* to couch instruction in entertaining forms.

Somewhere along the way, the Workshop learned that "entertaining" does not always have to mean "amusing," and nowadays its staff more often speaks of using "engaging" television approaches to attract and teach the child learners. *Sesame Street* was copied around the world by producers, some of whom assumed that the aim is always to amuse the viewing children. Actually, to engage the children with a comedy skit or or visual trick may work to teach some subjects some of the time. But just as useful, under the right conditions, is simply to allow television to serve as the prism through which the inherent appeal and fascination of a subject is revealed, without embellishments.

Thanks to the efforts of the Workshop and other dedicated production centers in the U.S. and around the world, proof that television confers value in children's lives, when it is thoughtfully conceived and produced, is no longer at issue. Later chapters explore with more detail the range of children's needs which have been addressed through television and the diversity of television forms that have been called into play in the process. Our only problem now, at least in the U.S., is to find ways to make this quality available in sufficient quantity—to go beyond demonstrations and occasional, usually short-lived, applications to develop a comprehensive children's offering.

In applauding the fact that the children's PTV schedule is now partly full we must not lose sight of the fact that it is still mostly empty. Why are we Americans so stingy in allocating a fair share of our invaluable daily television broadcast time to help educate our younger generation for the awesome responsibilities they will inherit? Put another way, why cannot the United States provide its number one natural resource—its children—with the electronic sustenance that television is uniquely capable of providing every classroom and home? Television is, after school and home, the country's most important teacher. What is more, as I will show in Chapter Seven—we can harness its potential for less than a penny a day per child.

Precedents abound elsewhere. A quality children's TV schedule is an institution in Great Britain and Japan. Youngsters in these countries benefit from a constant stream of fresh, new images and ideas available throughout their formative childhood years. An equitable portion of the total broadcast schedule in these countries is devoted to programs made expressly for children, and these programs are scheduled at times appropriate and convenient for child viewing. Both of these countries even strive to provide their children with a "microcosm" of the program varieties available to adults, including news, drama, sports, light entertainment, discussion, and how-to programming. Moreover, sufficient numbers of new programs are created each year to sustain a high ratio of new to repeat programming.

In Great Britain, for example, the BBC airs 785 hours of at-home children's television each year, representing 12.6 percent of BBC–1 program schedule. Of these, 590 hours, making up 75 percent of the total of children's shows, are newly produced each year.[14] Our own PBS, by contrast, carried just 87.5 new program hours in the 1984–85 broadcast year—a quite typical recent year—of new out-of-school children's TV fare.[15] Great Britain's population is one-quarter the size of ours, yet its yearly volume of new PTV programming for children is more than five times greater than our own. The BBC also creates educational programs for in-school use on a regular and stable basis.[16]

The Need in Education, the Opportunity in Television

In the meantime, education in our country is beset with a long-building crisis whose costs and consequences will be enormous. The dimensions of the problem were chronicled in no fewer than five commissioned reports and several individually authored books, whose co-appearance in 1983 fomented a major wave of national concern.[17] Former U.S. Commissioner of Education, Harold Howe II, has said of this "year of the reports":

> It is doubtful that American education has ever before received such a concentrated barrage of criticism and free advice. . . . What is even more unusual is that these outpourings are not just from academics worried about standards in the schools. They come from business and political leaders, from university presidents, from parents and students, and occasionally from educators themselves. The broad message is that the schools can and should be improved, particularly with regard to their academic function. The recommendations are legion and sometimes conflicting; no one can count their costs. Further, there is a frustrating sense among educational leaders about who should do what and how to start.[18]

Many feel that solutions must focus primarily on conditions in the nation's schools—on improving teacher recruitment, professional status and pay, on updating curricula, and on upgrading facilities, equipment, and materials. Many educators say that underlying all of these is the more fundamental need to strengthen the underpinnings of financial support. But another part of the solution lies in making fuller use of broadcast television for at-home learning. Television's unique contribution to this large task may reside in such factors as:

- its ubiquity;
- its nonthreatening, nonpunitive quality as a teaching medium;
- its ability to organize and present information in clear and memorable ways through animated graphics;
- its ability to depict live role models; and
- its nondependence on reading skill or ability.

The schools are being asked to do more than they can accomplish. As a result, each time this country has identified a major deficiency in children's education in recent years, television has responded as a supplement, to help provide a part of the answer—first to help meet preschool children's need for early social, emotional, and intellectual stimulation, and subsequently, in elementary school reading and in career exploration in science and technology. The most recent area was mathematics. But do we really need to wait for future reports to reveal that television also can help children understand history, geography, health, government, the arts, and simple skills for everyday living?

A measure of our crisis in children's home-and-school television is that we lack the level of assured funding that would allow us even to stand still. Funds with which to expand on or revise successful program series are almost totally lacking; funds to start new productions are in only slightly greater supply. With enough funds to create only one major new series every few years, we have had to learn to chase the most urgent education crisis of the moment.

Done without the benefit of supporting national policy, this ad hoc approach at least has given us a successful and highly visible era of demonstration activities. But we are moving far too slowly, and as we step from crisis to crisis, the ground gained crumbles away behind us for want of stable funding support.[19] This is regrettable, because

...ation which these productions address remain with ...tinuous attention.

...television can (1) *promote* useful activities, rang-
...ading to art and music to health and safety; (2)
...ren in skills and ideas ranging from school subjects to
...d economics to the harmful effects of dangerous drugs; and
...*inform* them about everything—world political and economic events, happenings in nature, career opportunities, and lifestyle trends and scientific discoveries which will affect their lives. It can start them off pursuing strands of life-long interests.

Well-planned television programs can help prepare children to find school, the workplace, the voting booth, and events in the larger world more interesting and comprehensible. Like teachers and textbooks, television can provide learning experiences that parents have neither the time nor, in most cases, the academic expertise to provide.

Looked at from every conceivable perspective, a hybrid, home-and-school schedule of children's television programming deserves to be supported. The special benefits to be realized range from social equity to educational cost efficiency. Many of these benefits hinge on what television can contribute toward filling children's lives with learning as a voluntary, everyday pastime.

Children's time is valuable, and parents need help in seeing greater portions of their children's time turned to productive uses. Educational television programs, regularly and conveniently available, can be an important part of the answer.

Children's weekday television viewing averages nearly 100 hours per month.[20] No one wants these children to watch more television than they already do; instead, what is needed is a useful alternative to the heavily adult-oriented program diet they now consume. What I am proposing is that at least 20 hours a month of thoughtfully crafted, age-appropriate educational fare be available as a viewing option for all children.

Like money contributed regularly to savings, a little of a child's time devoted each day to learning quickly adds up—and it soon begins to yield compound interest. Suppose we provide children with an hour each weekday of solidly educational or informational TV fare. An hour each weekday—260 hours per year—is equal to about a fifth of the total time a child spends in the classroom each year. It is also about one-fifth the amount of the time the typical child spends watching television each weekday.

Ten years of TV learning at the rate of just an hour is equal *in time* to two full school years. This is a ver amount of learning time which, if well filled, could sign our children's formative years.

One measure of the need for television as children's third educational institution—after school and home—is the complexity of the world today's youngsters will reside in and manage when their turn comes. Alan Pifer, who headed the Carnegie Corporation when it funded the Carnegie Commission on Children, points out that upon today's youngsters will fall the threefold responsibility of supporting the largest elderly population in our nation's history and providing the nation's productive work force, while rearing their own children.[21]

Readings of the future point to only a small fraction of the challenges with which today's young people must be prepared to cope. They will have to learn to refresh and retrain themselves through life-long learning. To a greater extent than ever before, education will no longer be seen as an activity to be completed early as preparation for life, but as a continuing activity throughout life. The need will be felt increasingly to provide another chance for those who fail or drop out the first time through.

Former U.S. Education Commissioner Dr. Ernest Boyer had this to say about the way in which television's unique strengths as educator came into play in one TV series:

> In the push toward strengthening academics, there is the danger that young people are gathering fragments of information without developing a perspective. The scope and drama of television can help remedy that. The series, *Connections*, for example, in tracing the roots of technology related how we live today to the long sweep of discovery and invention.[22]

Dr. Boyer went on to mention another very different educational application for the medium:

> Teenagers are confused about the future. Thirty percent of our high school seniors were still undecided early in 1983 about whether they were going to college, although that question pertained to a future only a few months distant. Public television, better than high school vocational counseling programs, could show teenagers what it is like to work at various occupations.[23]

Television's established role and value in helping children explore career possibilities is a key point in the rationale behind the creation the *3-2-1 Contact* science series. *3-2-1 Contact* was funded in response to our national need to see more school children develop interest in and consider careers in science and technology. It is designed to reach youngsters in their preteens, so that later, in high school, they will choose to enroll in the courses which will admit them into further study or work in science and technology. Without this high school preparation, a career in the field is closed to them forever.

Sesame Street, in the meantime, has become a kind of "omnibus" series, each year widening its scope by the addition of one or two new subjects—careers, computers, vocabulary, disabling conditions such as deafness and blindness, and promotion of book reading and library use, to mention only a few. In addition, CTW has created the outlines of a similar series for television's now forgotten early elementary (6- to 9-year-old) age group. This series concept has as its working title the *Sesame Graduates* series. The TV possibilities are at least as varied with these older children as in the case of *Sesame Street*'s preschool learners. Yet many worthy programming ideas have failed to get off the ground in recent years for want of adequate funding support, and there is no assurance that the Workshop, in spite of its excellent fundraising record to date, will succeed in forming a new consortium of funders to support this or any other new children's series.

Fine Educational Gems: Their Astonishing Cost Advantage

Children's public television in the U.S. today is stalled in a proving phase that began in 1969 with the first national distribution of *Sesame Street* and *Mister Rogers' Neighborhood*. When Newton Minow described television of the 1960s as a "vast wasteland," it is certain that in the children's area, a wasteland it was. Since that time, children's television has emerged as an educational resource of proven potential. Yet, still with us are all the same in-built, systemic shortcomings in America's television institutions which encouraged Joan Cooney and Lloyd Morrisett to found CTW in the first place as an independent force in the field. Under their leadership, the Workshop proved a vision of home-and-school television which seems to have everything going for it, except—so far—to have sparked the wider growth of the field which the Workshop had anticipated as the sequel to its widely acknowledged and highly visible successes.

Sesame Street has been a paver of the way and a model. It has been copied widely, not only in terms of surface appearance but in the unique way in which it was—and is—created: through a three-way collaboration of TV producers, subject-matter planners, and specialists in research on children's educational television.

All that this great success story lacks is a happy conclusion. Not that things have gone all that badly. In that erstwhile wasteland, now, at least, we can see in one small corner, standing out here and there on the landscape, a few gems and strings of gems of real value. Their presence makes us even more painfully aware of all the gaping holes where other gems might be.

As we survey this scene, we have to ask what conditions are responsible for our failure up to now to achieve the next major milestone, that of creating at least a minimally adequate, comprehensive children's television schedule, to supplement young peoples' education through an activity in which children already spend thousands of all-too-often wasted hours.

It was Joan Cooney who first described her vision for *Sesame Street* as "a Tiffany jewel." She used the ambitious metaphor to express her dream of seeing the children's corner of the wasteland eventually filled with other jewels, measured by *Sesame Street*'s high standard of combined entertainment and education. The problem with gems, Joan always knew, is that they come with a price tag, and the more massive they are, and the better their quality, the greater the cost.

It is true that television is costly, especially when to garner a voluntary child audience we have to match the technical and artistic quality children are accustomed to seeing on competing channels. Yet, even so, education through broadcast television makes abundantly sound economic sense. U.S. Commissioner of Education in the early 1970s, Dr. Sidney Marland, said of *Sesame Street* and *The Electric Company* that they are probably the best educational investment the government ever made.[24] And still today, the cost for the six million target-age preschoolers who tune in regularly each week to *Sesame Street* comes to just a penny per child per program viewed.[25] Factored across a whole year, programs like *Sesame Street* become the sort of cost-efficient bargain available nowhere else in education. The cost for *The Electric Company* when it was produced in the early 1970s was also just a cent a day per elementary school-age child reached.[26]

No complex economic analysis is required to appreciate what an extraordinary educational bargain broadcast television can be. So great is television's educational cost advantage that a few calculations, which anybody could make, literally on the back of an envelope, convey the point dramatically and well. For the 1986–87 school year we laid out an estimated $22.42 per school day to educate each child in grades one through twelve.[27] Compare this with the very large amount which could go each year to support children's PTV programs if we could somehow raise *just one cent per day* for each of the nation's 42 million children who fall in the age range of two to thirteen years.[28] The amount would be a rather astonishingly large $153 million—or more than five times the small and unstable annual amount of less than $30 million spent currently, from all sources, on public children's television.[29]

As a nation, we currently spend at the rate of about 12 cents per year per capita on programming in children's public television.[30] By contrast, our nation's projected $170 billion combined elementary and secondary school bill in fiscal 1987 translates to about $713.00 per capita.[31] Seen in this light, the yearly amount needed to markedly improve our children's educational television diet is miniscule. The amount which I propose (in Chapter Seven) to be minimally adequate for this purpose is $62.4 million.[32] This expenditure is easily afford-able: it requires less than six-tenths of a cent a day on behalf of each child in the population.

One prefers to believe that the key to a great surge forward in children's home-and-school television is not mainly one of achieving the necessary policy breakthrough in principle, since few issues of national self-interest can be so clearly argued from the standpoint of the need, the available but underused resource, and cost-efficiency. More complex, both from a policy standpoint and from a standpoint of practicality, is the question of how to collect and channel the dollars needed to support a quality offering of children's weekday out-of-school informational and educational TV programs.

Individual parents, no matter how wealthy, cannot buy for their children the best in educational programming that television has the potential to offer. There is no store from which to purchase or lease 260 hours—a weekday supply for a year—of age-appropriate edu-cational TV cassettes. Nor is cable TV the answer—not if we want to be able to reach all children with planned education, and not if we want to reach more than but a fraction of all children within the reasonably near future. So far, cable has not spent the extra amounts needed to incorporate a solid educational emphasis in its children's services, and it has little competitive reason to do so. It offers a service of unique value simply by offering "something" for children at times in the schedule when otherwise there is nothing. Cable's limited reach is another problem, especially in its tendency to exclude the poor by wiring first in wealthier neighborhoods.[33] Moreover, as much as a quarter of the total population will not yet enjoy even the option to subscribe to cable by the end of this century.[34]

The commercial broadcasters have their "collection" mechanism, in the form of advertising fees. An innovative mechanism is needed by which to better support children's informational and educational TV programs. Applying principles of sound business economics, it may be seen that we are able to realize dramatic, not merely marginal, cost advantages when we make use of nationally broadcast television as a force in children's education. Our economic folly if we fail do so is revealed in the following additional illustration. A small children's learning book which costs $1.49 will give, perhaps, as much as five hours of benefit. Yet for just $1.49 per child, we can supply every child in the country with 260 hours per year of age-appropriate, televised learning.[35] A full hour each weekday, week in and week out, for each of three child age groups. In this example, the ratio of television's cost-advantage is a little more than 50 to 1, assuming that every child watches every program.[36] Television's advantage is still 25 to 1 if only a very conservative 50 percent of the nation's 2- to 13-year-olds view each program.

There is no shortage of educational needs and certainly no lack of program ideas. Moreover, the public television signal today is available in nearly every U.S. household, and every station could and should make abundant space available in its schedule to serve children. But there is a great shortage of funding, which can only be met with substantial government participation.

The future of children's educational television depends on our government leaders' awareness of our national interest in this important, too-long-neglected area, and on the care they take in shaping a policy for long-term action. The answer lies principally with Congress and the Administration.

Sixteen years ago, we did not know enough about television's usefulness as a children's at-home teaching medium to be able to justify (much less help guide) the formation of national policy to set up permanent funding support for the activity. Today we do. One reason is that CTW and its supporters have set out deliberately in the field to demonstrate a wide range of educational uses, and these have succeeded. But another important reason is that we have created a model approach for designing programs which pulls together effectively the collaborative talents of producers and academics. As a result, we can say with some confidence today that we know how to go about the process of innovation itself. This is accomplished through the use of what we now call the CTW Model for program planning, research, and production. What this model is, what it has done, and how it has done it—these are a part of the later chapter on the Children's Television Workshop.

As a society, we did not anticipate television's potential educational benefits for children in advance, so a Children's Television Workshop had to come along to prove those benefits, time after time illustrating the medium's educational effectiveness and cost-efficiency. In this manner, we have demonstrated for children's television in the U.S. what first-generation television viewers in Japan and Great Britain never had reason to doubt.

Now the demonstration phase is complete. Every future new children's program or series will have to stand on its own individual merits, but justification for setting up a comprehensive educational service will never be more clear.

2 | *Commercial Television: How and Why It Fails Children*

Broadcasting, television and radio combined, was in 1987 a $30.6 billion-a-year business in this country.[1] Television alone accounted for $23.3 billion of this amount. The source of this revenue is advertising. Television may be described in traditional terms as a business in which advertisers pay the networks and the stations to insert commercial messages into the programming. But the business reality from the industry point of view is that a part of the fees paid by advertisers is used to insert program material into the vacant slots between commercials. Looked at either way, the important point is that the chief commodity bought and sold in television is audiences, not programs.

The average thirty-second-long prime-time television announcement in 1985 cost $100,000 (spots on a top-rated series cost $200,000; low-rated spots averaged about $80,000). An estimated 120 million people watched the 1987 Super Bowl telecast. Thirty-second announcements during that event cost $600,000.[2]

The rate which the networks charge is based on the number of people watching a particular program (as determined by rating services like the A.C. Nielsen Company), and, to a much smaller extent, the demographics and estimated purchasing power of that audience.

The effectiveness of television advertising is quite unprecedented. It is qualitatively different from print advertising and from radio advertising as well. During the 1930s and 1940s, the advertising community was skeptical that television would ever develop into a useful

19

marketing tool, particularly when the cost and complexity of producing TV commercials was taken into account. The rates charged by the networks prior to the mid-1950s were very modest, but even so advertisers were reluctant to invest in the new medium.

That situation changed overnight in 1955 when CBS revamped the old radio quiz-show format by offering participants big money prizes. The networks' first effort was called *The $64,000 Question*, and it was sponsored by a small and virtually unknown cosmetics company called Revlon. The fact that *The $64,000 Question* and the other quiz shows that followed in its wake were enormous ratings smashes was never particularly important. However, the fact that this one show enabled Revlon to leap from obscurity to total market dominance before its competitors even knew what had hit them was an American business phenomenon that the broadcasting and advertising industries would never forget.

Television advertising grew into a craft quite unlike anything that had come before. By the late 1950s it was already a cliché to say that the ads were better than the programs. As indeed they should be, when it is not uncommon for a thirty-second commercial to cost more than the thirty-minute program it sponsors.

The cost-efficiency of producing extremely expensive TV commercials has always been justified by their effectiveness as selling tools. And even costs approaching a million dollars for a single sixty-second spot do not seem excessive when one realizes that a single national airplay can cost as much as the original production. However, their very effectiveness in marketing, and the resulting necessity for so many competing producers of consumer goods to invest heavily in TV advertising, means that between producer and consumer a major new cost is added on to the price of the goods and services advertised on TV—a cost in excess of $23.3 billion in 1987.[3] This cost is recovered in the only way it can be—by adding it on to the price of the advertised goods. This additional cost is the "hidden tax" that Americans pay for their "free" television. Just how high that tax really is can be seen by dividing the sum realized annually by broadcasters in the airing of TV commercials by the population of the U.S. The resultant figure is the per capita cost of advertising:

$$\frac{\text{total cost of TV advertising } (\$23.3 \text{ billion})}{\text{population of the U.S.A. } (239 \text{ million})} = \text{per capita cost } (\$97.49)$$

If we take it as given that, ultimately, the cost of TV advertising is passed through to the people, then it is valid to compare this cost with what people pay for public television. In two other leading industrialized countries, Britain and Japan, public broadcasting is supported through a yearly television receiver tax levied on all set owners. In per capita terms, the Japanese in 1985 supported the largest public broadcasting system in the world for annual cost equal to around $11.93 per person.[4] And Japan's population is only half the size of ours. Britain has only one-quarter as many people as the U.S.—yet the entire BBC is supported at a per capita cost of only $16.14.[5]

In both cases, the actual cost to the consumer is much less than the extravagant $97.49 per capita expenditure which must be lavished in order to support our "free" commercial broadcasting system. By contrast, we paid only $5.41 on a per capita basis in 1987 to support all of U.S. public broadcasting.[6]

How and Why Advertiser-Supported Television Fails Children

In television's infancy, a period that coincided with the postwar "baby boom," TV broadcasters eagerly put children's programs on the air. They did this for three reasons: first, to attract the young families that were filling suburbia, families who were the prime target of both TV manufacturers and TV broadcasters; second, to fill up the otherwise useless time slots of early morning and mid-afternoon with inexpensive program material; and, third, to demonstrate their public-service orientation to the FCC, Congress, and the American people.

By the 1970s, all three of these reasons had become irrelevant to the broadcasting industry. From that point on, it was simply a matter of inevitable statistics writing themselves into programming schedules.

Table 1 reflects the accelerating decline of children's programming on American television. From a high of 32 hours and 45 minutes in the average Monday to Friday period in the 1954–55 season to five hours in 1970, the decline could not be more dramatic. It is as if the whole audience had disappeared—except that the audience did not disappear. Only the programming for that audience disappeared. Why?

The three great assets to broadcasters of children's programming

Table 1. Children's Programming on New York City Network-Affiliated TV Stations

	Hours and Minutes		
	Weekdays	Saturdays	Sundays
1948 to 1949	20:00	none	5:25
1951 to 1952	27:45	10:00	9:45
1954 to 1955	32:45	13:00	8:30
1957 to 1958	19:15	9:15	11:00
1960 to 1961	17:15	15:00	6:45
1963 to 1964	11:00	15:00	6:15
1966 to 1967	12:30	19:00	6:45
1969 to 1970	5:00	17:00	5:45

Source: Action for Children's Television.

had become liabilities. Television ownership had reached saturation level, so special programming to entice potential set buyers was no longer necessary. Besides, the America of the 1970s was no longer made up of the young suburban families that had characterized the immediate postwar period. The early morning and mid-afternoon time slots previously occupied by children's programming were becoming increasingly lucrative for other purposes.

The mid-afternoon slot was being taken up more and more by soap operas, a programming form that is extremely cheap to produce. Soaps were growing from a small-scale cult to a national craze, and, of course, as the audience grew so did the advertising revenues and the value of the time slot. Today, soaps bring in enormous advertising returns.

A similar process was taking place with the early-morning time period. All three networks were putting greater and greater emphasis on developing news and feature programs for the 7 to 9 a.m. slot. NBC's *Today* program, developed by one of television's most original programmers, Pat Weaver, had been successful since the 1950s, and for about twenty years had the field nearly all to itself. However, when CBS and ABC also began to develop early morning news and public affairs programs, the pressures on the children's shows that had previously occupied the time slot became very great.

But while this was happening, broadcasters began to make a startling discovery: *kids do not buy very much.* Perhaps they could be counted on to influence mom in the selection of a breakfast cereal, and from Thanksgiving to Christmas there would be a predictable period of hysteria, when it seemed that the entire world belonged to toy manufacturers and retailers. But for the most part, children—especially preschool children—are terrible consumers. They do not have headaches or heartburn, they do not buy beer or soap, they do not take vacations in Florida, and they are without exception shamelessly indifferent to how quickly a car can accelerate from 0 to 60 miles per hour.

The buying patterns of America's three-year-olds are designed to give admen ulcers—and if there is nothing to sell to kids, then what is the purpose of creating programs for them? Increasingly, broadcasters began to realize that the very concept of children's programming flies in the face of the central principle that governs the television industry in this country: *not to sell programs to viewers, but to sell viewers to advertisers*.

Consequently, broadcasters resorted increasingly to a unique (if radical) solution to the problem of the poor competitive economies of weekday children's programming: they simply stopped creating it. Throughout the 1960s fewer and fewer programs for young people remained in the weekday schedule; among those that lingered, nearly all had been on the air for at least a decade.

By 1974, the Federal Communications Commission, in response to a petition from Action for Children's Television, and subsequent public hearings, had put the industry on notice to self-regulate in the children's area, under the threat of an imposed minimum requirement if it failed to do so.[7] A key issue had been the inadequate provision for children in the weekday schedule, in the hours before or after school. Five years later, in 1979, the FCC released a task force study which reported that no net improvement had taken place in the children's schedule during the ensuing five-year period.[8]

The task force characterized the industry's scant weekday provision for children at the time as a case of "market failure," and went so far as to speculate on why such a market failure should have occurred: children simply are not a very desirable target for television advertising.

Two straightforward numerical facts will help to underscore the industry's economic self-interest in the matter. First, children age thirteen and under make up only a sixth of our population; and, second, these children account for a still smaller 3 percent of television's total yearly advertising revenues.[9] Yet, these children are 42 million in number—more than half as numerous as the total population of even the largest European countries (England, France, West Germany, Italy), and they number four to five times the total population of Sweden. As child advocate Marion Wright Edelman has said: "These children are a sixth of our population; they are all of our future."[10]

In its historic, December 1983 decision, the FCC ruled against any imposed provision for children. The industry response? Cancellations were inevitable, culminating in the removal of one of the longest-running and most highly respected children's programs ever aired, *Captain Kangaroo*, in the early 1980s. When that happened, there were no regularly scheduled weekday children's shows left on any of the commercial networks.[11]

Children's programming of *any* kind, let alone of high quality, has become almost invisible on weekdays outside of public television and independent (i.e., non-network-affiliated) commercial stations. It is true that the networks produced, and continue to produce, a number of children's weekday "specials" each season. Some are excellent. But they can never replace the regularly scheduled children's offerings that have fallen by the wayside.

It could be argued that this development is neither good nor bad—simply the unfolding of market forces that have been freed from intervention and regulation. It is also true that the program with which CBS replaced *Captain Kangaroo*—an expanded version of the *CBS Morning News*—is an important and praiseworthy broadcast.

Therefore, when one discusses the decline of children's television on the commercial channels, the point is not to ask "Who is to blame?" It may well be true that no one is to blame, although personally I cannot condone many of the networks' practices and choices. The point, rather, is simply to acknowledge the inescapable conclusion that if one is interested in children's television—and one of the premises of this book is that all of us should be—then commercial television is not the place to look for a solution.

Considered from the narrowly profit-oriented investors' and station managers' points of view, it is only sound business practice to schedule adult fare in preference to children's, when adult advertising produces much greater profits. Those who take the active opposing position hold that narrowly construed business interests should not be the deciding factor in shaping children's commercial TV. They accuse the industry of hiding behind the provisions of the First Amendment.[12] And they say the industry violates the letter and spirit of the Broadcasting Act of 1934, in seeking to escape its responsibility toward children.[13] These advocates build this case on the fact that space in the broadcast spectrum is scarce, and that it is a public and not a private resource. They point out that the authority under which the commercial stations are granted license to use the public airwaves for their own profit—namely the Broadcasting Act of 1934—requires that these stations program "in the public interest, convenience and necessity."[14] Children, these advocates say, are a special group, whose unique needs as children are not met by adult programming. The advocates conclude that commercial broadcasters, therefore, have a special obligation to serve children.[15]

Anyone reading the FCC's 1974 Report and Order—which in effect tells the industry to self-regulate or be regulated on the children's issue—would conclude that the FCC, at that time, was in broad and essential agreement with the advocates' case in the matter.[16] Issued five years later, the 1979 FCC task force report evinces more of the same mood.[17] Nor is the FCC of the 1970s the only body in government to side with the advocates. The U.S. Congress in recent years has prepared a bill which would override the FCC's December 1983 ruling against ACT's petition. Specifically, it would require that each commercial licensee carry an hour and a half of programming for children each weekday.[18]

We have waited almost twenty years since the Boston-based Action for Children's Television was formed in 1968 to spearhead advocacy for an improved children's TV offering. Why has no substantial improvement been forthcoming? The answer has little to do with the question of television's usefulness in children's lives. Instead, it has to do with the way the institutions of television operate in our country.

Everywhere in the world, wherever television exists, it operates within each country's unique traditions, visions, values, and vested interests. Nations vary greatly in their different approaches to media control. In most of the rest of the world, PTV came into existence before commercial television, to establish a firm pattern of public service expectations among the populace.

Differing National Traditions, Visions, Values

By looking at the telecasters' responsibilities toward children in Britain and Japan, we are able to see an instructive counterplay of different national traditions, visions, and values in broadcasting. Each broadcasting organization throughout the world takes on its own unique look and function, depending on the vision and purpose which gave rise to it and which it serves. A U.S. study group, convened to look at practices in children's television worldwide as background for this book, was reminded by former BBC children's producer, Joy Whitby, that, as she put it, "You can't unscramble your egg." Her caveat served as a useful reminder that we cannot expect to import other countries' practices intact, oblivious to our different traditions and values. Where their practices are seen to be superior to our own, they inspire us to seek improvement, but this improvement must be consistent with our own circumstance and values.

The systems of broadcast organization of the U.S. and of Japan have common roots in times of national economic crisis. Nevertheless, the very different approaches the two countries took in solving their respective problems launched them early along importantly divergent pathways. The U.S.'s heavy commercial domination, where many other industrial countries chose to nationalize radio, telegraphy, and telephony, owes much to the efforts of Herbert Hoover while he was Secretary of Commerce in the mid-1920s. By the time the Broadcasting Act of 1934 was passed, the U.S. was functioning under a radically different Administration and philosophy of government; yet the country was still deeply in the midst of the Great Depression, and in no mood to see the government build a national broadcasting capability, when the commercial world was able and eager to do the job.[19]

By this time in 1934, the British and Japanese system of taxing radio owners each year existed as a precedent of long standing, which the U.S. could have followed, except that Americans do not like such dedicated individual taxes at any time, and especially not during an economic depression. A strong tide of opinion developed, nevertheless, in favor of establishing a separate public broadcasting system. The powerful industry lobby successfully quelled this movement at the time by pointing to all the (then) unsold airtime on each station, which it said it would be only too pleased to make available for public service uses.[20]

By contrast, propitious timing and the events of history gave rise early to a strong public broadcasting system in Japan. Devastation caused by a massive earthquake in the Tokyo area on September 1, 1923, had all but depleted the Japanese national treasury. The great amount of public confusion which surrounded the event underscored the need for a national system of radio communication, and Japan's prompt response was to impose a yearly tax on individual owners of radio receivers to set up and operate the NHK, the country's national broadcasting organization.[21] Japan now also has four nationally networked commercial TV systems. Yet, in spite of this, the NHK continues to receive support at a level 30 percent greater than that which flows from all sources combined to support U.S. public broadcasting.[22] This is true even though Japan has scarcely more than half the U.S. population base to draw upon to provide this amount of support.

In Britain, the obligation of the broadcaster is seen differently. Britain has a dual system: the publicly supported British Broadcasting Corporation, financed by individual householders through a monthly TV-set license fee, and advertiser-supported Independent Television (ITV). Unlike the case in the U.S., both the publicly sponsored and the advertiser-supported systems by charter operate directly in service to the public interest.

There are four TV channels in Great Britain: two for the BBC, and two for the commercial stations. The BBC has been in existence since 1922; commercial broadcasting has existed in Britain only since 1964. The second commercial TV channel began service as recently as November 1982.

In Britain (indeed, in most advanced countries in the world), "public interest" is defined differently than it is in the U.S. The result is striking differences in the actual operation of the two broadcasting systems. Nowhere are these differences more sharply evident than in the treatment of the child audience. Both commercial and noncommercial British television give their children a decided advantage over ours. A key factor is control of broadcasting practices.

The Federal Communications Commission in the U.S. was created by an act of Congress in 1934. Its primary purpose is to ensure that every broadcaster in the country operates to serve the public "interest, convenience, and necessity." American broadcasters, and the FCC by tacit acquiescence, have interpreted this clause in the Communications Act to mean that the "public interest" is defined as "that which interests the public" that is, attracts the largest possible audience. A very convenient definition, indeed. The industry argues that the more people who watch a program, the more it conforms with a broadcaster's obligations to the Government and the people.[23]

For the noncommercial BBC, "public interest" was defined by its first chairman, Lord John R. Reith, as the mandate "to inform, educate, and entertain."[24] Specifically, this means that the BBC is obligated to create and transmit programs of high quality, to diverse audiences, for many purposes. The BBC must provide serious drama, but it also must provide light entertainment. It must produce accurate, impartial news and documentary programs, but it also must produce shows for children. Its obligations to its English audience are balanced by its obligations to Scots and Welshmen. In short, it must guarantee program diversity. Popularity is recognized as one criterion of quality, but not the only one.

The British commercial TV companies are regional businesses engaged in the combined enterprises of TV production and advertising. Yet the commercial TV companies are obligated to produce programming according to precisely the same definition of "public interest" as the BBC. They too must commit themselves to a policy of high quality, program diversity, and production for specialized as well as general audiences. In addition, in return for the privilege of making money through their use of the public airwaves, they are obligated to fulfill specific requirements, which include among them:[25]

1. They must pay a fee, by formula, which can amount to as much as 20 percent of their revenues, to the exchequer.[26]

2. They must schedule commercials together, in clusters, at specified periods throughout the broadcast day, for a maximum of six commercial minutes per hour. No program may be sponsored; all commercials must be "spot" ads, without any connection to programs.

3. They must produce programming to fill a schedule dictated to them by the IBA (Independent Broadcasting Authority). Specific program *content* also is controlled by the IBA but, in actual practice, is left to the individual stations and producers. The ratio between different types of programs must conform to strict and closely monitored standards, and all material is subject to review and revision before airing. Roughly 38 percent of the schedule is devoted to "informative" programs (i.e., news, public affairs, adult education, religions, etc.), 32 percent to "narrative" plays and feature films, and 8 percent (195 hours in 1983,

of which 130 hours were newly produced) to children's programming.

4. Balance, diversity, accuracy, and good taste are among the minimum requirements that the IBA sets for British commercial stations. Adult programs scheduled to air before 9 p.m. must be free of content that is not suitable for children's eyes.

5. All television companies in Britain must pay an annual fee to support the Independent Broadcasting Authority, which governs them and owns and operates the broadcasting system used by them.

6. All sideline activities of the commercial broadcasters must be approved by the IBA.

It is possible to construe these obligations as government interference in what should be rightfully considered private enterprise, but that is not so. These obligations are nothing more than the normal exchange inherent in any contract. Indeed, that is the key to this whole issue: *the license to broadcast is a contract between the broadcaster and the people, who own the electromagnetic spectrum.*

It is instructive in this regard to look at the children's program requirement imposed upon Britain's commercial (ITV) companies by the IBA. The *IBA Annual Report and Accounts 1984–85* lists the following transmission schedule of children's fare. The figures reflect the weekly average of programming on the combined two ITV channels for the year ended March 31, 1985:

	Duration Hours:Minutes	Percentage of Total Transmission Schedule
Preschool Education	2:02	2.0
Chidren's Informative	2:45	2.5
School Programs	6:51	6.5
Children's Drama & Entertainment	7:53	7.5
Weekly Total	19:31	18.5

When we consider the benefits these mandated programs contribute to the quality of British children's lives, and when we add to that the further contribution made by BBC-TV, we must ask why, with a population half that of the U.S., Britain provides children with a larger and more equitable schedule of informational and educational programs on both the commercial and the noncommercial side than we do. To find the answer, we don't have to seek farther than to examine the two very different kinds of contracts that were allowed to develop in the respective countries between the broadcasters and the public.

Although the two countries have much in common, the U.S. and Britain have adopted strikingly different practices in broadcasting. We have taken a laissez-faire approach. We can trace our differences in this regard to broader national differences in balancing free enterprise against government regulation. But we also can see that in Britain, the BBC's advantage in preceding commercial television was enormous.

Joan Cooney, cofounder and head of Children's Television Workshop, believes that we would have shaped the whole television enterprise in this country very differently if we had understood earlier what we know today about its remarkable public service capabilities. She points out that television burst into the American scene so rapidly (about 80 percent of American homes acquired television in a single decade in the 1950s), and with such unanticipated possibilities, that under commercial domination, we allowed the field to grow out of the public's control. Nobody took care to design the nation's broadcasting system with an eye to providing either the controls or the revenue-producing mechanism necessary to ensure that a proper balance of public service applications would flow from the field's inherent structure. Today, the fact that the industry exists in the U.S. as a powerful vested interest makes reforms extremely difficult to institute. The best we have been able to do up this point is to patch together a separate, poorly funded public television enterprise as an alternative means of providing for children and other groups skimpily served on the commercial side. Born in the shadow of commercial television, U.S. public television can never rise to the same position of esteem as either Britain's BBC or Japan's NHK, nor match their range of public services.

In Great Britain, Japan, and Sweden, people first received television by paying for it directly, through a receiver tax. They could see what they were getting, and they demanded a good return for their money. No part of the fee was to be given or withheld according to the strength of the commercial broadcasting lobby (for there was none; noncommercial TV developed first), or the degree of station ownership among members of Parliament. Broadcasting monies were dedicated exclusively to broadcasting in the public interest, and could not be used for any other purpose. The only directly political part of the process was in the establishment and adjustment of the license fee—and this was an openly debated event, with too much public participation for narrow self-interest to prevail.

Of course, in the American context at least, the whole idea of a license fee is obsolete and unwieldly. As we saw in the last chapter, television is ubiquitous in this country. Virtually *every* American household owns at least one television set. Therefore, a license system which differentiates between TV owners and non-owners would simply be a cumbersome nuisance. Besides, no American politician could ever impose a fee for what people tend to believe they receive for free. Such a proposal would be political suicide, and the death rattle would bring relief to the scores of lobbies who have a vested interest in the perpetuation of our inequitable system of broadcasting.

The central point of the European and Japanese system of license fees is not the fee itself, or the manner by which it is collected, but rather a means to assure adequate and sustained support to quality television, while emphasizing the public service obligations of the broadcaster.

It is commonly perceived that the European countries have state-controlled broadcasting monopolies, while ours is a free enterprise system. This perception is wrong on two counts.

Most advanced countries have a dual broadcasting system, with some stations supported by taxes, and others by advertising revenues. More importantly, *neither the American nor any other broadcasting system follows a free-enterprise pattern.* There is no country in the world where one can start or operate a broadcasting station without prior government permission. To do so would be a physical impossibility because of the scarcity of space in the electromagnetic spectrum. Choices must be made, and the ratio of applicants to operators will always be high. The question is not "Shall government have the power to license and regulate broadcasters?" Government already has that power, everywhere in the world. The question is rather, "What kind of contract shall exist between the broadcaster and the government?" The government gives the broadcaster the right to use the spectrum; that is, the right to use public property for his own private gain. What should the broadcaster give in return to the people?

The Public Desire and Commercial Television: Our Weak Quid Pro Quo

In Great Britain, as here, the commercial broadcaster is given the right to make very large profits by selling air time to advertisers. Noncommercial British television (the BBC) is given the right to collect a license fee from every television owner in the country. But a contract always implies mutual rights and mutual obligations. Without these, it is not a contract.

Therefore, the British view is that by imposing certain restrictions on broadcasters, the government is not exercising undue influence or excessive control, but rather simply receiving something of value in exchange for value given. This contractual concept of an exchange of values is completely separate and apart from the issue of freedom of expression. Translated into American terms, this means that First Amendment guarantees should not prevent the people's representatives from demanding full value from the private use of public property.

The American system of broadcasting, as administered by Congress and its administrative creation, the FCC, gives away a valuable resource, without getting anything of agreed-upon value in return. It is simply a bad contract, and anyone who has watched British TV or the NHK in Japan knows just how bad it is. In theory, broadcast licenses in this country are for a period of three years (the current administration wants to expand this period to seven years), and are subject to the test of "public interest" at renewal time. In reality, of course, renewal is virtually automatic. We have had television for more than forty years, and in that time, both actual industry practices and the mood of the FCC have moved in the direction of allowing the children's lot to be decided by the forces of the marketplace. No regulatory or legal action of any kind ever has—or likely ever will—be taken against a station for not including suitable children's programming in its broadcast schedule.[27] We should keep trying, of course; but what of children's unserved needs in the meantime?

Why do we permit our government to give away such a valuable resource? Why do we not demand fair value in return? There are many reasons, not the least of which is the enormous financial and political power of the broadcasting lobby. But the main reason why this imbalance can perpetuate itself is that we Americans are living with a myth, the myth of "free" television. In reality, we are paying much more in higher prices for advertised goods than we ever would with a fixed and open license fee. But myths, particularly myths that serve powerful vested interests, are hard to break.

In a curious way, the cable industry has had to deal with this myth as well. An enormously lucrative cottage industry has grown up in this country in the last decade: the production and sale of illegal dishes and decoders to steal cable signals. Respectable, middle-class families who would not dream of shoplifting do not hesitate to steal cable programs. After all, is not a television program something that one normally gets for free?

We in America have allowed ourselves to be lulled into the belief that our television is free. This belief has cost us dearly. By allowing advertisers to pay all of the costs (and reap all of the profits), we have relinquished control over the most important communications medium of our century. This is tragic, not only because we could have just as easily created a system which allowed for high profits while still maintaining impartial, public control but also because the commercial system of broadcasting as it has evolved in this country gives us poor program quality and higher consumer prices. It has also given us a strangely irrational nonprofit broadcasting service, unlike any other in the world. The distortions engendered by the three major networks create and maintain a warped framework for the system that was designed to be its antidote: American public television.

Television production costs are high all over the world, yet in larger countries, the audience is very large, so the cost per viewer is very small. Certainly, in a country as populous as the U.S., the cost-efficiency of television as a medium for either entertainment or education justifies the high expenditures required to achieve top quality in programming. This cost-efficiency should work to the benefit of both viewers and producers, perpetuating a system where high quality can be obtained for reasonable cost. As we have seen, whether this quality is obtained through license fees or through advertising revenues is not the primary issue. What is important in any television system is that the producers accept clearly defined responsibilities to the viewers, who must maintain ultimate control of the system.

Today, we hear from the FCC that we must relinquish control. The FCC was empowered to regulate broadcasting in the first place on the grounds of spectrum scarcity. But this issue has become clouded. A new phenomenon has arisen, and is being seized upon to relieve the industry and the FCC of all need to meet their responsibilities to the public, and to children in particular. With the advent of cable, home videocassette recorders, video discs, direct broadcast satellites, and other manifestations of the "new technologies," the argument is now being made that there is no more scarcity.[28] Television signals are no longer limited to the narrow spectrum of standard UHF and VHF signals, and consumers can now choose among an unlimited array of choices.

Close examination of those "unlimited" choices, however, will quickly reveal just how limited they are.

Over-the-air broadcasting is the predominant medium through which television programs reach American consumers. That is true today, and it will most likely remain true at least through the turn of the century and probably well beyond. As of 1986, cable reaches just over 40 percent of homes, but the once-promised cornucopia of unlimited program choices has not arrived. Most of the services devoted to culture or esoteric programming went out of business within a year or two of their inauguration,[29] and the once-ubiquitous term "narrowcasting"—that is, providing program material for every audience, no matter how small—is heard much less frequently, as the euphoria of cablecasting's halcyon days is replaced by the business realities inherent in providing a long-term (and easily canceled) service.[30]

Since 1975, when Time, Inc., combined satellite relays with cable delivery to create the immensely successful Home Box Office, the penetration of cable has increased rapidly. Just as with broadcast television during its great period of growth (1946–55), the cable companies have created programming schedules designed to appeal to as many viewers as possible. For the most part, this means first-run movies, sporting events, entertainment specials, and pornography, but smaller and more specialized services can be included as well. Warner-Amex offers a children's channel called Nickelodeon, which is available to 40.5 million cable-equipped homes (about 46 percent of the country's TV households). The Disney organization and others have created additional children's cable services.

How long services for children like Nickelodeon will be around is open to question. As cable penetrates a higher and higher percentage of homes, the need for a "loss leader"—either as an enticement for people to buy the service, or to help the company win lucrative community franchises—will decrease. Revenues to support a dedicated children's channel will be increasingly hard to come by. Advertisers will be reluctant to sponsor such a channel for the same reasons that they are now reluctant to sponsor over-the-air children's programming: the audience does not have enough buying power to make sponsorship sufficiently lucrative.

In the U.S., the current growth pattern for cable, overall, simply fails to support the FCC's contention that it affords a viable marketplace alternative to a regulated broadcast TV offering for children. The problem is not that many people cannot afford it. Although that may be a factor, it is completely overshadowed by a far larger reality, which is that cable will not even reach more than about 75 percent of American homes within this century.[31]

Broadcast television remains both the advertiser's and the educator's medium of choice, simply because it is ubiquitous, where cable is not. And it is too early to know how successful cable will be in attracting either the mass or the quality of buyers for it to become the alternative that can live up to the FCC's claims.

But in the interim—for fifteen years? twenty? longer?—the FCC's scenario is to leave kids admittedly shortchanged while we wait for the wispy "marketplace" promise to be fulfilled.[32] Why not turn the FCC's logic around, and require that children be served by the existing commercial broadcasting system until these promised marketplace alternatives become realities?

Of the other "new technologies," only home videocassette recorders show any sign of becoming larger than a fringe phenomenon. These videocassette recorders can get their material from three sources: over-the-air broadcasts, bought or rented cassettes, and when used in conjunction with a camera as a new form of home movies. Over-the-air broadcasts and the rental of popular movies are by far the most prevalent forms of VCR use. In short, the VCR's great advantage is that of control over viewing time, for it allows one to see programming at the hour one chooses. A small market of educational cassettes for children is emerging, but it hardly enlarges the available pool of program choices at all for children from lower socioeconomic circumstances, because of the prohibitive costs of owning the machines and leasing or buying the programs.

The "new technologies" have indeed affected the American family's program choices—but not at all in the way that broadcasters and the FCC would have us believe. The sudden and astronomical leap in productivity of information storage, computing, and telecommunications technologies, and the way in which previously separate industries have increasingly overlapped, necessitated major revisions in how those industries would do their business. The major change, of course, was the transformation of AT&T from the world's largest regulated monopoly into smaller but competitive information vendors. Increased productivity made deregulation of the phone company one viable method of stimulating growth in telecommunications. Whether this was the wisest course (for there are many dissenters to the divestiture of AT&T and universal deregulation) will be known only in the years to come. But one thing is clear. This process of deregulation has very little applicability to the sale of entertainment on television, and no applicability whatsoever to children's television programming.

The commercial television networks, with the acquiescence of the FCC, are simply using the deregulatory climate in order to rid themselves of a public service obligation they no longer wish to bear. In their view, since the child audience is of only marginal importance to advertisers, children should be of only marginal importance to the broadcast industry.

3 | The FCC: The View from Beneath the Sand

"No broadcaster has ever had his *license* imperiled on a children's programming issue. . . ."[1]

—FCC Chairman Mark Fowler
February 11, 1983

The Federal Communications Commission is the regulatory arm of the government that is empowered to oversee the activities of broadcasters. Created in 1934, it grew out of various legislative efforts to regulate broadcasting that go back to 1912. Why were these regulatory bodies needed? Because the number of frequencies that can carry radio and television signals is limited, without regulation competing stations would constantly interfere with each other. The listener would hear nothing but chaos.

Therefore, some form of impartial regulatory body was needed to decide two questions: (1) At which frequencies can specific stations operate? and (2) How is a choice to be made among the competing applicants for a particular frequency? Since the number of would-be broadcasters almost always outnumbers the available frequencies, some objective criterion must be established to allow one applicant to be chosen over another.

Answering the first question is fairly easy, since that is simply a technical matter. Answering the second question—or attempting to— has opened up one of the most complex and heated legal debates of this century.

The debate centers around two realities. The first is the *scarcity* of broadcasting frequencies. Since only a certain number of radio or television stations can be on the air at one time without mutual interference, others, by definition, must be excluded. This makes broadcasting entirely different from publishing a newspaper or mag-

37

azine, since, in theory at least, there is no natural limit to the number
of competitors in that marketplace of ideas. Since the First Amendment to the Constitution clearly prohibits the government from any
form of press regulation, a mechanism had to be found that would
control the selection of applicants, but not the content of their
programming.

That mechanism is the concept of "Public Domain." The Broadcasting Act of 1934 holds that the airwaves belong in perpetuity to
the people of the United States, and that they can never pass into
private hands. However, the government can license selected applicants for renewable periods of three years, and those applicants may
use the public airwaves for their private gain, provided that by doing
so they are responsive to "the public interest, convenience, and necessity." How they are to provide such public interest service, and
who is to decide how good a job they are doing are the two questions
which have formed the crux of the debate.

The second reality, after scarcity, is broadcasting's immense popularity. We tend to take this for granted, but on close examination
it reveals itself to be a phenomenon unlike any other. Both radio in
the 1920s and television in the late 1940s literally exploded into our
lives, quickly becoming indispensable. Before the American public
had a chance to understand the potential of TV for public service, it
became totally dominated in its early years by powerful commercial
interests. One would think that the same would hold for many modern
conveniences, but that is not true. The telephone, for example, took
over seventy-five years to penetrate just 60 percent of American
homes. TV reached 90 percent in scarcely more than a decade.[2] In
fact, there are more TV sets in America today than any other kind
of appliance (except radio, of course). More TVs than refrigerators,
telephones, or washing machines. More homes have television sets
in the United States than have indoor plumbing.[3] By any standard,
broadcasting is a basic necessity for the vast majority of the American
people. There are countless stories of families who lost all of their
possessions in the Great Depression, but who refused, under any
circumstances, to relinquish their radios. Further, Americans are vo-
racious consumers of broadcast fare. The average household in 1986–
87 tuned in to television for seven hours, seven minutes a day.[4]

All of this makes television one of the most profitable industries
in the world. Leaving aside, for the moment, the still somewhat
hypothetical question of competition from cable, satellite, cassette,

and videodisc, the fact remains that in the vast majority of instances, a license to broadcast is as good as a license to print money. Protecting those profits, and the regulatory climate that nurtures them, is the primary task of commercial broadcasting's trade association, the National Association of Broadcasters (NAB). The NAB, with its considerable resources to support research, legal services, and publicity, and to lobby Congress, makes Lilliputians of the advocates who say children have a right to share more fully in the bounty that results from the commercial development of the broadcast spectrum.

When Children's Rights and an Industry's Profit Objectives Collide

Criticizing the poor quality of commercial broadcasts has always been a popular pastime in this country, reaching its peak in 1961 when the then FCC Chairman Newton Minow denounced the entire TV industry as "a vast wasteland." My point in raising this issue is not to join the chorus of TV critics—there are already so many of them that they surely do not need one more voice—but to examine this issue of television "quality" and see how it affects our children.

Most television programs, in terms of substance, are very bad. Most books, newspapers, and magazines are also very bad. Quality is rare in any medium. The difference between bad books and bad TV is twofold: bad books are protected in absolute terms under the First Amendment, whereas First Amendment protection of television programs is more limited; second, bad television can do immeasurably more harm than a bad book. This is particularly true of bad television programs aimed at children. At a time when over one hundred million people can be viewing a single TV program, the potential for distortion, misinformation, and damage is enormous.

That is precisely why we have always had a tradition in this country of making children an exception under the law. As far as television regulation and First Amendment arguments for a "hands-off" policy are concerned, the tradition of establishing special legal sanctuaries for children has precedents that go back to the founding of the Republic.[5] The FCC's antagonisms to regulation of any kind and the agency's corollary dictums about the righting influence of marketplace forces must still acknowledge reality.[6] And reality shows us, in the most unambiguous way possible, that children are not being served equitably, as they deserve to be, by suppliers in the marketplace of broadcast television. This is why exceptions to our current deregulatory policies are needed.

We saw in the last chapter that when television first started proliferating in the suburban homes of postwar America, the networks offered a strong children's schedule.[7] In fact, they offered many excellent programs for both children and adults. During that period, from 1946 until around the time of Eisenhower's first election, the networks did everything they could to encourage consumers to buy TV sets. But eventually the growth rate of TV sales would have to start flattening out. And when it did, TV set buyers would no longer be the prime target. Now it was the turn of a new group to be given priority: the advertisers. Good taste, public service, and educational programming were becoming luxuries which the networks found themselves ever less eager to promote.

As a result, there were many bad and offensive programs aimed at children during the late 1950s and 1960s. They were bad on many counts; indeed, excessive violence, stereotypical (if not outright racist) portraiture, and exploitative advertising were merely the most visible offenders.[8] By the late 1960s, abuses had become so flagrant that a number of parents and educators banded together to form citizens' action groups in an effort to control, or at least slow down, the tidal wave that washed over children every Saturday morning. Most noteworthy of these groups was the Boston-based coalition of concerned parents that called itself Action for Children's Television. ACT was founded in 1968, and dedicated itself to pressuring stations, the networks, and the FCC to make improvements.

Slowly, some of the offensive practices were curbed. Violence in children's programming was diminished.[9] By industry self-regulation, hosts were no longer permitted to hawk merchandise in a way that made the commercials indistinguishable from the regular program content. Blacks, women, and Hispanics, while seldom represented as three-dimensional characters, were at least no longer simply the worst of the old stereotypical encrustations.[10]

In 1970, ACT lodged a protest with the FCC citing the commercial TV broadcasters both for their lapses in providing an adequate children's program offering and for their abuses in advertising directed to children, and calling for regulated reforms.[11] The FCC took up ACT's protest as a formal petition, and after much study and many hearings issued its landmark 1974 "Children's Television Report and

Policy Statement."[12] The Policy Statement left no room for ambiguity about the obligations broadcasters have to children. The responsibility broadcasters have to children and to the American public as a whole is the public interest standard as set forth in the U.S. Broadcasting Act of 1934. The language of the Act is broad: it charges the FCC to license each broadcaster to program "in the public interest, convenience, and necessity." As ACT president Peggy Charren has said: "These seven words are the hook upon which ACT hangs its entire program for change; without the public interest standard, Americans would lose their best legal argument for a responsible children's television service."[13]

The Policy Statement acknowledged the special status of children, and broadcasters' unique obligation to them. It noted children's need to be educated and television's value as a means to help meet this need. It described two specific problems—and suggested solutions to both. On advertising, the FCC favored full compliance with the industry's own limits on the number of commercials in children's programs, and elimination of host selling and its subtle variants by which television characters exploit children's allegiance to them to sell products. On programming, the FCC suggested that there should be a larger schedule of children's programs, including ones designed to educate and inform rather than just entertain. It also suggested scheduling improvements so that children's programs would not be shown only in the early morning television "graveyards." Both sets of guidelines were voluntary, but the FCC warned broadcasters that if they were not implemented the FCC would reconsider its options, including direct regulation.[14]

The FCC's statement left no room for ambiguity about the obligations broadcasters have to children. It stated clearly: *"We believe that they [broadcasters] clearly do have such a responsibility."*

The statement goes on to outline the specific areas of broadcasters' responsibilities, as viewed by the FCC. It is worth quoting at some length:[15]

"As we have long recognized, broadcasters have a duty to serve all substantial groups in their communities, and children obviously represent such a group.

"Moreover, because of their immaturity and their special needs, children require programming designed specifically for them.

"Accordingly, we expect television broadcasters, as trustees of a valuable public resource, to develop and present programs which will serve the unique needs of the child audience. Children, like adults, have a variety of different needs and interests. Most children, however, lack the experiences and intellectual sophistication to enjoy or benefit from much of the non-entertainment material broadcast for the general public.

"We believe, therefore, that the broadcaster's public service obligation includes a responsibility to provide diversified programming designed to meet the varied needs and interests of the child audience.

"In this regard, educational or informational programming for children is of particular importance. It seems to us that the use of television to further the educational and cultural development of America's children bears a direct relationship to the licensee's obligations under the Communications Act to operate in the 'public interest.' "

The 1974 Policy Statement, therefore, was a clearly articulated delineation of broadcasters' responsibilities to children. There was only one thing wrong with it. It bore no relationship whatsoever to reality. While the FCC was busy promulgating the responsibilities and obligations of broadcasters to children, reality was dictating that fewer and fewer of those responsibilities would ever be carried out. There was a clear conflict between what the FCC determined was in the public interest and what the broadcasters were convinced was essential to their well-being.

The commercial TV industry was told in essence in 1974 to self-regulate in the children's area, or face an FCC-imposed requirement. Four years later, in 1978, an FCC task force measured the progress that had been made. The results were issued in a five-volume, detailed 1979 staff report. The report concluded that broadcasters had complied with the advertising guidelines but not with those on programming. The report noted a slight increase in programming, but this was attributed mainly to an increase in the number of independent stations. No increase had occurred in the amounts of educational and informational programming. In defiance of the FCC's threats, the commercial TV industry had decided to stonewall on the children's programming issue.

The FCC had sought voluntary compliance in an effort to forestall the thorny business of deciding on an issue that the commercial broadcasters were prepared to resist with all their considerable resources and on constitutional grounds. What the FCC got for itself instead was a stand-off.

The FCC's response? A prolonged period of inaction, which extended well into the tenure of the new Administration. The FCC simply stuck its head in the sand, as if to pretend the problem did not exist. ACT finally had to appeal to the courts after twelve years to force a decision on what had become the longest-running petition not ruled on in the FCC's forty-nine-year history.

The FCC's attempt to prevail by threat of regulation was never a strong alternative. The inherent weakness of the approach is revealed in the fact that under heat from the FCC in the 1970s the broadcasters instituted a code to guide practices in advertising to children, only to rescind the code and absolve themselves of its restrictions in the 1980s, when Mark Fowler and his fellow deregulators took over at the FCC.

When the Commission finally did rule in 1983 to deny ACT's petition, the wide public outcry that might have been heard in another time was muted, as this one small issue became lost in the deluge of news about the Administration's wide-ranging deregulatory policies. Within the great tide of deregulation, the FCC's ruling on children's television was hardly more than a glass of water in the face. When major businesses both inside and outside the communications field were being restructured in fundamental ways, the kids didn't stand a chance. More than a decade of foot-dragging had paid off for the TV industry, as deregulation became the new trend of our time.

If there were ever a doubt about the commercial broadcasters' position in the matter of children's television, that question, at least, has been put to rest. They have shown that they will take a hard line and maintain an unpopular, adversarial stance to protect the extra profits they realize by programming for adults instead of children. The broadcast industry perhaps experienced some degree of threat in the late 1970s, because it hedged its position at that time by providing a token offering of clearly education-oriented, "pro-social" programs for children (the name coined at around that time to describe programs which are geared to children's social and emotional adjustment). But the networks promptly dropped most of the programs in their already sparse offering of informational and educational features in anticipation of or soon after the FCC's 1983 ruling.[16]

It was December 22, 1983, when the Federal Communications Commission formally ratified its indifference to children's interests and ruled that broadcasters would have no imposed obligation whatsoever to schedule weekday program time for the child audience.[17] Scrooge himself could not have come up with a nastier Christmas present.

The FCC's Report and Order in the matter reiterated the special obligation broadcasters have to program for children, but left it to the broadcasters themselves to interpret the specifics of that obligation.

The commercial broadcasters' position was inevitable. It was, and is, systemically rooted. It is not the result of some nefarious conspiracy on the part of greedy-minded robber barons, nor of any per se effort on anybody's part to deprive children. The actions of the industry's executives are driven by the desires of faceless stockholders, who expect them to show the best possible profits. The situation continued to deteriorate because economic realities would not permit any improvement from within, and because the FCC had neither the power nor the political will to enforce any of its own recommendations.

While Congress Stalls, the Hot Potato Cools

The issue is not closed yet. The principal remedy proposed in the ACT petition was to require that each commercial station set aside a minimum of one and a half hours each weekday for children's informational and educational programming. By denying ACT's petition, the FCC effectively tossed the problem into the hands of Congress, which has the power through legislation to override the Commission's ruling. Congress now has "inherited" all the many thorny issues raised in both the ACT petition and the FCC's ruling on it. Among these are issues which come under the provisions of the First Amendment.

The commission itself has always been split on the question of its authority, under the First Amendment, to promulgate any regulations or suggestions dealing with program content. It is entirely predictable, indeed certain, that one has merely to suggest certain perimeters of content suitable for children to be met by a phalanx of Washington lawyers, all wearing T-shirts emblazoned with "First Amendment" written out in Gothic script.

ACT's petition attempted to confront the First Amendment issue of censorship and control over program *content* by confining its recommendations largely to the area of program *scheduling*. I say "largely" because attached to ACT's proposed hour-and-a-half weekday scheduling requirement is the additional requirement that the programs in this weekday schedule should emphasize information and education in their content. Some of the broadcasters go further to argue that an imposed schedule requirement for children would in itself constitute a form of control over program content.

Whatever action Congress takes, it will set a precedent with even larger implications. A quite real possibility is that the industry will be relieved perpetually of any special responsibility for children. This prospect is a particularly hard one to swallow, when we consider that other countries—Japan and Britain especially, but many others as well—do require broadcasters to fulfill a special responsibility to children while still guaranteeing freedom of expression. It *can* be done, and it has. We in America, however, have not been successful in differentiating between those two entirely separate areas. Consequently, the First Amendment remains the Janus it has always been: our most vital and treasured protection against tyranny, but also our most over-used shield for all kinds of shoddy excuses.

To the FCC's dubious credit, it acknowledged in its denial of the ACT petition that there is a valid claim to be made in behalf of children—that they do deserve to have their own special programs within the overall context of television. I say "dubious" because the agency's assertions as to how an ample provision for children is to come about are easily seen to be grounded on half-truths and empty promises.[18]

The head of the agency, Mark Fowler, decreed that "market forces" alone would determine events in the industry. According to the new doctrine, only direct, free, and totally unregulated competition within the broadcasting industry will ensure the survival of the First Amendment. To reconcile this marketplace approach with the admittedly just demand that children be served, Fowler's and the Commission's answer to ACT and the wider American public argued that we have only to look at the totality of television delivery systems to see that the solution already exists—almost.

Mr. Fowler addressed the issue of children's programming in a speech made at Arizona State University on February 11, 1983. He said, "In advancing a marketplace approach to broadcast regulation, I realize that not every program need can or will be met by commercial broadcasting." He went on to state that the resulting gaps, in children's programming specifically, will be met by cable and cassette—but only if we (a) wait long enough and (b) put into the mix an expanded contribution from public television!

Here, by the chief architect's own admission, then, the alternate forms of video technology upon which the Commission's supply-side logic depends are, in their current state of development, inadequate to the task.

The Commission's 1983 ruling cites the currently scheduled amount of children's PTV programming—in excess of 1200 hours per year— as evidence against the need for a regulated industry requirement. But why did the Commission take no note of the fact that in a typical year, more than 90 percent of this amount consists of programs from previous years played in repeat?[19] When the FCC refused to impose a modest, 390-hour-per-year weekday children's schedule on the commercial television stations, it gave no heed to the fact that no more than around one hundred hours of new children's programming had been produced for the PTV out-of-school children's schedule in any recent year.[20]

The FCC's ruling calls on public television to make up for the industry's lapses in the children's area. From which sources it will receive the funding to undertake such a responsibility is a question that Mr. Fowler and his fellow Commissioners leave unanswered.

Some legislators do not agree with the FCC's tactic of acknowledging a deficiency and then, in effect, simply turning its back on the matter. A House bill introduced but not voted on in 1983 would have stipulated the minimum amount of children's programming that would meet the special obligation of broadcasters to children. Parallel bills introduced in the House and the Senate in 1984 and again in 1985 and 1986 proposed legislation that would override the FCC and require commercial TV broadcasters to schedule seven hours each week, including, in these earlier versions, an hour each weekday of children's informational and educational programming.[21]

A 1988 version of the bill, incredibly, contains no weekday children's offering. Yet we know that in the near future, more than three million children will be born in the U.S. each year. Quite possibly, they will be deprived tomorrow in the same way their counterparts are today. We shall turn again to consider the need and prospects for a legislated requirement in the final chapter.

In the meantime, how does public television's offering for children relate to the responsibility of commercial TV? To rationalize the "marketplace solution" promulgated in the FCC's 1983 Report and

Order, the Fowler FCC tries to lessen the burden of responsibility on the commercial side by calling attention to what public television does for children.

Lessons from Abroad

Is public television the answer? Do we want to create complementarity between commercial and noncommercial broadcasting? A look at the relationship which exists between the two sectors in Great Britain and Japan may provide some helpful insights on this point. If there is a clear and immediately useful lesson to be learned from the Japanese situation, it is that we must *first* make adequate provision to meet children's educational and informational needs elsewhere and, only then, perhaps, allow commercial broadcasters off the hook on these responsibilities.

In Japan, as compared with the U.S., public service and profitability are even more sharply the separate and distinctive functions of public and commercial broadcasting. Public television is better supported in Japan than perhaps in any other country in the world,[22] and partly as a result, no regulatory body exists to compare either with our own FCC or Great Britain's IBA. The commercial stations attempted early on to mount an education service as a profit-making activity, but gave up on the effort when they were unable to make it pay.[23] One of the four nationwide commercial networks which operate in addition to the two nationwide noncommercial networks in Japan calls itself the "family" network. Most of its programs are not vastly different from those found on the other three commercial networks, but the strategy of pitching to a "family" does tend to make sound business sense where five channels (two public and three commercial) are competing for the general audience.

We see the same market phenomenon in the U.S., when in the largest cities, served by the greatest number of channels, one station decides to program to a different audience than the others. This marketing strategy accounts for the occasionally seen weekday children's programs played on the independent (i.e., non-network) commercial TV stations.

The NHK aims the programs on its very strong "first channel" toward a general audience, and dedicates the second largely to educational programming for narrower audience groups. Thus, the

NHK's second channel assumes most of the responsibility for tying television in to the nation's education agenda.

NHK television substantially preceded commercial television, and it is perhaps partly for this reason that attitudes about public service programming on Japan's commercial stations are so relaxed. Another contributing factor may be that all the commercial networks were started by newspaper groups, who were accustomed to operating in a laissez-faire tradition.

Japanese children are well served by the NHK. They receive both in-school instruction programs, and lighter, often broadly informational and educational programming for at-home viewing. The commercial stations schedule mostly cartoon animations for youngsters. No Saturday morning cartoon "ghetto" exists, comparable to our own, for the simple reason that all Japanese children attend school on Saturday forenoons as a part of their standard, five-and-a-half-day-a-week class schedule.

Partly because Japanese children are already so heavily schooled (nearly all school-age children enroll in *jukyu*, or private, after-school tutoring for upwards of two hours each weeknight over and above their five-and-a-half-day school week), and partly because the NHK already provides well for them, a current of public sentiment exists to require of commercial television only that it provide light forms of diversion. Many feel that TV performs a public service by providing escapist fare to help offset the stresses put on many Japanese children by the "education mother." (This is the name by which the Japanese refer to mothers who exercise what is perceived to be an unhealthy amount of zeal in their efforts to push their children along academically.)

Great Britain presents a different pattern. There, as in Japan, they support two public TV channels, and both antedate the appearance of commercial television. They are operated by the BBC which, like the NHK, is supported by a monthly TV-set tax, levied on every household with a television. As reported earlier, the Japanese paid $11.93 and the British $16.14 per capita to support public television in 1985.[24] But because Britain has less than half Japan's population, the BBC receives roughly half the annual levy enjoyed by the NHK.

Both the NHK and the BBC are heavily centralized, which allows them to take advantage of the extraordinary efficiencies which come with targeting for national audiences. Both countries' PTV systems claim to provide adequate regional programming, as well.[25]

Strikingly unlike Japan, however, Britain established commercial television as virtually a mirror image of the BBC. A major factor in delaying commercial television's arrival in Britain had been the widespread repugnance many Britishers felt toward commercialization of television in the U.S. They had grown accustomed to the quality standard set by BBC-TV, with its proud reputation as the world's premiere public service broadcasting organization. The result was to create in Britain a very different form of commercial television, one which, in the words of British TV historian David Glencross, "was set up to anticipate and control what was held to be the unrestrained excesses of commercial television as reported from the U.S.A."[26]

Today, as it has been since the beginning, British commercial television (ITV) is operated—not merely regulated—by the IBA, a quasi-independent agency set up by the British government, which holds commercial television to the same public service obligation that is mandated upon the BBC. But the term "public service" has a different connotation in Britain than in either the U.S. or Japan. Defined initially by the BBC, when it provided the only TV service available, public service embraced the entire spectrum of program varieties, ranging from the most serious to the lightest. This philosophy still shapes the BBC children's schedule, which its managers describe as a "microcosm" of the program forms available to adults. Thus the BBC children's schedule contains a mix of forms, ranging from light (animated cartoons) to the more serious (news, drama, documentary).

By the IBA's requirement the commercial stations must schedule roughly the same amount of program time for children as does the BBC, and these programs must reflect a designated balance of light and serious fare. For 1985, the ITV stations were required to produce and carry each week (in hours:minutes): 7:25 of children's drama and entertainment; 3:31 of children's informative programs; 2:32 of preschool education; and 6:55 of school instructional programs.[27] The IBA has right of prior approval over all children's programs that are to be broadcast on a commercial station.[28] Commercial television is organized on a regional basis, and regional broadcasters have lost their licenses to competing groups for their failure to satisfy the IBA's strict programming requirements.[29] One of the IBA's standards is that nothing may be aired prior to 9:00 p.m. that is inappropriate for child viewing.

It would be misleading to draw too-sharp distinctions in comparing the commercial and noncommercial sides in either Japan or Britain. The point is to describe general tendencies, not to suggest that these are absolutes. With this caveat in mind, the following valid and useful generalizations may be drawn.

Japanese television shows us a model of a largely compensatory relationship between the commercial and noncommercial sides. The NHK carries the mantle of responsibility—and public accountability—for ensuring that television serves the entire range of children's needs. Commercial television in Japan is largely free to function as a hands-off, market-driven, advertiser's vehicle. In the children's area, it carries occasional light entertainment.

By contrast, Britain presents us with a largely duplicative model, in which public service (broadly defined) is incumbent on both sides— as the raison d'être of the one, and as the imposed and enforced mandate of the other.

To summarize further, putting the U.S. into the picture, we see that Japan's children are served well by television. A well-supported system of public TV carries the burden of providing serious fare, both for home viewing and to advance the national education agenda. Commercial television provides light programming for children as an alternative. British youngsters are treated to the entire spectrum of light and serious fare on both the commercial and noncommercial sides. Only the United States leaves children poorly served through both public and commercial TV. The exception is that preschool children are substantially well served in the U.S. on the side of public television.

But this one bright spot is due, not to the effective workings of "the system," but largely to the efforts of independent, outside program funders and producers. Moreover, it is not a stable and in-built function of our major U.S. television institutions but is subject to the ability of special organizations like CTW to come up with most of the new funding year by year.

Our FCC tilted toward a compensatory model in its 1983 decision against a regulated children's schedule, when it called upon public television to provide a part of the overall solution. But is this what we want? It seems to suit Japan. It would seem not to suit the British. Yet, somehow, both countries manage to make available a rich spectrum of choices for their children. Both countries allocate an equitable amount of time on television for children every day, and both of them substantially renew their children's menu from year to year.[30]

Commercial broadcasters in the U.S. provide our children with a weekly dessert feast on Saturday mornings. Meanwhile, PTV tries to provide a balanced diet in everything it offers, but operates hand to mouth on a beggar's budget. Cable currently is stronger in the U.S. than in Japan or Britain, but it is our medium of choice only if we are content to provide sustenance to less than half our child population. And, in any case, U.S. cable companies do not try to provide curriculum-oriented programs tied to our children's highest priority educational needs. Their "education" offering is strictly education with a small "e."

A compensatory model is espoused by Fowler and the FCC in the Commission's 1983 Report and Order on children's television. The order specifies no imposed minimum of children's programs on the commercial side, and says public television should make up the resulting deficiency. This model most closely resembles that of Japan, but with one important difference: Japan first provided well for children on its public television system, and set in place a mechanism in the form of a dedicated annual TV-set tax to ensure that children, along with all the rest of its population, would enjoy an abundance of the benefits television affords. Only later was commercial television allowed to grow up along laissez-faire lines.

Why Should Public TV Take Commercial TV off the Hook?

The FCC's 1983 ruling was totally arbitrary. It took as its implicit premise that children are not adequately served, not even when all the forms—broadcasting, cable, cassette, and videodisc—are thrown together, and came to the conclusion that we should, therefore, rely upon public broadcasting to take up the slack. Starting from the same premise, we can conclude as readily that commercial broadcasting, therefore, should be required to increase its children's provision in the manner proposed by ACT.

The FCC's lone dissenter in its 1983 ruling, Commissioner Henry Rivera, had the following to say on the arbitrariness of the ruling:

> My collegues on the commission believe that the free market is a panacea and will take care of children. But it's fairly clear to almost everybody who ever studied the issue that the marketplace is bad as far as children are concerned. Broadcasters sell audiences to the ad-

vertisers, and children don't buy pantyhose, beer or cars. So a broadcaster given the choice is not going to program for children but for
adults. And that's what happened. Why should children be relegated
to either PBS or independents? Adults aren't. The reason is that children don't have a lobby. They don't have the political muscle to go
up and visit Capitol Hill and say they're not going to stand for it.[31]

Commissioner Rivera found the ruling arbitrary also on two other
grounds: that it lacked an adequate data base for its assertions on
how well the marketplace provides for children, and that it departed
sharply and without proper explanation from the FCC's own prior
position on the children's issue. For more on his views, see Chapter
Seven.

The FCC's course of action would codify public television's role as
a compensatory institution, whose function is to cover for commercial
broadcasting's omissions. The desirability of program diversity for
children is sufficient reason to shun such a compensatory arrangement. But why should the lapses on the commercial side be made up
for at the public's expense, when the public service responsibility of
these broadcasters is the law of the land? Even the FCC's 1983 Report
and Order reiterated the principle that the commercial broadcasters
do have a special obligation to serve children's unique needs.

So we have a case in which both the special need of children and
the special obligation of broadcasters to meet this need are unarguable. All we lack is the will so far to impose compliance upon a
recalcitrant television industry through mechanisms that already
exist—the FCC and Congress.

We don't enforce the public interest standard which is a legal obligation tied to every broadcaster's renewable license; yet I believe
Americans would be outraged if they thought the laws that govern
broadcasting in this country contained no special provision for children—no sanctuary, no requirement of age-appropriate informational
and educational programs, no special television schedule to which
children might repair.

With all due respect for the First Amendment, we nevertheless are
a nation that in its deepest traditions believes in legal sanctuaries for
children—in our child labor laws, in exempting minors from obligations entered into by contract, and in setting up special laws for
non-adults with special juvenile courts to administer them. The special
protections children thus receive include the provision that they be
spared the penalties we mete out to adults for criminal misconduct.

But an FCC in 1983 bent single-mindedly on deregulation never even contemplated a special exception for children. "Maybe sometimes it is that we want Johnny to play baseball," Chairman Fowler once lamely quipped.[32] Okay. Fine. Let's have a provision for that, too. We can only be grateful that that same type of marketplace mentality does not hold sway among all who look after our nation's community libraries.

Fowler's comment in fact plays to our ambivalent feelings about the great amount of time children spend in viewing television. Which is ironic, because that of course is the whole point in looking for a regulated children's provision from commercial television in the first place—to see that more of children's TV viewing time is spent productively.

Certainly, we should not shrink from regulating as a knee-jerk reaction. There is regulation, and there is regulation. Perhaps regulations which allow already profitable industries the protections and privileges to grow fat and lazy at the consumer's expense do deserve to be disassembled. But surely regulation to give children a fair shake on weekday television deserves to be looked upon as a different matter.

The children's television issue in the U.S. crosses two separate and important agendas. The one engages questions of how to manage a public resource when it is licensed over for commercial development and use. The other is very different. It is concerned with how to make full and effective use of television within our larger scheme of providing for children's education. I submit that by pursuing both agendas vigorously, we can bring into existence not a *duplicative* overall system like Britain's, nor a *compensatory* system like Japan's, but a *complementary* program offering, widely diverse in form and content.

The rare best of what we see for children on U.S. commercial TV is equal to the best of the children's programming we see on television screens around the world, as attested to by occasional awards won in worldwide competition. And as I illustrate in an examination of exemplary children's programs in later chapters, the range of subject matter and formats which can be treated with imagination, creativity, and insight is almost limitless. We must, therefore, acknowledge that only by encouraging the widest possible diversity can we hope to realize any kind of high vision in children's programming. The way to foster this diversity is to let commercial and public television each shoulder a share of the responsibility.

Our failure to support the noncommercial side in meeting its share
of the need only makes all the more grievous the fact that the commercial networks—CBS, NBC, ABC, and their affiliates—today air
zero hours of regularly scheduled children's programming each weekday. The little programming that appears on weekend mornings and
as occasional weekday children's "specials" falls within an incredibly
narrow range.

Even mindless cartoons viewed in moderation are not per se bad
for children. Done sensitively, they provide amusement and a harm-
less diversion, and perhaps at times a useful escape from everyday
pressures. The concern comes when there is little diversity, less creativity, and almost no attention paid to the ideal of creating a well-
balanced, regularly scheduled, child-oriented offering.

Children's programs look very different from each other all around
the world, depending on whether they are of the uncompromised
friend-of-the-child variety, which aim to meet children's real needs,
or are of the friend-of-the-merchandiser variety, which too often
exploit and through hyped advertising gull children and mis-educate
them to be cynical of the intentions of the adult world toward them.
Yet not only do Congress and the FCC fail to exact a well-bargained
quid pro quo in behalf of our children but they allow them to be
exploited by refusing to establish a balance of information and educational fare.

The fact that we in the U.S. exact so small a price in return for
U.S. commercial television's use of the public airwaves has been an
important part of the advocates' case not only for regulated reforms
but for other proposed remedies. In the category of "other proposed
remedies" has been the suggestion that each U.S. commercial TV
station be required to choose between the alternatives of scheduling
a well-balanced offering of children's programs at convenient and
appropriate weekday viewing times, or paying to help support the
weekday PTV children's schedule.[33]

If cable and cassettes were *real* supply-side possibilities, they might
be reasons to relax regulatory pressure on the broadcasters. But they
are not. The facts as presented above instead bear out that these
program sources were called upon by the FCC as excuses for its own
inaction.

For parents in the U.S. today, scarcity in the children's television
"marketplace" is not some kind of abstract debating point, but an
everyday reality. There is no equating print publishing with television,

for example, where children's fare is concerned. The need for TV regulation comes, simply, because parents are stuck with a supplier who enjoys a privileged position, and leaves no choice to the public—the legally stipulated owners of the airwaves—but to take what is offered or be without. The time to put right this topsy-turvy arrangement is long overdue. It's too bad we didn't get it right in the first place and keep it going right all along. Neither did the Australians get it right at first. Like us, they took a permissive approach and allowed commercial television to emerge to become a powerful antagonist. But then, recently, they instituted effective reforms. It can be done.[34]

If we truly want to create a rich and varied programming schedule for our children, with quality and diversity as our guiding principles, we should act to improve children's programming from all the available sources: public television, commercial TV, cable, and all of the new technologies—from direct broadcast satellite to videodiscs and videocassettes. Only by committing ourselves to quality all across the spectrum can we truly fulfill the vast potential of television as an enricher of children's lives.

I believe that goal is both worthy and realistic, and that we as a nation ought to commit ourselves to it. I know, however, that we are far from articulating such a commitment at the present time. If past is prologue, then judging by our limited action over the past two decades, the outlook for children's television on public TV is not bright. However much the will, talent, and dedication may be there, the money is not.[35]

The outlook for children's television on the commercial networks is virtually non-existent. Without fair, strong, and consistent pressure from Congress, the networks will never commit the resources or airtime necessary to create more than a scant offering of quality programming for the child audience, scheduled at times that are friendly to the commercial system's needs, not to those of our children. As we have seen in our overview of television systems in Britain and Japan, quality in children's television can be ensured when national policy mandates that broadcasting be *organized and managed* as a public-service activity, with fair and equitable treatment of all audience groups.

Scheduling at convenient times for child viewing, balance between new production and repeats, and programs geared to narrow age groups are all fundamental prerequisites for any "vision of quality."

None of those prerequisites will develop on our networks without strong regulatory pressures, and the United States—alone among advanced industrial nations—has no means of ensuring quality airtime for its young people. The Federal Communications Commission has traditionally been weak and unfocused, even under previous administrations, when the government assumed an activist role. Since the inauguration of President Reagan in 1981, the little FCC pressure which once existed has now evaporated altogether.

American commercial television's "vision of quality" for the child audience turns out to be the snow and static of a non-existent signal. The FCC's "vision of quality" is nothing but a shrug.

4 | *Public Television: A Tug-of-War for Scarce Funds*

Critical to an expanded new phase in children's public television is a stable supply of adequate funding. The public television signal is available to 98 percent of the nation's households, and the PTV stations for the most part are willing hosts. But for reasons to be examined, our PTV service on its own is powerless to take its children's offering beyond the current inadequate start-up phase. It was powerless, on its own, to fund this start-up phase in the first place, and it lacks the financial resources to sustain continued production of even the best of the program series created for its child constituents through the initiatives of outside funding and producing organizations.

A major part of the problem is that, overall, public television in the U.S. is drastically and chronically underfunded. This impoverishment affects all program areas. The U.S. alone among the industrial countries of the world leaves public television reliant on outside groups to fund, directly and individually, substantial numbers of its programs. This external program support is essential life-blood that makes significant PTV programming possible year after year. But it doesn't provide well for children. For instance, contributions to PTV from businesses in fiscal 1987 exceeded $160 million, according to the Corporation for Public Broadcasting, yet only three grants of more than $1 million from the business sector have ever gone to support programs for young children.[1]

The Need to Focus Out-of-School Children's Programs Mainly on Education

The principal outside underwriters of children's PTV programs in recent years have been groups with an interest in education, especially agencies of the federal government and large philanthropic foundations. This mechanism of external initiatives accounts for the fact that the U.S., to a greater extent than any other country in the world, focuses its out-of-school children's PTV schedule on national education priorities.

Japan and most western European states produce two quite distinct types of children's PTV programs. A school television service assumes the burden of educating children in school subjects. This leaves the producers of the out-of-school children's program schedule free to focus on a wide variety of extra-curricular matters. Programs for home viewing frequently are meant only to entertain. At other times, these programs may inform and educate, but only in the broadest sense. It is common, for instance, to see at-home programs which deal with children's social and emotional adjustment, drama and the arts, or popular debating issues. Others treat current events. But it is just as common to see even lighter fare: performances of popular music, reports on sporting events, and arts and crafts demonstrations to spark do-it-at-home activities. Invariably, two separate departments in these countries' public television organizations divide the responsibility for children's school and nonschool programming.

Against this background, we can see why CTW's invention, the children's home-and-school hybrid, is an innovative TV form, unique in the entire world. Of the home-and-school hybrid it can be said that necessity was the mother of the invention. The hybrid makes sense because we lack an adequate PTV offering in school and out of school, and because the hybrid variety works well in both settings at the same time. CTW's example shows how public television here and around the world can economize, at least some of the time, by serving school and home with the same programs.

The home-and-school hybrid cannot answer all programming needs in these two settings, but it has worked repeatedly in the U.S., and to a greater extent than anybody anticipated. Our best-known examples are *The Electric Company*, with its emphasis on reading skills, *3-2-1 Contact*, which teaches about science and technology, and *Square One TV*, which introduces mathematics. *The Electric Com-*

pany as the first of the genre set a formidable standard for its successors to live up to. It was viewed for many years on a regular basis in schools by an estimated three million children, while another three million viewed it after school in their homes. The series quickly became the most-used TV series in our nation's schools, and it sustained this distinction for many years; moreover, it did so well beyond the time in 1976 when it was no longer renewed on an annual basis. This was a remarkable achievement in itself. But perhaps most extraordinary is that at the same time the series performed successfully in the at-home setting in competition with popular forms of commercial TV programming.

In producing these and other like series, the U.S. acquired an invaluable legacy of experience in methods of program planning and pretesting. The larger legacy includes, in addition to these state-of-art advances in planning and research, high credibility among parents and educators.

Looking at our past successes in fundraising for these children's PTV programs, it is important to ask why, in spite of the clearly established need and opportunity, the U.S. has not created a policy to fund more.

The Need to Fund Children's Out-of-School Education Programs Independently

A part of the problem is systemic with public television, rooted in the competition for scarce resources which tends to stifle efforts from within the field to develop narrowly defined areas of programming excellence.

The next solid step forward must be to go beyond creating occasional programs to build up a comprehensive PTV children's out-of-school schedule. But the only way this can come about is to allow the growth of the children's service to surge ahead of that in other worthy PTV program categories. If this cannot happen—if the children's schedule on PTV must be restrained by tying its fortunes to the slow and uncertain growth of public television overall in this country—we will remain stuck for the remainder of this century and beyond in what already has been a far-too-prolonged early proving phase.

We could look to public television itself to allocate a greater share of its resources for children, and I will argue later that we should. But the best the field can contribute on its own, with its limited financial means, is not very much more than it does now.

The answer is to look beyond the institutions of public television to see how outside advocacy and funding might contribute to creating a substantially improved PTV children's offering. This undertaking is hampered by countless forces, which range from the way we value children to sensitive organizational issues in public television. Some are relatively easy to see; many defy our efforts to measure their influence. For example, how do we assess the extent and effect of apathy toward public television, caused by our false impression in this country that commercial television broadcasting comes for free? Or how much of our crisis of neglect can be traced to our attitudes as a society toward children and their upbringing?

CTW's president and cofounder, Joan Cooney, believes parents in America just do not care enough about their children. A sobering thought. If they did, she feels, they would demand and receive much more for them from television. Her partner in founding CTW, Lloyd Morrisett, chides the government for its shortsightedness in failing to build on its own cost-effective educational successes in children's out-of-school television. Morrisett's point affirms that one goal in improving children's public television can be to advance the nation's education agenda. In other words, this goal need not be advanced exclusively on grounds per se of increased funding for public television.

Another factor, I believe, is the absence of a concrete proposal by which to spark a national dialogue, to help concerned parents and other advocates and policy makers become better informed and more clearly focused in their support. There is a critical need to engage the participation of educators, journalists, lawmakers, corporate and foundation decision makers, and interested parents, who must understand that without their informed involvement and support, fine quality television for children will come to a dead end.

Each time CTW succeeded during the past twenty years in the ordeal of generating another large pool of dollars from yet another consortium of backers to create a major children's series, its staff has wondered if it might not be giving genesis to just one more in a soon-to-be-extinct line of dinosaurs. Other children's PTV program producers have fared no better, but, in fact, always worse. This is not the way we should be funding fine children's educational programs. The dollars are undependable and always too few.

To illustrate more clearly the hurdle which future funding represents, it will be useful to set up as a reasonable objective and a point of reference a working idea of the program need in the children's area, and the budget required to meet it. We may then look at the current and potential sources of funding to locate the most promising among them.

A crucial early step is to acknowledge realistically the limited funding role which public television itself can play. A look at the growth and current structure of American public television will show why it is that although the idea makes sense as an activity largely for public television, there exist fundamental obstacles to its emerging principally by and of public television. We begin to appreciate the difficulty of expanding the children's PTV schedule when we realize that the three-hundred-odd stations of public television together support less than a quarter of the PTV children's program offering.[2]

Public television grew to exist at all in this country not as a matter of national policy but because many people and organizations helped to nourish it. In no area more than in children's programming is there a clear need to nurture its capacity to add diversity to the available viewing choices, and to act as a counterbalance to commercial television. Today, no less than at any time in its development, PTV will require major assistance through outside initiatives in planning and funding if we are to see the children's area become a comprehensive center of excellence. Education is the justification for doing so. With our nation's education system in a state of perpetual deficiency,[3] there is a natural marriage to be made, to link the education need and the PTV opportunity.

Public Television's Slow and Tenuous Growth

In the months before the Communications Act of 1934 was approved by Congress, one of the proposals then pending was to allocate 25 percent of the radio spectrum for educational, nonprofit stations. The proposal was defeated, largely because the commercial broadcasters assured Congress that they had plenty of unused space on their stations, and they would be happy to donate significant chunks of their airtime to worthy causes in the public interest.[4] And, for a time, they did. However, there was never any guarantee about reserving that kind of public service airtime beyond its initial period, and as the demand for radio advertising grew, airtime for public service purposes diminished.[5] Its withered remnant can be seen today in the occasional thirty-second Public Service Announcements (PSAs) that radio and TV stations sometimes broadcast.

The issue of "public service" lay dormant until the FCC put a three-and-a-half-year "freeze" on all TV station allocations in late 1948. The growth of television had been so explosive that chaos was developing among competitors for the increasingly lucrative FCC licenses.[6] In 1952, as the freeze was coming to an end, one of President Truman's FCC appointees, Frieda B. Hennock, led a successful campaign to have the Commission set aside 242 channels for educational television.[7] Unfortunately, most of those channels were in the hard-to-tune UHF band.

This allocation was one of the few times the FCC took a bold initiative toward the creation of a public service-oriented broadcasting entity. The political reasons for this action were ingenious. If the scheme worked, and a national network of educational stations came into being, the FCC would look very good. If it did not work, the allocated channels could always be reassigned to commercial licensees. Commercial broadcasters were not unhappy with the arrangement. Two hundred forty-two channels had suddenly been removed from the hands of potential competitors, and were being allocated in a way that did not constitute any kind of threat to the networks.

Important as this accomplishment was, no method of funding the educational system that had just been created was anywhere in sight. Public television was born with the right to a spot in the broadcast spectrum, and nothing more. Commercial television was saved from any kind of responsibility either to its audience or to an educational television network that existed in name only.

In point of fact, "public television" was not born with that name at all. It grew first to be National Educational Television and its chief sustaining activity for the initial decade and a half—until passage of the Public Television Act of 1967—was to provide instructional programs for schools and colleges in return for program and operating support, which came largely from state and local education agencies.[8]

Both *Sesame Street* and national networking came to public television in the same year, 1969. By the mid-1970s, a combination of government facilities grants, local support to help staff stations and produce classroom instructional programming, and nearly $300 million in grants from the Ford Foundation had created a public television presence which one PTV wag described as "something of a national embarrassment: too small to wield much of an effect and too large to be ignored." Commercial television was being seen in 97 percent of U.S. households, often on multiple channels.[9] A smaller 65 percent had access to public television (although public television, too, now enjoys near total nationwide coverage).

The Ford Foundation's goal had been to help build public broadcasting, and a part of its contribution went to support the first nationwide networking of public television programs in 1969. This opened the way for cost-efficient productions of high quality addressed to national concerns. For the first time, public television could attract serious attention from major program underwriters interested in reaching national audiences. In return for program funding, they could receive on-air institutional credit. For large foundations interested in education, here was a new, cost-efficient means to help them realize their aims.

Before this time, children's programs on public television had been the television counterpart of the one-man band. In each locale, where programs existed at all, they usually were written, acted, and directed by a single individual. The main performer in a typical 1960s production was more likely to be a teacher than a professional actor, and the studio set, more often than not, was a simulated classroom, filled with white children. The scripts were amateurish and frequently delivered in condescending tones.

Children's programming fared much better in the early days of British and Japanese television. Handed a monopoly on television broadcasting, Britain's BBC and Japan's NHK carried forward into their TV programming the same high standard of public service already established for radio. With no commercial competition, these two PTV organizations could substantially shape the expectations their viewers would hold for this popular new medium. In its program offering for children, the BBC's self-avowed aim was, and still is, to "uplift" children's taste.[10]

Large and stable revenues, the cost advantages of centralized national production, and adequate resources with which to build a permanent staff of dedicated children's television producers—all these allowed the BBC and the NHK to create some of the world's most admired children's television programs and to set a standard of public service which we in the U.S. could at first only look upon with envy.

Public television in this country was not created from a vision of quality such as that which inspired Lord Reith in Britain or the founders of the NHK. Its genesis was much more haphazard. Where Great Britain, Japan, Sweden, and many other countries impose yearly taxes on TV sets to support public service television, we in the U.S. long ago passed the point in our broadcast history when we might have instituted a similarly dedicated yearly receiver tax. What we have instead is a disjointed pattern of funding which virtually guarantees that the system is often in conflict with itself.

Overall fiscal year 1987 revenues for public television break down as follows:[11]

	Percent	Amount (*millions*)
State and local governments	22.4	230.5
Corp. for Public Broadcasting	14.3	147.6
Subscribers and auctions	23.7	244.6
Businesses	15.6	160.4
Colleges and universities	9.7	100.4
Federal grants and contracts	3.8	38.8
Foundations	4.0	41.7
All other sources	6.4	66.3
Total:	100%	$1,030.3

Public television today labors under two immense handicaps. First, there is no constant, long-term source of revenue. Every penny that the system raises is obtained on an ad hoc basis, often for just a year at a time, or one series at a time, or even a single hour at a time. Most of its program support comes earmarked for a specific purpose or program. This means that the funders—be they corporations, foundations, or government agencies—exert enormous control over the content in the PTV schedule by deciding which individual programs to sponsor. Each PTV station reserves the right to reject any program.

By contrast, in Britain, one of the cardinal principles of the *commercial* network is that no program can be "sponsored" in any way. All commercials must be in the form of "spot" ads, totally unrelated to and separated from programs.

U.S. public television's second handicap is localism, which is reflected even in public TV's name, although in a fairly subtle way. PBS stands for the Public Broadcasting *Service*, and not, as most viewers believe, the Public Broadcasting *System*. The reason for that is simple: there is no comprehensive system, let alone centralized management over resources and priorities.

The chief organizations in public television today are the Corporation for Public Broadcasting (CPB), a quasi-governmental agency, which channels and manages the federal government's appropriation to the field; the Public Broadcasting Service (PBS), which organizes and transmits nationwide, by satellite, a core schedule of programs; and 258 independent, station-operating organizations. CPB was established by the U.S. Congress and is dominated by presidential appointees. PBS, as a counterbalance, is a membership organization whose board and top staff are drawn largely from the PTV community. Each of the local, station-operating PTV organizations, in addition, is directed by its own autonomous board. These local organizations altogether operate a total of some 319 stations.

The Corporation for Public Broadcasting provides a degree of national-level leadership and coordination. Its limited province includes some power to balance the PTV program offering, to the extent that its small program fund allows. This fund was $37 million in fiscal 1988.[12] Meanwhile, the local stations try to ensure that the interests of their several separate constituencies are served. This is done through the programs these stations produce or purchase, individually, and by pooled purchases of programs through the Station Program Cooperative (SPC), which was set up expressly for this purpose. This cooperative mechanism has helped to make possible some of public television's most effective and memorable program offerings. At the same time, however, localism burdens the field and contributes to inefficiencies that have no counterpart in the more centralized systems of public television found in most other countries.

Public Television's Rootedness in Localism

The majority of noncommercial stations have priorities quite divorced from any production philosophy. They are preoccupied with acquiring program material at the lowest possible cost to serve their constituencies in the best way possible with scarce resources.

On the other hand, the major production centers—stations such as WNET–13 in New York, WGBH–2 in Boston, and WQED–12 in Pittsburgh—compete, each striving to attract as much program funding to itself as possible. This creates a certain amount of healthy rivalry among the big stations, but it also tends to make for a division of needs between the handful of major stations and the bulk of the system's licensees. Making the system even more complicated is the fact that the individual licensees fall into three entirely distinct classes:

1. stations licensed to a state or community agency;

2. stations affiliated with a college or university; and

3. stations licensed to operate as separate, nonprofit foundations.

The most visible stations within the system, those that operate as national production centers, all belong to the third category. However, the most numerous are those which belong to the first and second categories.

The two national entities, PBS and CPB—both headquartered in the Washington, D.C., area—are strictly limited in how they can influence the program schedule or the allocation of revenues. These national bodies further dilute centralized authority between their often-conflicting provinces. Further yet, the stations cooperate in acquiring programs within large regions of the country through four intermediate-level organizations.

This fragmented system of public television is much more expensive to maintain than one organized according to more rational and controllable objectives. As a result, we receive less for our money than we could be getting with a stronger balance of centralized management.

To see that is so, let us compare the annual budget and output of public TV with the corresponding figures of the BBC. In 1985, the BBC operating budget was $903.9 million. For that figure, British viewers got two nationwide television channels, three radio networks, one of the most respected comprehensive news organizations in the world, a shortwave service, and a host of ancillary publishing and educational products. More than 85 percent of the BBC product was domestically produced.

By contrast, our public broadcasting system had total 1985 revenues of nearly $1.1 billion—21 percent more than the BBC's. Yet, our system consists only of one national PTV network, one radio network (which reached less than 60 percent of our population), no shortwave service, and insignificant ancillary services. A comparatively large proportion of mainstay programs continues to be imported—especially the high-quality ones shown during prime time—and comparatively few domestically produced public television shows are sold as widely abroad.

The reason for the disparity between British productivity and our own is not hard to find. American public television never had the benefit of the kind of comprehensive vision and national commitment that attended the birth of the BBC, and that of many other national broadcasting services.

Our public television grew up fragmented, localized, and chronically underfunded because that is the only way that it could exist at all. In the absence of any comprehensive framework, or any broader national commitment to a "vision of quality"—and in the face of strong competition from advertiser-supported commercial television—it is a tribute to the dedication of public television's work force and supporters that it functions as well as it does.

The saddest irony here is that, despite television's $887 million share of all 1985 public broadcasting revenues, our public television system is drastically and chronically underfunded. More important, it is undependably funded, and funded in such a way that successes can rarely be repeated, while inefficiencies perpetuate themselves. This is the highest price of our piecemeal, ad hoc funding dilemma. The disproportionately large number of administrative personnel compared with the numbers of people actually engaged in program production would simply make no sense to anyone who had worked outside the American public television system. That disproportion traps managers and employees alike, creating cost structures that actually work against the system.

Our large population base makes us an ideal candidate for the management of a truly cost-efficient public television system, one that produces programs with all the diversity and quality that our nation can abundantly supply. The $887 million that public television cost in 1985 may seem high, especially when compared with what that money could buy were it more efficiently deployed. But it is still very little when one considers that most other advanced countries enjoy such a degree of public trust in their broadcasting systems that their citizens willingly pay a much higher per capita cost to support them. That public trust could be built because narrowly commercial television interests were not yet around and entrenched when public broadcasting started.

The following figures show the small per capita amount we pay to support public television, compared with other industrial countries:

	U.S.A.	Britain	Japan
Population	239	56	120
Public broadcasting revenues	$1,096	$904	$1,420

(All figures in millions, for 1985. Funding shown in U.S. dollars.)

This translates into per capita support as follows:

	U.S.A. (PTV)	Britain (BBC)	Japan (NHK)
Per capita support	$4.58	$16.14	$11.83

The meaning of these figures is very clear. For each American, our Public Broadcasting Service receives support of 1.25 pennies a day. British per capita support is three and a half times as great as ours, and Japan's, more than two and a half times our own. Indeed, if we supported public broadcasting at the same per capita rate as the Japanese, the amount generated would be more than 2.8 *billion* dollars—about as much money as the U.S. commercial TV industry earned in profits in 1985.[13]

There is nothing wrong with high profits for the networks. As a matter of fact, the Japanese have a dual broadcasting system in which commercial broadcasters are not tied to any substantial public service obligation and are free to earn even higher profits than their American counterparts. This happens because Japanese TV and radio stations have much higher concentrations of viewers than do their U.S. counterparts—1.25 million people for every TV station in Japan, as opposed to 350,000 for the U.S. The disproportion in radio broadcasting is even higher; 2.2 million Japanese for every radio station, as against only 30,000 Americans.[14] But at the same time, the NHK, Japan's public TV system, enjoys a level of public support and program diversity unsurpassed in the world.

What Is Needed for Children

The dollar amount required to build up and sustain a minimally adequate, research-based children's public service offering I hold to be approximately $65 million per year. This is a very modest target amount. The detailed rationale for this figure appears in Chapter

Seven. Three key factors in the rationale for this amount should be mentioned here, however. An underlying consideration is that with educational programming, it is necessary to provide a substantially renewed offering each year for each of three child age groups—including 2- to 5-year-olds, 6- to 9-year-olds and 10- to 13-year-olds. In this way, as children grow up, they encounter graded levels of subject-matter content, in keeping with their developing interests and understandings and their changing educational needs.

Two other key factors in arriving at the $65 million figure are the amount of schedule time to be filled and the amount of scheduling repetition children will benefit from educationally, or tolerate before switching channels.

To provide each of three child age groups with an hour of programming each day, 260 days a year, requires 780 schedule hours. Currently, we produce for PTV, on an undependable average, fewer than 100 hours.[15] Fortunately, we do not have to produce a full 780 hours a year to fill a 780-hour schedule. In fact, if we produce a fourth of that volume, or just under 200 hours a year—which is a little more than double our current output—and if most of this programming is of high enough quality to be used in subsequent years, to teach new "generations" of children, we can quickly build up a splendid, largely re-usable children's offering. We would still have a heavy rate of repeats, but not half as heavy as currently exists.

The $65 million-per-year budget requirement is an extraordinary educational bargain at just six-tenths of a cent per day (calculated on a 260-day year) for each of the 42 million children who range in age from two through thirteen years in the U.S.

We need more program hours, and dollars to produce them. Yet currently, nowhere is there an organized forum for wide public dialogue out of which to mold a national policy on educating children through television, including ideas on a structure by which to implement the activity. Somebody has to say how and by whom the entire enterprise is to be managed, to ensure a proper regard for priorities, efficiencies, and public accountability. It is clear that only by framing a national policy in children's television can we expect the requisite funding to be forthcoming.

Why Public Television Can't Afford It

An important limitation in PTV's funding role is the magnitude of the cost involved in mounting a minimally adequate children's schedule. The $65 million needed annually compares to the following in the current pattern of PTV spending:

- It is nearly twice the approximate amount of $35 million spent in 1985 by the stations themselves, through their Station Program Cooperative, to support all categories of programs in the national program schedule.[16]

- It is more than double the undependable $28.7 million amount which came from all sources in 1985 to support program production for the national PTV children's out-of-school program line-up.[17]

- It is nearly four times the approximate and undependable $13 to $14 million allocated in 1985 from within public television to support the national children's schedule.

It is inconceivable, in light of the above figures, that public television will dedicate the next $40 million of general funding it raises to support the children's schedule—or for that matter, half of the next $80 million it raises. Yet something at least close to this level of funding support is needed if our minimally adequate, hypothetical children's schedule is to be realized. A second part of the problem lies in the competition which exists within public TV for scarce resources.

This competition works against the possibility that, by the system's own efforts, funding for any one program or audience area will be allowed to surge ahead of that for others. The result is an incapacity to single out children's television, to allow it to thrive, and, more than that, to help it emerge among all program categories as an outstanding center of excellence.

PTV can contribute importantly toward a greatly improved children's offering in a variety of essential ways, but cannot—and should not—assume the sole advocacy role. One unwelcome result, should it attempt to do so, could be to generate pressure for the system to set rigid internal program funding quotas in the diverse program categories.

Inescapably, a great part of the initiative force required to develop a $65 million-per-year expenditure in the children's program category will have to come from outside public television. Where concentrations of excellent PTV programming have emerged in the past, they have been the result of external funding initiatives. For instance, the chief programming interest of the Ford Foundation, under former CBS news head Fred Friendly's guiding hand, was news and public affairs. The approximate amount of $300 million spent by the Ford Foundation represents the largest infusion of PTV funding from a single private source to date.[18] Another excellent recent example is the Annenberg/CPB project, through which $150 million in private philanthropy currently is being given in fifteen equal installments, by a single foundation, exclusively to support adult learning through the electronic media.[19] The Corporation for Public Broadcasting was chosen after the fact to administer this activity; CPB never could have risen above the leveling influence of the field's competing priorities to single out this one program area, a priori, as the target for a $150-million fundraising campaign—nor should it have.

There are many precedents in addition to the Ford and Annenberg examples already mentioned. For instance, oil companies have contributed hundreds of millions of dollars to support quality adult PTV programming.

Another example, less well known on the home screen but nonetheless important, is the large number of children's classroom TV series created through the independent Agency for Instructional Technology. AIT succeeded time and again at the remarkably complex task of generating up-front support for several classroom TV series by organizing nationwide consortia of state and local education agencies.[20]

The Children's Television Workshop has acted from outside PTV as the leading force in generating funds to support children's home-and-school programming. Only a fraction of these funds likely would have been available in the absence of CTW's efforts to locate and attract them to the field.

What Public Television Can Do to Help

Public television has a wide-ranging agenda to support, and it contributes importantly to children simply by scheduling and transmitting the children's out-of-school line-up. Even so, for our hypothetical children's schedule to become a reality, PTV must be willing to play more than the role of passive host. For example, the stations themselves could work to increase their own capacity to produce programs for the national children's schedule. Another alternative is to muster an increased contribution of program funding to help support outside initiatives. This increased commitment is important not only to give the field a say in its own destiny but also because a comprehensive children's schedule cannot come into being without support from every funding source with the interest and ability to contribute.

Just as CPB plays a vital role through its program fund in helping launch new children's initiatives, the stations play an important complementary role as one of the very few sources of follow-up funds to help keep already-proven successes on the air. CPB's 1985 Annual Report expresses that agency's belief that "educating our children is the most important thing television can do"; it cites its renewed dedication to support children's television for home and school use as its top priority; and it reports dollar commitments in this category of $6 million, $8 million, and $10 million, respectively, for fiscal years 1984, 1985, and 1986. This amount is divided between classroom and out-of-school programs. CPB's total 1985 program expenditure for all program categories was $29.3 million.[21]

The stations of public television help to support the national children's out-of-school TV schedule through their Station Program Cooperative (SPC) fund. Yet, considering that nearly all of the pooled station support for the national program schedule is channeled through this fund, the fund is regrettably modest. The total SPC expenditure for all program categories in 1985 was only $35.2 million; the amount allocated to support the national out-of-school children's schedule, a mere $6.65 million. A positive but modest recent development is that the SPC fund has shown good growth in recent years, following several years of 1 to 2 percent growth. These efforts by CPB and the SPC are important functions to be continued in the future.

We should seek for preferential treatment for children from public television to compensate for the current, overwhelmingly pro-adult bias in the contributions which corporations and foundations make to PTV. A practical rationale exists, also, from the PTV stations' own self-interested point of view, since a strong children's schedule is important in attracting the public's goodwill and continuing voluntary financial support. Children aged two through thirteen, taken along with their parents and grandparents, make up nearly half of the country's total population. When parents contribute to public

Table 2. Households Watching PBS in a Typical One-Week Period

Program Category	Estimated Number of Households Reached Once or More[a] (*millions*)
All programs	49.5
Children's programs[b]	15.9
Adult science	14.5
News and public affairs	12.3
Adult drama	8.8
How-to	7.4
Adult telecourses	1.4

[a]*Source:* A.C. Nielsen and PBS Research. The figures given are averages of 10 weekly measurements taken between October 1985 and August 1986, except for adult telecourses, for which category only five measurements were taken.

[b]WonderWorks is counted twice—both under Children's Programs and Adult Drama.

television the entire system is strengthened. The more attractive the children's schedule, the more likely young families are to develop early what may become a life-long habit of voluntary giving to help support PTV.

On the strength of viewing numbers, children are already PTV's most loyal, although far from its best served, viewing audience. The disproportionately large representation of children within the total PTV audience is clear in Table 2.

For the ten weekly rating periods included in the survey, the average number of households tuning to a PTV children's series is estimated at 15.9 million. Although children ages two through thirteen are only one-sixth as numerous in the general population as adults, the average weekly viewership for children's programs exceeds that for any adult program category.

Perhaps it is figures like these that have encouraged some in public broadcasting to assert, as I have heard them do, that children are PTV's one substantially well-served audience group. Yet, while programs for preschoolers are well represented in the PTV broadcast schedule, parents of elementary school-age children today will search in vain for as much as one hour of new age-appropriate PTV programming each week, on a year-round average, to expand their children's horizons. The 6- to 9-year-olds are an almost-forgotten group.

Meeting the Unmet Balance

CPB and the Station Program Cooperative are the two key sources of children's program funds in public television. Today, in combination, they provide about a quarter of the amount needed to support a $65 million-per-year funding level. They should do more, but most of the unmet $50 million must come from outside sources.

To develop this outside funding will require a major new approach. The funding pattern of the past is not one which simply can be extrapolated in its present form to meet a larger challenge, not even when the justification is to help serve a wider range of children's highest priority education needs.

A capsule funding history of CTW programs will help to illustrate the problem. CTW is an independent supplier of programs—mostly children's—for both public and commercial broadcasting. The Workshop's first creation, *Sesame Street*, received half its initial funding from a group of federal agencies, led by what then was called the U.S. Office of Education (now the Department of Education), and the other half from a combination of foundations, the Carnegie Corporation and the Ford Foundation, and the Corporation for Public Broadcasting. This series continues to be renewed each year, at a current annual cost in 1985 of nearly $10.3 million, but none among the original consortium of backers still contributes. One consortium group had to be assembled to launch the series and support it through its start-up years, and another to continue it in yearly renewals after that.

In 1985, 70 percent of *Sesame Street*'s nearly $10.3 million annual cost of renewal is borne by CTW, out of its own self-generated income, and the remainder by the stations in public television, through their national program fund, the Station Program Cooperative. The $10.3 million required that year to support *Sesame Street* represents more than a third of the total (largely undependable) amount spent that year on PTV children's series.[22]

A special problem in funding PTV children's programs is the unwillingness, or, often, inability of most of the currently contributing organizations to provide long-term support for a series beyond a few start-up years. Another type of hurdle lies in the fact that for each CTW series, a consortium of public and private backers had to be convinced, individually, to divert funds into television which, but for a well-argued series concept and carefully organized production plan, would have been directed to other educational uses—or, in the case of private corporations, to other public relations uses.

If we could find the formula that would allow other children's series to match *Sesame Street*'s success in spawning revenue-generating products as a dependable mechanism of self-support, much of our funding problem would be solved. But this part of the *Sesame Street* success story appears to defy duplication. Or, at least, no other educational series so far has been able to duplicate the phenomenon.

Most foundations find television's budgets overwhelmingly large in light of the limited amounts of money they have to spend. Foundations nearly always follow one of two funding strategies. Either they will fund activities which have a finite lifespan, because they meet some short-term crisis; or, to deal with areas of continuing need, they will contribute to help launch organizations which have a chance to become self-sustaining after a limited start-up period. Most U.S. foundations are careful to avoid involvement in highly specific activities which obligate them to provide follow-up funding over a long period. Their pattern in funding children's television is no exception. Consistent with this philosophy and approach, foundations sometimes will help to start a new children's PTV series, but cannot be counted on to provide the follow-up funding that is needed to keep a successful series in production over the longer term.[23]

Corporations cannot be counted on to give funds to support children's PTV programs. But when they do—and the ones which have can be numbered, literally, on one hand—most achieve the goodwill they seek in one or two years of initial funding.[24]

The agenda underlying past contributions by foundations to the children's PTV area has been education. Their aim has not been per se to help strengthen the children's PTV line-up. To illustrate, neither Ford nor Carnegie conditioned its funding for *Sesame Street* or *The Electric Company* on the distribution of these series through public television. The same is true for the contributions these two series received from government.

The emphasis given here to the home-and-school type of program, catered to national education priorities for children, is not meant to suggest a limitation on program diversity. On the contrary, it is meant to encourage opportunities for greater numbers of different program producers to create more varieties of programs on a wide range of educational (as broadly defined) subjects. Planned education simply happens to be the foremost area in which children's needs coincide with the interests of potential backers.

Planned education is a costly "extra" in children's television, which is one important reason why no other PTV system in the industrialized world gears heavily toward its own national education priorities in shaping its out-of-school children's schedule. Those systems abroad with the resources to create a comprehensive children's line-up prefer instead to serve their children through the less expensive "micro-cosmic" variety of children's programs alluded to in earlier chapters.

The focus on planned and tested educational outcomes in series such as *Sesame Street, The Electric Company*, and *3-2-1 Contact* came about in the U.S. only because organizations outside of public tele-vision—most especially, foundations, federal education agencies, and the U.S. Congress—took an interest in the educational uses of television.

Government's participation in funding these series is part of an overall patchwork of government funding to support PTV program-ming. One committee of Congress oversees the federal appropriation for public television per se, while others vote funds within specific program categories in keeping with their several different agendas. These dedicated funds have been channeled through such agencies as the U.S. Department of Education, the National Science Foun-dation, the U.S. Department of Agriculture, and the two National Endowments, for the Arts and Humanities, among others. In fact, for a time, *Sesame Street* and *The Electric Company* were mentioned specifically in legislation passed by Congress, with the funds admin-istered through the former U.S. Office of Education.[25]

In earmarked government funding for the field lies the greatest hope—indeed, perhaps the only hope—for a substantially expanded children's offering for play on PTV and perhaps other outlets. What I propose will not open the door to federal control over funding for all PTV program categories. We long ago established a dual system of government support for public service television programming, with the total contribution consisting in part of general support for PTV, and the remainder targeted to support specifically designated public or commercial programs. But for my proposal to be activated, we have to anticipate that this type of special government funding will not be triggered by just any kind of appeal: the agenda, I believe, has to be education. And, second, we have to understand that public television cannot be either the chief advocate or the main conduit for this type of special funding. PTV can go to only one federal funding trough, one time a year. It cannot lobby one congressional committee for general funding and at the same time approach several others for special, earmarked funds. This is not a rule foisted on public television by government, but a practice that protects public television's own keen interest in avoiding dedicated allocations directly to CPB by Congress to support specific programs or program categories.

If all this seems excruciatingly baroque, well, that is the nature of our public television system, and such are the penalties because we will not accord it better.

5 | The Prix Jeunesse and a Worldwide Vision of Quality

Adults in the U.S. have almost no opportunity to view outstanding children's programs made in other countries around the world. Yet it is important that parents, educators, and other interested individuals be aware of the variety of proven ways in which television at its best can contribute to children's social, emotional, and intellectual development. If advocacy is to be commensurate with television's potential, what is that potential? One way to explore this question is to review a selection of prize-winning entries from the only worldwide children's television awards festival for out-of-school programs.

Since 1964, a forum has existed for the sole purpose of honoring outstanding children's television programming from all over the world. This is the Prix Jeunesse ("Youth Prize") International organization, headquartered in Munich, Germany. Every two years, children's television producers meet to view and judge the work of their peers. The focus of the Prix Jeunesse is on general programming designed for the at-home audience. The counterpart in television for in-school use is the Japan Prize Contest.[1] The sole purpose of the Prix Jeunesse organization, and the events that it sponsors, is to promote excellence in children's at-home television throughout the world.

The organization's commitment to diversity is apparent from even a casual glance at a list of program winners in any given year. All categories are considered; the best of all categories are honored. Drama, light entertainment, documentary, public affairs, arts, and sciences—in short, any category that would appeal to an intelligent, well-educated adult—is open for exploration as a children's medium. The foundation is insistent on practicing the philosophy that there is no such thing as a single "ideal" children's program—there is only excellence, in all of its many and various manifestations.

An examination of the list of Prix Jeunesse winners since 1964 reveals that those countries in which a commitment to public service is embedded in broadcasting law and practice have a disproportionately large share of first-rate children's programming.[2]

But what is "first-rate" programming? Do any of us have the right to set ourselves up as judges on this issue? Do not expressions like "first- rate" and "excellent" reduce to a question of taste, and is not taste subjective?

I believe that areas of broad agreement are nevertheless possible, and that we can—indeed, must—make the effort to single out and applaud excellence in children's television. In doing this, we are not setting up arbitrary standards of culture or genteel acceptability. Diversion and romantic escape are essential to any child's psychological diet, and often are far better than condescending pedagogical homilies. The aim is not to define excellence once and for all, but to suggest by specific illustrations how limitless is the slate of possibilities admitted by the criterion of wide professional and public acclaim.

Quality Defined as Meeting Children's Diverse Real Needs

A key consideration which inevitably enters into our qualitative judgments has actually very little to do with specific program types, formats, or content. As we gather in a harvest of fine children's programming from around the world, one underlying criterion appears above all others: that quality is defined in terms of the extent to which it meets diverse real needs of children. A good program is not images and sounds coming out of a box. It must exist *through* and *for* its audience. How well can a TV show help a child understand the mysterious world outside—and the equally mysterious world within? And, not to be forgotten, How does it help children to enjoy themselves?

Programs submitted to the Prix Jeunesse as award candidates are ones which clearly do strive to meet real needs of children. A selective review of the winners therefore provides an indication of particular needs which various children's program producers—and the jurists— have perceived to be both worthy and amenable to successful treatment on television. As will be evident, winning entries truly are a varied lot. The search to identify underlying and unifying themes is actually facilitated by the great diversity apparent in national expressions, styles, and content, and in fact it is through this diversity that they become visible.

Children are often depicted in key, initiating roles—teaching a lesson of beauty to a school teacher, facing up to life's inevitable torments and traumas, taking off on wildly imaginative flights of fantasy, discovering compassionate feelings for the less fortunate, expressing pluck and resilience in the face of embarrassments and defeats, or learning to conquer their fear of cold or indifferent adults.

The quest for beauty, the strength to right a wrong, the will to prevail in the name of justice and fair play, the tenacity to remain courageous in the face of obstacles and to persist in making a wonderful dream into reality; to see and respect perspectives which differ from one's own; to take setbacks with equanimity and push ahead again; to take actions that one truly controls and understands; to dream while becoming more aware of reality; to be self-reliant and resourceful; to find one's place among family and friends; to observe well—for pleasure, learning, and understanding; and to become aware that, whatever problem or hurt one may experience, there are others who have known it, shared it, and care about it—all of these are among the values expressed in the Prix Jeunesse award-winning programs over the years.

One has only to express these values to see how rarely they are realized in our own children's programs. Indeed, one of the strongest arguments for quality children's television in this country is that it is needed to serve as an antidote to much of the product currently being aired. Quality programs, of the Prix Jeunesse calibre, would help to counteract some of the harmful and misleading impressions left with children from viewing shows that are created with little or no regard for what children will take away from the viewing experience. Indeed, the explicit aim of creating an antidote to poor-quality children's TV has been behind the production of many Prix Jeunesse winners.

Thoughtfully produced children's programs can also serve to allay the confusion and fear that often result when children watch adult programs. Adult news, for example, is a common source of distressing images and impressions. It is frequently misapprehended, but when it is accurately understood it is often the most upsetting. Kids are not just smaller versions of adults, and news programs which are especially catered to them can educate, and sometimes soothe, as well as inform. Material that will help them cope with upsetting and frightening content can be of special benefit when woven into the structure of a news program for children. But at the same time, children should not be deprived of the opportunity to have access to the news. Ignoring a problem is not the same as solving it.

Finally, one comes to that category of program, still distressingly large, which perpetuates stereotypes of ethnic or occupational groups, or of aged or disabled people.[3] Here, too, Prix Jeunesse-level quality programs are needed as an antidote. George Gerbner, Dean of the Annenberg School of Communications at the University of Pennsylvania, has shown through research that heavy consumers of television tend to accept TV's distorted version of reality as authentic.[4] Children are especially susceptible to this syndrome. Thus, the use of violence as an acceptable solution to conflict becomes first plausible, and finally inevitable—simply because that is how so many situations are resolved on television.

Gerbner's work, and that of other prominent social scientists, has focused much-needed attention on the potentially damaging effect of TV.[5] But social scientists who study the medium's effects on people are telling us with increasing clarity of the many ways which television can also be a positive, healthy factor in children's lives.[6] We see how this can be so when we look at award-winning programs. For example, children often generalize and draw conclusions from a single traumatic event in their lives. But when television focuses on the real needs of children, it gives them the means to broaden their vision, to share feelings and values, and to learn that a single event does not have to color one's whole outlook on life. As a healer, television allows children to experience a broad range of responses to all of life's experiences, whether joyous or troubling. In fact, that is itself a vision of quality: the ability of television to do things that parents and educators sometimes cannot. TV can be a marvelous instrument of compassion, able to meet the vital needs of children in a unique way. And there are times when it can do this better than anything—or anyone—else available in a child's world.

A Selection of Prize-winning Programs

I would like to illustrate this positive function of television by describing a representative sampling of Prix Jeunesse winners and letting the programs speak for themselves. Unfortunately, not only do we Americans produce a relatively minor share of outstanding children's programs ourselves but our youngsters almost never enjoy the chance to see the best foreign children's programs on our own airwaves. Contrast this with the viewing options available in our country for adults, where the finest programs from Britain and other countries have been a staple of public television for more than a decade, and we see yet another indication of how badly represented children's television is in America.

The Prix Jeunesse foundation divides all entries into three broad categories: "story telling," "information," and "music/light entertainment." This is to allow producers the widest possible range in which to explore themes of interest and value to children. And, for over twenty years, that is exactly what they have done.

The first thing that one notices about many of the Prix Jeunesse winners is that they deal with subject matter that would often be thought too grim, too uncomfortable—or simply too honest—for American television. While rich in imagination, these programs do not simply escape into a fantasy world; on the contrary, they are scrupulous about insisting that the world be looked at the way that it really is. For example, in 1978, the BBC Children's Programmes Department won a prize with a half-hour drama called *Michael*. The title character is a part-time truant whose "good" (that is, socially acceptable) behavior is as puzzling as his bad. Why does he avoid help while obviously hungry for contact? Within its compressed action, the play deals with separation, trust, and renewal.

The Dutch program *A Letter from Emmy* is even grimmer. Emmy is a girl who was seriously injured and disfigured in a traffic accident. The program details the lengthy, indeed torturous, process of physical and mental rehabilitation that she goes through. At no time does the program glamorize Emmy's tragedy; indeed, it makes clear at the outset that she will never fully recover. And yet by showing, simply and honestly, how one young person faces up to a terrible and painful event in her life, the show helps all children tap their own inner strength. Although the subject is grim, the treatment is honest, caring, and warm.

Similarly, the Norwegian program *But Glass Birds Can Never Die* treats the themes of death and grief for very young children—even those under the age of five. The narrator, who is himself an old man, talks to children about how all people grow and change and eventually die: if there were no decay, if real birds were made of glass, then there would be no life either.

The imagery of birds was used in a totally different way in a BBC program for slightly older children called *Think Again*, which introduces the concept of flight by examining the physical structure of birds. The program takes its title from the fact that it is designed to stimulate children to "think again" about the world that surrounds them. Each of the six programs in the series encourages children to look at the most ordinary, commonplace objects (a chair, water, milk, a leaf) and see that object with fresh vision—a vision that unlocks some element of truth, or wonderment.

Many programs deal with minority groups, the disabled, or others who could be considered disadvantaged or excluded from mainstream society. The Dutch program *Follow the Trail*, for example, follows the children of foreign laborers in Holland as they return to visit their native countries, such as Morocco, Turkey, Yugoslavia, and Greece. The purpose of these programs is twofold: to give the foreign children a sense of pride, by highlighting their own culture and customs, and to help integrate them into Dutch society by familiarizing Dutch children with their foreign schoolmates' backgrounds.

The British series *Vision On*, which began in 1972 and has been widely co-produced with other European broadcasting organizations, takes this understanding for minorities a giant step further. The program began as an experiment for deaf children—a purely visual presentation, without speech, that would express a wide range of ideas, attitudes, and feelings. The result not only was an outstanding success with deaf children but, because it had music, it quickly built a following among children whose hearing was normal. The strength of this program is threefold: it breaks down all language barriers, it trains children in the critical faculty of visual perception, and it encourages understanding for the deaf.

Understanding and compassion for all members of society is a key theme among Prix Jeunesse winners. The 1974 Swiss program *Claudia, Or: Where is Timbuktu?* deals with the relationship between a boy and his younger sister, who has Down's syndrome. The boy, Danny, goes through various stages of feeling for his abnormal sister, from latent antipathy to hate, before a series of circumstances forces him to confront her condition and its relation to his own life. The film stands as a warning to children against making unwarranted value judgments, and shows that there are certain things that can only be changed through a change within ourselves.

The Japanese program *Kuro Hime* (1968) brings children back into the realm of myth and fantasy. A young god, disguised as a dragon, plays an enchanted flute and protects the peace of the forest and mountain. When evil humans persist in killing the animals, the dragon-god destroys them all except for a young princess. The forest, now peaceful once again, echoes to the sound of the princess's flute.

The use of classical fairytales and myths in children's television today remains underexplored, especially in American television, although we find occasional excellent programs of this type from foreign countries. Our children are more likely to see shallow parodies of these than the originals. Yet Bruno Bettelheim, in his classic study *The Uses of Enchantment*, emphasizes the enormous importance of fairytales as a unifying element in the culture of a people. He maintains that the decay of these myths in our own culture has left important psychological and social needs unfilled in our children, and that the neat "logic" by which we resolve so many of our modern children's stories is artificial and unsatisfying; worse, according to Bettelheim, it weakens some of the most basic bonds by which a society defines itself and creates its own unique unity.

Children define the limits of their identities not only through the slow reshaping and adaptation of archetypal myths but also in their mundane interactions with the everyday world. How does a young child learn to get what he or she wants, for example, while still respecting the needs and wishes of other people? The 1982 Danish series *Mine and Yours* deals with the very complicated issue of ownership and sharing for children aged five to seven. Blending realism and exaggerated fantasies, the program helps young children find the right balance between their own fledgling egos and the outside world.

Books and Television: Their Co-existence in Children's Lives

Many of the Prix Jeunesse-winning programs are built around the complex visual imagery that television has made so much a part of all our lives. Indeed, as mentioned earlier, one program, *Vision On*, uses images only, with no sound at all. These children's programs have done much to expand the visual beauty and complexity of television as a medium, teaching a kind of "visual literacy" to children in the process; yet the question of when to use the television camera as a single, transparent lens and when instead to employ television's unique visual "language" is one which has occupied children's program producers for as long as there has been television—and it continues to do so.

The question first emerged in the medium's earliest years, when people began to worry that television might significantly displace traditionally valued children's activities such as lively play, family discussions, and book reading. The positive contribution television can make had not been well demonstrated, and so was not yet much appreciated as a countervailing consideration.

True to the pattern described by media guru Marshall McLuhan, who lived and wrote during television's formative years, early children's TV programs largely imitated earlier media. Among early Prix Jeunesse winners storytellers appear with only a minimum of props; hosts are shown seated in straight-backed chairs reading from books they hold in their laps; "talking heads" give lectures as a way to teach and demonstrations to encourage hobbies and crafts. These early efforts look primitive by today's standards; yet, they returned to their young viewers some of the valued experiences television was criticized for displacing.

One might believe, following the principles in McLuhan's writings, that the earliest children's programmers simply lacked the imagination to create new and unique television forms. Perhaps some did, but their recourse to children's books and literature has a more complicated basis than that. There was already a rich tradition in children's literature for them to draw upon. Television was just starting. Moreover, the number of program hours which must be produced to fill a year-long schedule is so great, and the programmers' means so limited, there was no possible way to fill all those hours with newly written material and sustain acceptable quality. Add to this what many producers saw to be television's democratizing potential: it could spread the benefits of book reading to the masses; it could strive to elevate all children's reading tastes while expanding reading interests; and it could perhaps help to encourage children who lacked the proper parental models to develop a life-long reading habit.

Today, television's role in relation to children's book reading is beginning to resolve into increasingly clear and productive forms. In the U.S., the *Reading Rainbow* series for elementary school-age children aims mainly to *promote* book reading. It presents "teasers" to spark interest in specific books, and by special arrangement with the nation's booksellers and librarians, these books are made abundantly available. But at other times the aim is simply to build positive associations with books and reading. Ultimately, of course, only reading can spark an innate desire to read, but TV promotional messages nevertheless have proved to be an effective catalyst. The fact that book advertising on commercial television is not economically viable makes book promotion to children as a public service on television all the more necessary and worthwhile.

Programs which focus on the acquisition of reading skills address the more fundamental point that an improvement in children's reading abilities helps to promote independent book reading activity. CTW's reading skills series, *The Electric Company*, is an example. This series pioneered in the use of sophisticated entertainment values to attract and hold a large, voluntary at-home child audience while teaching a basic educational skill.

The U.S. and other countries also have made beginnings—but only beginnings—toward laying up treasure stores of replayable programming based on classical literary (fictional and nonfictional) works of interest to chidren. This is another genre found among Prix Jeunesse prize-winners. But whether these be prize-winners or not, few would say that competently done television renditions of literary classics in any way trivialize or detract from the message of the written originals. And, in fact, just as exposure to fine books can foster selective taste in book reading, so watching TV programs of splendid literary quality ought to create an appetite for more.

Special services exist in some countries that alert subscribing teachers and librarians to upcoming out-of-school television programs, both commercial and noncommercial, which might serendipitously tie in to the school curriculum. Teachers assign viewing of these programs as "homework."

Less common, but interesting just the same, are the several patterns by which combined book-and-television offerings are made available to children. Books may be based on television programs, in which case the programs spark interest in reading the books. Or the pattern may be the reverse. With increasing frequency, a book and corresponding television program are co-released.

These, then, are the emerging pattens. They are strong directions to build upon. The relationship between television and book reading which they reflect is a far cry from that expressed in the sensationalized indictments against TV which one encounters from time to time, mostly in the popular press. We in America are in general very critical of television. We have a tendency at times it seems to become almost hysterical on the subject, and a great deal of nonsense has been uttered on how the tube will be the ruination of us all. Particularly silly in my view has been the notion that children are divided into two classes: a book-reading elite, and the great mass of young people whose minds are being rotted by unhealthy exposure to the electron beam of a cathode-ray tube. A corollary of this notion is that just because too much TV is clearly harmful, the less children see, the better. And if television could somehow be disinvented altogether, that would be better still.

The viewpoint does a disservice to children because it underestimates the enormous benefits that television can bring to children's lives. Television is not the antithesis of reading; on the contrary, used well, it can encourage and instill a life-long love of literature. This is something that other countries have known, and pursued effectively, for years.

Former Librarian of Congress Daniel Boorstin brings the historian's perspective to bear on this by pointing out what he calls "the displacive fallacy of technology." New technologies do not replace old ones, they simply change the environment in which the new and the old co-exist. Television, books, and computers each have useful roles in the dissemination of knowledge.

The Special Nature and Place of Programs Geared to Children

In short, the useful functions which television can serve through children's quality programming can be as diverse and as varied as the programs themselves. When we speak of shaping children's programming as a microcosm of adult programs, it is clear that this means much more than merely preparing scaled-down versions of adult television forms. News can be not only informative but also educational. Drama not only can entertain and delight but, in Aristotelian fashion, can instruct as well. Documentaries can "document" emotional states and the personal resourcefulness of their human subjects, as well as provide plain objective descriptions of physical and social events. And all of these possibilities can be achieved by talented and creative producers while sustaining high levels of technical skill and artistic integrity.

Children's television at its best, as the Prix Jeunesse winners have shown in so many ways, can be very good television indeed. Even so, the Prix Jeunesse's selection process fails to single out and award other valuable contributions which television can make to children. Some of these become apparent when we look at the range of activities carried out as a part of the comprehensive children's television offerings which many countries support. One of these is to acknowledge children who have made outstanding achievements in the performing arts. Lacking a special story angle, a presentation of this type is unlikely to win a television award. Yet special recognition is due children's programming departments that give child artists-in-training prominent television exposure as a reward they can strive for and cherish.

In Turkey, the children's television group not merely gives coverage to but organizes and carries out each year a national children's week, an official state function, as a special tribute to the country's young people. Britain's BBC conducts periodic fundraisers for charity which ask for small money donations to be given by children exclusively. Invariably these mount up to a sizable and genuinely useful sum, which then is given each time to a single cause, for example to help provide food for famine-stricken children in the Third World. The BBC contributes television coverage to vivify for its child audience both the need for the help and the concrete result.

Japan's national public broadcasting organization, NHK, takes special pride in pointing out the well-documented role television played in its early days in stemming the spread of polio among Japanese children, through a public information effort that was mounted as a part of a major governmental immunization campaign.

I alluded earlier to the value of co-releasing books and television programs. This highly desirable type of arrangement has become a well-established tradition with the BBC, which has maintained a rich flow of books in conjunction with *Jackanory*—itself a prime example of "storybook television"—and other programs.

As these examples convey, children's television affords many productive opportunities for synergistic interaction with other activities.

Children studying a particular period in history at school who simultaneously view a television program covering the same era will learn more both from their school lessons and from the television program than if they had engaged only the one or the other in isolation. Television's function in such a partnership might be either to do a broad sweep of the era or to dramatize in specific, human-interest terms how the large forces that shaped the period were played out in the daily lives of individuals.

A look at Prix Jeunesse prize-winners will fail also to register other achievements of children's program departments. There is no acknowledgment, for instance, for departments which give extended coverage to complex subjects through prolonged program series. Why should there not be an award category in which only programs from long-running children's series compete?

Blind spots or other limitations in the Prix Jeunesse award screening process are mentioned not to criticize per se, but to provide a more comprehensive vision of quality.

Another important but neglected category is that of programs which set out to encourage children to engage in post-viewing, follow-up activities. The possibilities are numerous: to encourage drawing, to give lessons on a variety of musical instruments (as has been done in Japan for many years), and to promote instructive hobbies, personal journal-keeping, pen pals, and participation in contests. Other possibilities include various forms of physical exercises, staging a neighborhood dramatic performance, raising plants, and carrying on family discussions on suggested topics.

One successful children's series gives math puzzles which are solved in later episodes. And U.S. public television's splendid *Zoom* series of the 1970s sometimes created entire episodes based on suggestions from its child viewers, incorporating the children themselves when feasible.

These are only a few of television's possibilities for children. There is always room for innovation, but we are well beyond the state of groping to seek an unknown potential, for we have seen that potential realized all around the world in many forms. We have only to harness it, to adapt it to our own needs, our own system—and our own children.

Acknowledgment ought also to be given to the capacity of children's programs to reflect and perpetuate different countries' prominent national values. Britain's emphasis on "storybook television" instills pride in a great literary tradition. Sweden's interest in world affairs and its sense of respect for children of foreign workers come together to sustain a prominent international focus in that country's television offering for children. And Japan, unique among the countries of the world, regularly produces *With Mama*, a television series especially for two-year-olds, ascribing the phenomenon to keen national interest in early education for young children. India and Cameroon, both countries with multiple languages and cultures, say they want to use television to help inculcate youngsters with a sense of national identity and unity.

All in all, there is plenty in these examples and the Prix Jeunesse winners to please the discerning eye. We in America have contributed to a compelling vision at times, but not nearly often enough. But when we have done so, the results have been uniquely our own, and very exciting. There is one Prix Jeunesse winner I remember with particular pleasure.

The year was 1970.

The program was *Sesame Street*.

6 | Sesame Street *and the CTW Vision of Quality*

One has only to say the words "educational television" in order to call forth for most people images of television at its deadliest. Who does not remember those early classroom instruction shows, each virtually indistinguishable from the next, with the camera pointed straight at a lecturer in front of a chalkboard?

To most people, *Sesame Street*'s major contribution is that it broke this image of dull educational TV once and for all. It did, and that is certainly important. But the contribution that the program makes to a vision of quality in children's television goes beyond its famed cleverness and high production values.

In 1969, before *Sesame Street* went on the air, the United States was not highly regarded as a producer of outstanding television programs for children. To be sure, there were occasional flashes of quality—Leonard Bernstein's *Young People's Concerts*, for example— but the bulk of this country's programming for children was inane, dull, insufferably condescending, and totally unrelated to the real needs of children. For the most part, the best one could expect was escapist nonsense; more often than not, what the children got over the air was potentially harmful. Children's television was held in such low esteem that the industry even coined its own pejorative soubriquet for it: "kidvid." And, for the first twenty-five years of television broadcasting in this country, kidvid it remained.

Then, from a clear and timely vision of a need and an opportunity, *Sesame Street* emerged to become a national—and international—

institution. From the very first, *Sesame Street* attracted favorable attention from parents and educators, and instant popularity among children. Both the acclaim and the popularity continue to grow. In 1987–88, its nineteenth anniversary season, *Sesame Street* continues not only as one of the most phenomenally popular television programs ever produced— adult or children's—but also as one of the outstanding success stories in the history of American education. *Sesame Street* reaches viewers of all ages and backgrounds, but among its primary audience—inner-city preschool children from low-income backgrounds—its penetration ranges from 93 to 99 percent.[1]

Sesame Street: *The Right Idea at the Right Time*

Each of CTW's four children's series received its funding as one small part of the nation's response to a newly recognized, urgent, and widely pervasive educational need, or deficiency. In this vein, *Sesame Street* has been described by Joan Cooney and Lloyd Morrisett—the two people who jointly conceived it, and found grants of eight million dollars in 1968 to launch its first season—as "the right idea at the right time."[2] The original proposal for the series illustrates the point.[3] The proposal points up evidence that many children, especially those of the poor, arrive at school ill-equipped by their home circumstances to grow and flourish intellectually in response to the demands of the classroom. This situation is only worsened in view of the finding that, by the age of five, more than half of a child's total, lifetime intellectual capabilities will have been formed.[4] At the time, the cost for buildings and teachers, including teacher training, to meet this important need would exceed $2.5 billion, and, even so, the classroom-based solution could not be made widely available for many years.[5]

In the meantime, television in 1968, the proposal continues, is ubiquitous, reaching into 97 percent of all U.S. households; yet, its overall quality is so poor as to have been characterized by former FCC Chairman Newton Minow as a "vast wasteland." The crux of the proposal is a section which tells how techniques used in TV advertising and entertainment, but untried in education, might be adopted or adapted to attract and teach preschool-age learners.

The vacuum filled by the *Sesame Street* series is even more apparent when seen against the backdrop of the societal events of that decade. The civil rights movement had inspired foundations, federal agencies, and the public at large to seek answers to the social and economic plight of the black minority. The Head Start movement had emerged out of, and further fueled, public awareness and outrage at the inequities in educational opportunity across ethnic groups and socioeconomic levels. Everywhere—in the news, in demonstrations in the streets, in administrative organizations, in Congress and federal agencies, in schools and colleges, and in the workplace—could be seen new concern about the cycle of poverty with its shameful harvest of joblessness, homelessness, and illiteracy, and its denial of job skills and, consequently, of hope. Ears were open in those days as never before or since to proposals for helping to break that cycle, at least in part, through a new emphasis on social programs geared to children.

A children's television series, broadcast nationwide, could reach children not privileged to be sparked to learning through other experiences. It had to appeal to all children, or it would not survive. But for children of low-income circumstances, it would be special— it would provide a conceptually and verbally rich learning experience, and important early exposure to school-related skills, all of which, we know, are less available to them in their homes than to their middle-class peers in theirs.

Ford Foundation grants to help launch public broadcasting were approaching the twenty-year, $300 million mark, at which level they peaked, and were phased out, by 1972. At the same time, two other nationally significant events in children's television were in the making: the advocacy group, Action for Children's Television, was formed, and the original round of research on violence in children's television was launched by the office of the Surgeon General.[6] Clearly, *Sesame Street* might in one stroke help to address an urgent need among preschool children; demonstrate and help to promote an improved standard of quality in children's television; and strengthen and diversify the public broadcasting system.

Add to this the fact that here was a new tool, hardly tried. Television ownership had reached 90 percent of all U.S. households only ten years before. Twenty years before, that number had been scarcely 10 percent.[7]

One after another demonstration of television's scope and impact had caused the nation—and the world—to be aware of its influence and potential powers. The first nationally televised debate among presidential candidates had proved that one evening of prime-time exposure not only could interest unprecedented numbers of individuals in the political process but might make or break a presidential candidate.[8] In 1963, an entire nation sat before their televisions transfixed by the events surrounding the assassination of President John F. Kennedy. The unprecedented role of television, in reassuring a distraught public and in presenting real-time documentation of the ensuing events, was so striking that it became, itself, a subject in the news.

We had witnessed on-the-spot coverage of man's first walk on the moon, and had looked back upon ourselves from a moon's-eye view as a big blue, brown, and white marble hanging "over there" in space.

Telstar I, the world's first geostationary communications satellite, launched in 1962, had only shortly earlier made possible instant international TV news coverage, complete with the astonishing new capacity to intercut in real time between cameras located oceans apart.

Another action of the Ford Foundation, completed in 1969, was to fund the formation of a network, making it possible for the first time to interconnect the stations of public broadcasting. These at that time numbered 130, and through their combined signal coverage, they could reach perhaps 60 percent of the nation's TV households.[9] (This compares with more than 315 stations today, able to reach 98 percent of all TV households.) This networking was the key to outside funding which the PTV community needed. The ability to offer prospective underwriters national exposure and the efficiencies of centralized productions enabled PTV to forge major new opportunities.

The door was open to a marked improvement in programs made for children. *Sesame Street,* and, a short time later, *The Electric Company* and *Zoom,* among others, emerged out of this opportunity. Children's Television Workshop rapidly grew to become the main outside supplier of children's PTV programs. Meanwhile, the PTV community directed its own attentions largely to the priority of creating a strong new evening schedule for adults. National networking gave the field a chance to expand beyond its beginnings in the world of instruction to develop a unique service and role in the home.

Sesame Street's Accomplishments

Different observers, reflecting different priority interests, might disagree on *Sesame Street*'s most significant contribution. As a member of the original team, I believe its chief contribution has been to facilitate the transition from home to school for many "generations" of children aged three through five years, which is, of course, precisely what it sets out to do. Since its inception, *Sesame Street* has treated a range of subject areas, nearly all meant to contribute to one aspect or another of young children's school preparedness. These have ranged from prereading and number skills to constructive forms of social interaction, to simple reasoning and classification, and knowledge about the physical and man-made worlds.

Additions have been made to *Sesame Street*'s curriculum each year, sometimes due to a breakthrough in thinking about how to treat a difficult or sensitive topic and, at other times, reflecting new priorities in preschool education.

The series' now extensive curriculum for and about the disabled is an example of an area which was developed only gradually, having not been represented at all in the earliest seasons. Several different insights helped convince the Workshop it could present disabled individuals on *Sesame Street* without inadvertently doing harm. One was to realize that the physically or mentally disabled could appear on the street without any explicit comment or explanation. CTW had been concerned that if special comments were given, no matter how objective and supportive, preschool viewers might assume that disabling conditions are something bad, which need to be explained or, worse, excused. Subsequent CTW experience confirmed that a useful positive approach in programming for children of this age is to give no explanation at all, but simply to show everybody relating to everybody else, on everyday matters, in warm and simple human terms.

Another breakthrough came in realizing that a major part of *Sesame Street*'s contribution to benefit the disabled could be to encourage the non-disabled members of the audience to give up stereotypes and relate to the disabled in accepting, sensitive, and supportive ways. This insight helped the Workshop to see how, in directly benefiting the disabled, it could provide an indirect learning experience of special value to all children.

A clue to the power of positive portrayals made without any explicit comment was *Sesame Street*'s effectiveness in similar presentations of blacks and whites, on the street, engaged in the simple events of everyday living. The same approach was used later to introduce Spanish language and culture.

Reaching the Audience

With two viewing opportunities a day in most communities of the U.S., *Sesame Street* regularly achieves near-saturation levels of penetration into homes where two- to five-year-olds are available to view it.[10]

The *Sesame Street* audience grew rapidly over the series' initial year on the air, and gradual additional increases were logged over a period of several years after that.[11] Many factors are responsible for these increases. An initial barrier to audience size, quickly overcome, was the absence of any previous, regularly scheduled public television offering for preschoolers. The *Sesame Street* viewing habit had to be built from scratch. Mothers had to help the children find the channel, but first, they themselves had to know about it. Moreover, they had to be willing to adjust their activity schedules around its time of availability; for many, a part of their daily routine consisted of viewing popular daytime programs on competing channels. To give over the *Sesame Street* time period to their preschoolers, mothers and other caretakers would have to like the series and believe in its value for the children.

Efforts were undertaken to publicize the series and its benefits, especially in low-income neighborhoods containing large black and Spanish-speaking populations, and to the disabled. To promote wider and more effective utilization by these groups, CTW created the department of Community Educational Services before *Sesame Street* first went on the air. For more than fifteen years, the many activities of this outreach department were implemented through field offices strategically located around the country.

During one summer alone, it enlisted the participation of 7500 Neighborhood Youth Corps participants in a total of thirty, mostly urban locations. All the participating youths were between 14 and 18 years of age. They were trained first to view along with pre-schoolers, then to provide them with activities aimed at reinforcing the program's educational objectives. Over the years, scores of similarly innovative outreach activities—always linked in to organizations able to pick up, support, and carry on the work—have helped to establish the series' strong and loyal viewership.

Early in the history of the *Sesame Street* series—before it went on the air—the problem arose of how to convince the public television stations to carry it at favorable mid-morning and mid-afternoon times for child viewing. The barrier to this convenient scheduling was the long-standing tradition of instructional service offered by the stations to local schools and colleges in return for needed financial support. When early signs indicated that the stations might not clear the most suitable times, including especially a key morning hour, Joan Cooney began an extensive tour, which took her and a key staff aide all around the country, to explain the educational values being designed into this as yet unknown series, to try to convince groups of station managers and their constituent local school administrators that their support for this investment in preschool education fell properly within their mandate and interests.

They were convinced. By the time of the series' second season, *Sesame Street*'s daily two-play pattern was firmly established. An important reason is the uninterrupted year-round availability of the series. The 130-program format, chosen to allow year-round availability, was pivotal in bringing PTV's after-school children's program block into existence. Today, the time period is a firm, if not yet firmly funded, tradition.

Evaluating the Contribution of Sesame Street

Plans to conduct a major follow-up study to evaluate the teaching impact of *Sesame Street* were an integral part of the initial project proposal. The two questions in the minds of both the backers and the producers were how much this television series could accomplish, and what part of the impact could be measured. Key members of the Workshop's production and research staffs held higher ambitions for the series than we thought it prudent to announce publicly.

One of the country's largest educational measurement groups, the Educational Testing Service (ETS) of Princeton, New Jersey, contracted to conduct a major national evaluation. The results of the ETS study were highly gratifying to the backers and the Workshop. Most encouraging was the finding that significant learning gains were made by the test children in all three target age groups—that is, three-, four-, and five-year-olds— and by children in both middle and lower socioeconomic groups. ETS also found that those who watched more learned more.[12] Moreover, separate, independent studies carried out in the early 1970s on adaptations of *Sesame Street* produced in Mexico, Germany, and Israel confirm that even a brief, six-month exposure to a series in the style of *Sesame Street* can bring about measurable learning gains.[13]

An independent re-analysis of the ETS data later concluded that parental encouragement to view was a significant factor contributing to gains in achievement scores. This analysis, carried out by Dr. Thomas Cook and his associates, found that in comparisons between the two different test groups set up by ETS (one in which parents were asked to encourage viewing, and one in which they were not), the children in the former outperformed those in the latter.[14] A likely factor in this learning advantage, I believe, is that children in the "encouraged" groups may have watched more shows.

The second main question taken up in Cook's analysis of the ETS data is whether or not *Sesame Street* narrows the academic achievement gap between children from middle- and lower-income circumstances. The goal of narrowing this gap is alluded to in the original *Sesame Street* funding proposal; but it was reviewed and reconsidered before the series' first season aired. The consensus of key staff and advisors at the time was that a television series available to all children could not be expected to serve as a vehicle for "compensatory education." This is the name applied to efforts such as Head Start, whose goal is to make education benefits exclusively available to children from lower socioeconomic backgrounds. The series did nevertheless set out right from the beginning to emphasize areas of instruction thought to be of special value to low-income, minority children.

As Joan Cooney frequently and publicly made clear, in statements which predate the appearance of Cook's study, the Workshop's goal through *Sesame Street* and *The Electric Company* is to help ensure that a maximum number of children from all backgrounds achieve the crucial level of literacy required to gain employment and to pursue further study. Nevertheless, the two series make a special effort through portrayals of strong, minority role models to reach out in their appeal to minority children. They do this also through an emphasis on elements of black and Spanish-speaking culture. This is done because members of these ethnic minorities are disproportionately represented in the lower socioeconomic group.

I make these points simply to establish that when Cook *et al.* re-examined the data to see whether *Sesame Street* did or did not narrow the academic achievement gap, it was their goal for the series they were testing, not a goal or a claim by Children's Television Workshop.

Educational Testing Service has a chapter in the Cook *et al.* book which makes this point and reviews the entire complex issue more thoroughly than is possible here. Cook and his colleagues in any case conclude that they lack adequate data to support a position on the narrow-the-gap question.

The evaluation studies done to date are all regrettably but necessarily limited in scope. They show at best only what could be shown of *Sesame Street*'s full impact by tests covering a fraction of the series' carefully stated education objectives, and administered after a limited (less than one year) exposure by viewing children. In fact, the ETS studies assessed the achievement advantage of viewers contrasted with nonviewers after only a six-month period of exposure. Yet, we know from survey data that children grow up watching *Sesame Street* the year around over a period of three to four preschool years—and, indeed, that they continue to be occasional "check in" viewers for several years after that.[15] As a result, the highly encouraging achievement gains found to date quite plausibly may reflect only a small fraction of the series' true contribution to preschool children's social, emotional, and intellectual growth.

Also, results from the A. C. Nielsen television ratings company show that, for the country as a whole, growth in viewership was gradual over those first two years tested by ETS.[16] The anticipated effect of greater viewership in later years would be to increase the series' effectiveness.

A suggestion of *Sesame Street*'s teaching potential when viewed with high regularity in controlled circumstances is provided by a study carried out in Mexico, where children in preschool classrooms were assigned individually, at random, to be either "viewers" or "nonviewers" of *Plaza Sesamo* (the Mexican version of *Sesame Street*) over a six-month broadcast season. Tests were given to both groups, before and after the six-month viewing period. The results showed a significant learning advantage in favor of the viewers over the nonviewers on tests in each of six subject-matter categories. Moreover, viewers outperformed nonviewers on three tests given to see if the viewing children were acquiring certain generalized skills in addition to those which the Mexican producers set out to teach directly.[17]

A second study done by the Mexican research team set out to compare achievement gains for children from middle and lower socioeconomic status. It is inconclusive due to the fact that many parents of the lower socioeconomic children took the children with them to the fields while the show was on the air. As a result, these children viewed an average of fewer than 20 of the 130 programs in the series.

Sesame Street in the U.S. in 1976–77 reached about six million 2- to 5-year-old children in a one-week survey period. If we let that stand for the yearly preschool audience, and count all the preschoolers reached in the years since, that represents some 126 million child-years of at least once-a-week viewing. Anything with the opportunity to affect so many children should be held accountable, and for *Sesame Street* (or any other CTW series) this accountability inevitably goes much farther than merely to show tested outcomes.

CTW's accountability for *Sesame Street* initially consisted of answering to the federal agencies and foundations which supplied its backing. Their representatives were invited to attend all key planning seminars as observers. They received regular reports, and could ask questions at any time. In addition, in the early years, a national advisory committee of about forty prominent individuals met quarterly to review and comment on all aspects of the planning, research, and production.[18] Upon CTW's incorporation, in early 1970, the Workshop's management began to answer in all its affairs directly to a board of trustees which today numbers fourteen members. The public, the press, and the station managers in the PBS system are additional constituency groups to which CTW responds in creating its children's television productions.

The CTW Workstyle and Aims

Among *Sesame Street*'s innovations, one of the most important, I believe, is one that viewers cannot see, one that does not deal with *Sesame Street*'s content, but forms the basis of its philosophy and management.

Until *Sesame Street*, U.S. children's programs were created either by entertainers or by educators. The programs of the former focused on diversion, those of the latter on teaching. It was widely held that these two professions are by nature incompatible, and that any attempts to force a working relationship between them could result only in friction and wasted effort.[19] The Workshop had to test that cliché, and surmount its limitations, or it could never accomplish its goal of linking at-home television to the nation's education agenda.

Sesame Street did not start out as a program about a group of likable people and zany Muppets in an urban neighborhood. It started out as an idea by Joan Cooney that the best educational TV program would also be one that was witty, entertaining, and fun. To translate this idea into a working program concept, the Workshop chose 250 specific and carefully-defined learning goals.[20]

From the outset, the only chance CTW had of reaching those goals—or any goals—was to tie the educational research and the creative writing together. The Workshop was determined not to be just a production factory churning out TV programs, but a research laboratory dedicated to devising and validating methods of teaching children more effectively. Thus it created a management model that would allow the two hitherto segregated groups of writers and re-searchers to work together productively. The steps and procedures involved in this working relationship define the "CTW model," as it has come to be known. The model is emulated by many production centers around the world.

A typical early planning session involves a three-way discussion among producers, researchers, and subject-matter specialists, and aims to create a precise and detailed list of desired educational ob-jectives. These are defined in such a way so that they can later be tested and then measured against a program's original expectations. Television segments are then devised with the aim of meeting those objectives, and nearly always in such a way that education and en-tertainment are intertwined.

The fulfillment of these objectives is always complicated by the sheer volume of material to be produced: in some cases, 130 hour-long programs each year. And, of course, those 130 hours are pro-duced to a very high and sophisticated professional standard. To meet these standards, CTW employed more than thirty-six North American film animators for *Sesame Street* alone. From the beginning, the pro-gram attracted an extraordinary group of talented guest artists. Zero Mostel illustrating the concepts of "big" and "little" with an unfor-gettable pantomime created a television classic. In fact, *Sesame Street* contains many segments that qualify as TV classics.

Clearly, a special kind of organization was needed to accommodate this television model. Within the educational TV system as it existed in the mid–1960s, scores of smaller community and college-affiliated stations were struggling to put on the most limited kind of program-ming with inadequate funds, while the larger stations in major population centers such as New York, Boston, and San Francisco tried to create a limited national programming schedule of culture and information programs for adults. *Sesame Street*'s aims and organization would not fit within any of the existing structures. The initial $7.2 million outlay was, in fact, the largest sum ever spent on a single noncommercial program up to that time. Research alone accounted for 8 percent ($576,000) of this first-season expenditure. For such sums to be spent on a show for preschoolers was unheard-of—and, for some at least, unthinkable. The series' backers agreed there would have to be a new organization, insulated from competing priorities, and free to recruit top-rate producer talent.

Strong pressures were brought to CTW to tone down its vision, lower its sights, and produce a more modest offering for less money. But as documented in Richard Polsky's history of the transactions leading up to *Sesame Street*, Joan Cooney and Lloyd Morrisett refused. Either the series would be produced the way it should be, with talent and money to fit its ambitious goals, or it would not be produced at all.

It was an extraordinary gamble. A part of the reason why it worked is that all who were involved were willing to submerge their individual egos in deference to the urgent need and unprecedented opportunity. Far from being put off by starting with assigned educational goals, most of the show's writers and producers looked on those assignments as fascinating challenges to their creative abilities. For the outside educational advisors and the staff researchers, the experience of seeing academically-stated objectives translated time and again in creative ways by outstanding animators, musicians, filmmakers, and puppeteers was exhilarating. The task of helping to focus, and often to reshape, the directions of that fine talent was both delicate and rewarding.

The Workshop's philosophy and approach soon could be summarized in just a few statements. The organization would:

1. establish and use television as a significant tool to address urgent educational priorities;

2. create a fusion of education with entertainment on a scope unmatched by anything previously attempted in the children's area;

3. demonstrate the educational cost-efficiency of programming which is budgeted, planned, and produced well enough to attract a large, voluntary audience of home viewers;[21]

4. devote unprecedented effort to identifying precise educational goals, making extensive participation of expert consultants and advisors a key element in this activity;

5. develop the formative research process, involving pre-broadcast child testing with revisions of the experimental production elements, as a central activity in new series design;[22]

6. create a management model whereby effective three-way collaboration between researchers, subject specialists, and television production specialists run smoothly;

7. give special emphasis to the needs of low-income and minority children;

8. promote a widespread awareness of television's potential to teach children effectively, to include, whenever possible, innovative community outreach activities, to help ensure that a series' potential is understood and taken advantage of by those who might benefit most from it; and

9. widely disseminate what is learned in the areas of research, project planning, and production.

These organizational goals and procedures have been applied repeatedly in other CTW productions, including *The Electric Company* and *3-2-1 Contact*.

The Origins of CTW's Home-and-School Hybrid

The Electric Company and *3-2-1 Contact* are CTW-produced TV series for children of elementary school age. Like *Sesame Street*, they were designed to attract large out-of-school audiences. But unlike their preschool predecessor, they could expect a significant in-school viewership, and, as a result, they were created to be a new kind of home-and-school hybrid. Both series further illustrate how television can be tied to needs of children in which our whole society has a stake.

Around 1969, "the reading crisis" was recognized as an urgent problem of national scope; in 1971, *The Electric Company* became available over the air to more than 85 percent of all U.S. households.[23]

Right from its first year, it was being viewed each week by an estimated 6.5 million elementary school-age children, with roughly half of this viewing taking place in schools.[24] It was intended to be a teaching supplement only, but enjoyed outstanding popularity among teachers, according to independent nationwide surveys. These surveys showed that in its first weeks on the air, it was being used in 23 percent of all U.S. elementary schools, and by just a year later, this figure had increased to 34 percent.[25]

The series became the most used television program in the history of U.S. school television.[26] Sidney Marland, then Commissioner of the U.S. Office of Education, was so impressed with its documented reach and educational impact that he described it along with *Sesame Street* as "the best educational investment ever made" in this country.[27]

A major evaluation study of *The Electric Company*, carried out over a two-year period by Educational Testing Service of Princeton, New Jersey, established that, after six months, viewers of the series had made significantly greater reading progress than nonviewers in 17 of the 19 reading skills tested.[28] A school system in Lincoln Heights, Ohio, made the series the focus of a system-wide effort to cope with a long-standing problem of reading deficiency. By a special closed-circuit arrangement, *The Electric Company* was made available for use by teachers at any time throughout the entire school day, and in only one year, the reading test scores of the children who viewed it, as indicated on standardized reading tests used extensively nationwide, advanced, on average, by 2.3 years.[29]

The Electric Company was designed initially for 7- to 10-year-olds who were experiencing difficulty in learning to read, but it soon came into extensive use also in first-grade classrooms, as a means to introduce reading. Partly because it appeared in PBS's after-school children's program block, it has always attracted a large preschool viewership (more numerous, in fact, than its audience of school-age viewers!).

To make the series useful for remediation, CTW drew upon the unique capabilities of television. Important among these are:

- the non-threatening and non-punitive nature of televised instruction;
- the possibility to view in one's own home, where there is no stigma attached;

- the availability of animation techniques to attract the learner's eye to the print, refined with the use of a special eye-movement measuring device;[30]

- the capacity through humor to attract a large, voluntary audience of learners;

- the capacity of attractive, live characters and popular music to create positive associations with reading; and

- freedom to repeat brief lessons exactly, but in ways that avoid boredom, in order to provide for reading practice and reinforcement.

The Workshop also relied once again on the CTW Model, with its emphasis on submitting experimental productions to child testing and revision.[31] One strand of experimental production and research—the eye-movement studies mentioned above—sought effective ways to entice children to notice and read the print on the screen. Many production techniques were tried, among them, telling a joke right up to its one-word punch line, then printing that on the screen so it could be read by the viewing child; zooming in on and animating the print; and asking children to read a single word on the screen before it "self-destructs"—which the word then always did do, after a few seconds. Most important of all, the research demonstrated that many of these innovative presentational devices really did work as intended.[32]

These techniques, and others like them, aim to entice children into an active role as readers, and, to this end, they depend on the use of television capabilities not available through the use of the static, printed page.

Another line of experimentation in the design of both *Sesame Street* and *The Electric Company* is concerned with eliciting not just visual activity and involvement but vocalization—actual reading aloud in response to the televised presentation. So successful are the producers in inventing these techniques that one may frequently observe children in classrooms reading out with great animation, aloud and in unison, whatever is printed on the screen. Music and special sound effects, resources only rarely called into play by teachers in the classroom, are the key ingredient in many TV segments that successfully entice children to read aloud.[33]

It is true that *The Electric Company* could not be geared to reach each learner at his or her individual reading level, but it nevertheless could and did present skills which were new to some learners, while providing useful practice and review for others.

Not the least of the special advantages realized in the case of *The Electric Company* was television's ability to incorporate always the most up-to-date and best-validated approach to reading instruction known at the time. Because the series was to reach so wide an audience in such an important subject area, CTW recruited the nation's foremost reading researchers along with classroom practitioners to form its permanent advisory board.[34] The early 1970s was a time of volatility and change in this country's approach to reading, and during the several years in which it was renewed, *The Electric Company* could boast of being ever on the forefront. Textbooks, which must be used six years or more if schools are to maximize the return on their investment, are comparatively slow to reflect change.

Television is the only experience easily available to all children after school and in summertime which affords them an opportunity to review or catch up on school subjects. *The Electric Company* was designed in ways which were intended to ensure its usefulness at these times. For example, following *Sesame Street*'s lead, each of its six production seasons consists of 130 programs. Presented at the rate of one each weekday, this number exactly fills out a six-month season. One full repeat then fills out an entire calendar year. The resulting year-round availability not only provides a convenience to children and their parents but encourages regular viewing and gives the PBS stations the year-round presence they need when filling a time period for children (or for any audience).

The Electric Company matched *Sesame Street*'s achievement, proving once again that TV can make learning of school-related skills a voluntary daily pastime among children.

The series went off the air after a fourteen-year run in 1985 due to a combination of factors: it had been eight years in repeats; the need in phonetics had abated somewhat due to improvements in schools; a new, wider focus on the teaching of reading was emerging. And perhaps the stations of PTV surprised themselves a bit when they allocated too few votes to sustain it.

The *3-2-1 Contact* series answers a very different problem of learning and motivation, and, as a result, it taps into different ones of television's special capabilities. The series was created in the late 1970s because the U.S. had fallen behind as a nation in preparing large enough numbers of children well enough to fill the demand for specialists in science and technology in the workplace. If children do not begin to prepare early—by the ninth or tenth grade at the latest—the door to a career in science and technology is closed to them forever. Many teachers in the upper elementary grades of school are ill-prepared to spark the kind of curiosity and interest that can put children in touch with the wonders of the world and the fascinating ways in which scientists go about looking at them. Yet, without this spark, too few children elect the high school courses needed as pre-requisites to choosing science and technology as majors in college.[35] The problem is especially acute in the case of girls and members of minorities, both of which are greatly under-represented in careers in science and technology. This fact was a special concern among the series' funders, and was among the considerations causing them to choose television as one part of an overall solution.

Career demand is not the only factor which gives us a national stake in educating young people in science and technology. As citizens in a participatory democracy, our children will grow up having to cope wisely and well with societal issues involved ever increasingly with science and technology.

Yet, to say that television is a useful means to help build children's interests and understandings in this critical field is not to say that television can solve the whole problem, or even very much of it. In the face of a problem of such magnitude and complexity, nobody can expect television to play more than a modest, supplementary role. What makes television an important part of the solution, nevertheless, is the nature of the problem itself.

Children's intellectual growth in grades three through seven is characterized by a rapidly unfolding capacity to understand, coupled with a similarly expanding awareness of the world. We find children for the first time in their lives preoccupied with their own status and role, likes and dislikes. These are the years when they develop favorite subjects, and areas of individual reading interest.

Most important, as they begin to think seriously for the first time about what they might be and do in life, each does so with an emerging strong sense of what is realistic for him or her, individually. But during this malleable and impressionable period, children are highly prone to make tragic career miscalculations as insidious stereotypes come into play, such as those associated with their sex, or their race, or with the educational history or economic circumstances of their family. Children become the victims, also, of our culture's stereotypes about what life is like for someone working, for example, in the field of science and technology. The classic image is that of the white, middle-aged male in a lab coat bent for long, tedious hours over his instruments and test tubes.[36]

In the face of all this, television is able to depict a convincing array of live models to enrich children's understanding. It can do this by showing people actually engaged in their daily work activities as they pursue many different kinds of careers.

Clearly, the longer term answer lies in gearing up the schools through course development and teacher training. But to accomplish these activities requires first the will and support, and then the time for publishers and teacher-training institutions to do their respective parts.

In January 1980, three years before the problem received significant national attention, *3-2-1 Contact* made its debut, nationwide, on public television.[37] Of the more than $10 million required to launch this series' initial 65-program season, $5.5 million came from federal agencies which were five years ahead of the rest of the country in recognizing the problem, and at the time still lacked the policy-makers' interest and the resources needed to mount a more comprehensive response. These agencies—the U.S. Department of Education and the National Science Foundation—at the time redirected discretionary funds (that is, funds not expressly earmarked for television) to support the series. The remainder of *3-2-1 Contact*'s support came from a combination of sources, including United Technologies ($2 million), Corporation for Public Broadcasting ($.67 million), and CTW itself ($2.5 million).

A large part of television's special role in this case was to respond rapidly and on a nationwide scale. But television stands apart, too, in that eventual improvements within the schools, by contrast, will vary in quality and availability from classroom to classroom and region to region. Nationally broadcast educational TV programs are equally available to all children.

3-2-1 Contact in 1987 consisted of 205 half-hour programs, created over a seven-year period. Programs follow weekly themes, among which are communication, heat and cold, fast and slow, big and little. The typical half-hour program contains three to four mini-documentaries. These are films, shot out in the field, that show engaging adult professionals in science and technology doing interesting things and looking at what they are studying or building in interesting ways. The films feature as role models people from all age, sex, and ethnic groups. A small regular cast of youngsters appears frequently in a studio setting to provide a "home base," grounded in the child's familiar perspective. As a way to bridge from this familiar cast and perspective to people and events in the real world, each documentary film features one or more of the regular cast members, who is seen out in the field, on location, engaged in direct exchanges with scientists and engineers as they carry out their work. These attractive young cast members exhibit a lively curiosity, point out linkages to their own interests and everyday experiences, and show genuine and spontaneous appreciation for the ingenuity of a technological device or the importance of a scientific study.

Television like this, well planned and executed, featuring attractive role models and realistic situations, has a capacity to involve and convince which few elementary school teachers, on their own, backed up only with print materials, can possibly match or exceed. The point, however, is not that teachers and books and broadcast television should be in competition, but that each has something unique and of value to contribute.

So powerful and open-ended is the television medium, from the producers' point of view, that great care must be taken to use it in ways that motivate without misleading children. Sensitivity to this point led to very different approaches in the two cases of *The Electric Company* and *3-2-1 Contact*. To achieve its full effect, each had to attract the largest possible voluntary viewing audience. *The Electric Company* posed a particular challenge, because it had to entice children who were experiencing reading failure to return again and again, voluntarily, to a screen filled with print. There was no way to conceal the program's serious educational intent.

The series also had to avoid condescending to its target audience of problem readers, or else risk attaching a stigma to viewing. The producers' answer was to couch the series in a "gutsy" type of humor, people it with an adult cast, and script it with so much wit and skill that the reading never would be experienced by its child audience as the remedial drill and practice which, in fact, it actually was.

All indications are that the series did very well. Surveys covering both home and school settings prove that the series attracts and holds its audience as intended.[38] Although we do not know precisely what accounts for this high child appeal, I feel sure the use of classic, vaudevillian humor, geared to the children's own level, is an important factor. I believe that children also respond from an innate desire to learn.

Unlike other forms of remediation in reading, television eliminates the onus of failure and the threat of punishment so commonly experienced by that half of all children who find learning to read a struggle.[39] The contrast with what sometimes goes on in the classroom reading circle—a very medieval type of learning situation—is striking. Slower-learning children, when pressed by turns to read aloud, do so haltingly and often showing clear feelings of distress and self-denegration. The practice is counterproductive. Struggling learners experience no such distress while watching *The Electric Company*. Televised teaching is nonthreatening and nonpunitive—just the qualities a faltering learner can appreciate and respond to.

Whereas *The Electric Company* focuses on demotivated children, *3-2-1 Contact*, by contrast, deals with the not-yet-motivated. Children may come to *3-2-1 Contact* with stereotyped views of science, along lines of sex, race, and socioeconomic status, but at least they will not yet have experienced personal failure in studying science. Although some will have acquired negative associations with the word "science" itself, they are still eager, nevertheless, to learn more about the innumerable specifics of science.

Nowhere has the democratizing effect of broadcast television been more clearly apparent than in the case of *3-2-1 Contact*. At an early stage in its planning, the CTW researchers went to schools to talk at firsthand with sixth-grade children who were singled out by the teachers for their keen interest in science. They talked with all children eventually, but from this particular group, they learned that the series could not be designed at a level of depth and intricacy which would satisfy these budding science whizzes. These children already possessed exactly the background of knowledge and interest which the series' backers and science advisors wanted to see *3-2-1 Contact* impart. So CTW shaped *3-2-1 Contact* instead to help spark the large majority who possessed only marginal interest in the field.

To ignite this spark, the series draws upon a capability of television with which many seem to find fault—namely, the relatively effortless accessibility of its messages. Television sometimes is berated because it imposes little demand for effort upon the learner. Even the professional educators sometimes argue that, because television viewing is a "passive" rather than an "active" experience, it cannot possibly impart much useful learning.[40] I take a sharply opposing view. I think TV can be an active and demanding experience. Second, I look upon television's often nondemanding quality as an important teaching asset when the aim is to introduce children to an unfamiliar field and to bring to them their first taste of something which they might wish to explore more fully, later, through other means.

The Longest Street in the World

Subsequent to *Sesame Street*'s success, CTW was able to formulate some additional goals as well. It internationalized the concept. *Sesame Street* was found by recent count to be playing in seventy-three different countries. *The Electric Company* and *3-2-1 Contact* still further extend the Workshop's presence throughout both the English-speaking and the non-English-speaking countries of the world. In addition, *Sesame Street* has been recreated in eleven other languages, with CTW participating as co-producer. *3-2-1 Contact* so far has been co-produced in three other languages. Serendipitously, *Sesame Street* also was found useful as a means for teaching English overseas, and for this purpose, was carried for ten years in Japan, in its original, unmodified form.

This worldwide distribution has caused *Sesame Street* to be characterized by journalists, whimsically, as "the longest street in the world."

Table 3 charts the history and current status of foreign language adaptations for *Sesame Street* and *3-2-1 Contact* as of 1986–87. It shows that *Sesame Street*, in adaptation, has been available in some co-producing countries long enough to have served many successive "generations" of preschool children.

Further extending *Sesame Street*'s reach, the Latin American version has been distributed throughout nearly all of Mexico, Central and South America (except for Brazil, which produced its own Portuguese version), and the Kuwait-produced version has played in more than half of the twenty-two Arab-speaking countries.[41]

Completing CTW's international distribution picture is the circulation of other, less well-known CTW programs. One of these is a two-hour animation special, presenting one of the late C. S. Lewis's

Table 3. CTW International Co-productions[a]

| | *Sesame Street* Adaptations | | | |
Title	Co-producer	First produced	Seasons produced	Current status
Sesamstrasse (German)	Norddeutscher Rundfunk	1971	6	In broadcast/ in production
Vila Sesamo (Brazil)	TV Globo	1972	3	
Plaza Sesamo (Mexico)[b]	Televisa	1972	3	In broadcast/
Sesamstraat (Holland and Belgium)	Nederlandse Omroep Stichting and Belgesche Radio en Televisie	1976	6	In broadcast/ in production
1, Rue Sesame (France)	Télévision Français 2	1978	2	
Barrio Sesamo (Spain)	Radio Television Española	1978	4	In broadcast
Iftah Ya Simsim (Kuwait)[c]	Arabian Gulf States Joint Program Production Institution	1979	2	In broadcast
Sveriges (Sweden)	Sveriges Television	1980	1	
Rechov Sumsum (Israel)	Instructional Television Center	1982	2	In broadcast
Sesame (Philippines)	Human Settlements Development Corporation	1983	1	
	3-2-1 Contact adaptations			
3-2-1 Contact (France)	International Televisa Distributors	1979	1	
3-2-1 Kompass (Germany)	Metropolitan Import-Export	1981	1	
3-2-1 Contacto (Spain)	Radio Television Española	1982	1	

[a]Effective as of the 1986–87 broadcast year.

[b]Includes 17 Latin American countries.

[c]Includes several Arab-speaking countries.

seven classic children's tales. The seven as a group are known as *The Chronicles of Narnia*. This particular one of the seven is titled *The Lion, The Witch and the Wardrobe*.

CTW also produced and distributes a series of thirty programs, each half a minute long, titled *Betcha Don't Know*. Originally produced as occasional inserts for NBC television, this brief series provides answers to some of the questions children most frequently ask.

Other CTW productions distributed internationally as well as in the U.S. include two *Sesame Street* Christmas specials and an hour-and-a-half-long special titled *Big Bird in China*, shot in mainland China. This special, in addition to having played domestically and elsewhere in the English-speaking world, has received wide play in mainland China. Two additional Workshop productions, both for family audiences, are *Health Minutes*, a series of fifty, minute-long television messages on health, produced in and widely distributed throughout Latin America, and a made-for-TV movie of *Beauty and the Beast*, starring George C. Scott and Trish Vandevere.

The story of *Sesame Street* recreations abroad will one day make an excellent book in itself. Each country participating in this process of international co-production achieves a level of program quality and quantity not otherwise affordable. In this way, all the cooperating participants benefit, and CTW is no exception. Income over the years from *Sesame Street* adaptations has contributed importantly to keeping the U.S. series on air. The resulting new U.S.-produced materials are then made available for use abroad, thus completing the cycle, to the advantage of all.

Some may question whether this one series, whose curriculum and cultural elements were designed for a U.S. child audience, can be valid for so many different countries. But international co-productions of *Sesame Street* are far from being merely dubbed-over versions or simple copies of the original. Instead, they substantially recreate the original to reflect each adopting country's own educational goals, characters, and cultural setting. The typical pattern is for a country to create a six- month broadcast season, of 130 half-hour programs, each consisting 50 percent of segments on lease out of CTW's current segment inventory, and 50 percent of program elements newly produced in and by the adopting country. CTW's role, in addition to that of providing program segments, is to provide training and technical assistance in subject-matter planning, research, and production. These types of support are made available to the extent of a country's need and desire for them.

Elements produced by an adopting country reflect educational goals set up by that country's producing organization, in consultation with prominent local experts in early childhood education. An adopting country's curriculum typically includes a combination of educational goals from the U.S. *Sesame Street* and new goals reflecting its own children's unique needs. The resulting series is, of course, presented entirely in the local language.

These international adaptations of *Sesame Street* are often important for what they displace as well as for what they provide. Because programs in the *Sesame Street* mold cost more than other children's program forms, the intent of the adopting country, invariably, is to upgrade its children's offering. This aim may be manifested in a variety of different ways. One typical area of improvement is in production technique. In some cases, for instance, a children's department which has done little more than to dub or subtitle imported cartoon animations expands into script writing and creation of original music, animation, and studio elements.[42] In addition, most of the co-producing organizations abroad have had no prior experience in setting educational goals, and so are participating for the first time in a collaboration among subject-matter experts, television researchers, and television producers.

The CTW Model

The steps in the CTW model serve, basically, to organize the collaboration of diversely talented team members.[43] Through the co-production process and other means, the model has been widely adopted internationally. Some co-producers who learned to apply it in creating adaptations of *Sesame Street* later re-applied it to create their own new, goal-oriented series.[44] A critically important feature of the model is that it does not dictate either the subject matter or the cultural content of a television program which has been designed by following it.

Figure 1 presents the steps in the CTW model. The model in its most elaborate form is not a recipe that can deliver guaranteed success. One review of its applications mistakenly assumes that the Workshop's ambitions for the model are greater than they ever were.[45] But the model does describe a prudent set of management and research steps by which to improve any educational series' chances of success, which is all any plan or approach can reasonably be expected to do.[46] The important first step, *to plan curriculum objectives* for a series, is a collaborative activity involving television producers and researchers, along with outside subject-matter experts. The initial goal planning for *Sesame Street* was done by conducting

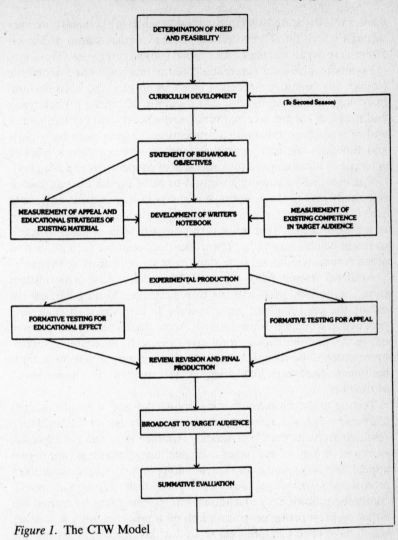

Figure 1. The CTW Model

five curriculum seminars, each lasting three full days. Each was attended by television producers, writers, and animators, authors of children's books, academic experts, and teachers and parents of preschoolers, among others. Around twenty-five people, in all, attended each of the five workshops.

The next step is *to write a comprehensive and detailed goal state-*

ment. Precisely stated goals are crucial to achieving planned outcomes through television. Those defined for the original season of *Sesame Street* were organized under four broad subject categories. These are: (1) symbolic processes (prereading and number skills and geometric forms); (2) cognitive processes (such as sorting and classification, matching, embedded figures, and rhythmic patterns); (3) reasoning and problem solving (clues, events, sequences); and (4) the natural and man-made worlds (with subcategories ranging from body parts and functions to tools, machines, and structures to work roles of community members and the processes of cooperation and fair play).

The aim in educating efficiently is to build on the existing knowledge and skills of the learners, and the next step in creating *Sesame Street*, accordingly, was *to test the existing knowledge and skills of target-age children*. One point is to pitch the level of the instruction so it will be challenging but not frustrating. Another is to know how much emphasis different important learning objectives will require.

Audience testing, following the CTW model, is done in two distinct steps, or phases, each with its own purposes. Testing carried out during the pre-broadcast phase is done to help shape or revise the production while it is being created. Accordingly, field testing carried out in this phase is called "formative" research. By contrast, follow-up research done to assess the educational effects of a series after it has been produced and aired is referred to as "summative" evaluation.

Testing to establish the existing knowledge and skills of potential learners, which was referred to earlier, is only one of the formative research steps in the CTW model. Another is *to test the television likes and dislikes* of the target audience, using measures of program appeal. Similarly, studies of experimental productions are undertaken *to evaluate instructional strategies*.[47] These tests of program appeal, comprehensibility, and educational effectiveness may be carried out either on pre-existing programs or on pilot programs for a new series which have been produced expressly for this purpose of testing and revision. Both approaches were taken in creating the original *Sesame Street*.

Careful planning and research is a price which must be paid to achieve high program quality and effectiveness. When large expenditures are being made on an innovative new production, backers appreciate the degree of extra insurance which is provided by formative child testing and revision. In the CTW model, these are a built-in part of the early planning and production process.

Formative research to support decisions in program design began at CTW as an experiment in its own right. Nobody knew at the beginning what contribution child testing could make to help guide improvements in *Sesame Street*'s—or any other series'—structure and elements. There was no professional community of practicing formative researchers and no body of recorded practice. Research done to improve television commercials was proprietary and unavailable, and, anyway, methods for testing the older audiences which interest advertisers would not work with preschoolers because they involve introspective judgments and coordinated responses beyond young children's development and ability. With modifications, a few of the already existing research methods could be adapted, and some general learning principles could be applied, but for the most part the CTW research team was obliged to approach each new question as an essentially new problem to be solved.

Joan Cooney describes the formative research for *Sesame Street* and *The Electric Company* as the key factor which made these productions unique. Joan also once wryly described the collaboration of researchers and producers as "a marriage worth keeping intact—for the sake of the children."

The term "presentational design" describes what CTW's formative research is about. Formative studies over the years have focused on the controllable elements of the presentation responsible for such outcomes as attention and interest, comprehension, active participation, and identification with role models.

In general, we have been interested in better understanding the contribution the moving image can make in advancing children's social, emotional, and intellectual development.

Today, the Workshop's audience-testing methods have been expanded to include the use of sophisticated computer programs and eye-movement measuring devices.[48] But one ingredient never changes—the need for creative interpretation by researchers who understand television in relation to children's thinking and learning processes.

The Future and CTW's Home-and-School Hybrid

CTW invented a form of children's television which is unique in the world, a home-and-school hybrid which presents expertly planned education content within television's engaging entertainment and documentary forms. Where other countries dedicate equitable portions of their comprehensive PTV schedules to children as a matter of fairly allocating scarce resources, CTW had to raise special funding in the U.S. to create *Sesame Street* and, later, *The Electric Company, 3-2-1 Contact*, and, in 1987, the new math series *Square One TV*.

Chronically inadequate funding throughout U.S. public television forced the Workshop to seek a rationale and agenda which would make children's television attractive to backers from outside public television. To raise the financial backing for its three children's series, CTW had to invent a new genre of home viewing fare, one whose main agenda is education.

More often than not, the funders for CTW's series have been mainly interested in the education needs of children, and have been interested in television only to the extent that it is a cost-efficient and ubiquitous means for helping to meet those needs. As a result, we are the first major industrialized country in the world that funds children's out-of-school television for the express purpose of helping to meet urgent national education priorities. As we chart the future of children's television, we should not lose for our children's sake this innovative form with its unique educational advantages.

In CTW's early days, producers of children's programs in other countries sometimes were baffled—and apparently, on occasion, threatened—by the emphasis on planned education in the Workshop's out-of-school children's shows. Those who were threatened didn't like the precedent; they didn't want to be held accountable on educational grounds, and they most emphatically did not wish to complicate their lives by working in collaboration with education professionals. I believe these concerns and a position of strong international visibility in children's television at the time are the basis for the curious flap put up by the BBC Children's Programmes Department in the early 1970s when CTW went to explore their using *Sesame Street*. (*Sesame Street* has since played repeatedly to a successful reception by children and their parents in Britain.) Today, both *Sesame Street*'s emphasis on education in at-home children's television and its reliance on collaborative planning and research are better understood. As a model, it is appreciated especially in developing countries where education resources are scarce. But more than that it is highly regarded wherever there is a concern to see the educating potential of television exploited to its fullest.

So far, we in the U.S. have not done as well as we ought to have done to develop this proven form of education supplement. *Sesame Street* went on the air in 1969. From the time when *The Electric Company* premiered in 1971, it was then nine years before the next new CTW series, *3–2–1 Contact*, saw air in 1980. The fact began to be apparent at CTW in the mid–1970s that, in spite of the excellent public reception and tested educational effectiveness of *Sesame Street* and *The Electric Company*, the government was not going to follow through with continuing and expanded support for the genre—even while it was describing these two series as the best educational investment our government had ever made.[49]

Each of CTW's four children's series reflects a carefully considered, multi-million dollar investment in helping to meet a major educational deficiency through television. Each has succeeded in the eyes of the public, and, in spite of persistent insufficiencies in funding, each so far has earned for itself a prolonged presence in public television.[50]

Collectively, these series, along with other quality offerings, such as *Mr. Rogers' Neighborhood, Reading Rainbow, The Voyage of the Mimi*, and the dramatic specials for older children contained in "WonderWorks," are the beginnings of what could become a much expanded form of everyday learning activity and should become a virtual fixture in American education.

It is no simple matter to explain why government has failed so far to institute a policy that will provide America's children with rich out-of-school learning opportunities through television. I have alluded earlier to barriers inherent in our broadcasting institutions, and in the visions and values on which they are founded. Other specific barriers are explored in the chapter which follows. Some of these are rooted in vested interests, others in outmoded traditions. One of the largest perhaps is the public's sense of powerlessness to affect what broadcasters—commercial or noncommerical—offer up for children. My own belief is that when a mechanism is found by which to express the public's desire in the matter, the barriers will be surmounted. Wide public discussion and participation are indispensable. We turn now to explore specific paths of action open to us.

7 | Conclusions

Has television for America's children come to a dead end? Our success in creating a new kind of hybrid, home-and-school medium has demonstrated television's capacity to become children's third institution for learning surpassed in importance only by the family and school. Children's time is valuable. Every child's TV-viewing day could be filled with an hour of carefully planned, age-appropriate educational programs for less than a cent per child per day.[1] The benefits during our children's crucial early years for growth and learning could be enormous. The interplay with school learning would enrich both experiences.

The proving phase has shown us the way. We have demonstrated repeatedly, since *Sesame Street* received its initial funding of $8 million in 1967—twenty years ago—that television has an important dual educational role to play, to support and complement the efforts of the schools. Major program series created and aired during this twenty-year proving phase have responded with distinction to one after another in a succession of national educational crises. In fact, every time a major educational deficiency affecting young children has come to light in these twenty years, television has been called upon to provide a part of the solution.

All the ingredients to create and air a full schedule of high-quality educational shows for children are in place. America has the expertise, the production capability, the pedagogical and research skills, the audience, and the need. Public television has abundant air space, and might be prevailed upon by parents and outside underwriters to become a willing host. Parents, children, and educators have shown great enthusiasm for all the fine quality programs so far made available.

Thanks to the many outstanding successes of the past twenty years, we have fashioned our own unique national vision of quality. Why, then, have we lacked the will to carry it through? Why is our government so short-sighted in failing to create the national policy and provide the funding to make full and effective use of the most cost-efficient teaching medium ever invented—broadcast television?

The great flaw in our success story is that PTV's finest home-and-school programs for children still are only funded, when at all, one by one, on an ad hoc basis. Only through relentless and exhausting fundraising efforts have organizations like CTW pulled together consortia of backers in government, foundations, and, sometimes, corporations on a series-by-series and a year-by-year basis. Long-term funding to expand or continue successful and deserving series is in even more drastically short supply. Many splendidly conceived proposals for urgently needed programs simply do not make it.

As a result, more than 90 percent of the programming in the weekday PTV children's schedule in recent years has consisted of shows played in repeat.[2]

Unquestionably, we in the U.S. share with other industrial countries a high regard for the benefits which children's television at its finest can bestow. There exist, nevertheless, vast discrepancies in the extent to which we as compared with other countries realize television's potential for children. These differences spring from variations in the way we and these other countries have formed our television institutions—in the different provisions in the laws establishing them; in the order of appearance of commercial vs. noncommercial television; in the immediacy of public participation in funding our respective broadcasting institutions, ranging from directly paying a TV-set tax on the one extreme to indirect funding through advertising or general taxation on the other; in the extent of oversight and penalization to ensure that public service benefits are realized, on the equitable basis, to meet the legitimate needs not only of the majority but of special audience groups; and in having or not having a well-articulated national policy to reap television's benefits in service of children and education.

The lapses we countenance in our own television institutions are seen in cross-cultural comparisons to be woefully shortsighted, or even bizarre. For instance, the Japanese Broadcasting Corporation, NHK, reports that in 85 percent of all Japanese schools, every classroom has a color television. The NHK reports further that each year 97 percent of all classrooms in Japan make some use of NHK's school television service. Yet, by contrast, the U.S. Department of Education places almost no priority whatsoever on television's development and use to advance learning for America's children. The bizarre part is that where another country's provision for the use of television in education is so vital and so far advanced, we are utterly without any well-informed, long-term, or dependable policy to guide our own educational uses of television, and this is true in spite of the unarguable fact that U.S. schools are drastically and chronically burdened by performance demands that exceed their capacity to deliver, and that television languishes as a proven but neglected cost-efficient ally.

It is fitting that we begin exploring a minimally adequate PTV children's schedule that places children's needs first, and, only then, keeping in mind the same high standard, turn to explore an agenda for legislated regulation on the commercial side.

The Shape and Cost of a Minimal Schedule

The schedule most likely to attract funding support must be modest—minimally adequate to serve all children aged two through thirteen—and, I believe, must consist of programs geared to our most urgent national education problems. Moreover, for each educational outcome sought, television must be seen to be more effective, and substantially more cost-efficient, than any other means available. This high standard is well within broadcast television's capability.

The schedule which will be proposed here in detailed outline calls for a multi-year program build-up, in phases, eventually yielding a one-hour weekday schedule, year round, for each of three child age-groups: 2- to 5-year-olds, 6- to 9-year-olds, and 10- to 13-year-olds. The scale of yearly funding support is $62.4 million. Although modest, this amount is about double the current expenditure from all sources for children's PTV programming.[3] Anything more ambitious to begin is unrealistic; anything less ambitious short-changes children by drastically under-utilizing this powerful educational resource.

This yearly budget, as shown below, will buy enough programming at today's rates to continue the preschool service and provide a quarter of a full year's schedule each for 6- to 9- and 10- to 13-year-olds. By simple arithmetic, this yearly program build-up rate will fill a year's schedule for each age group in four years. "Simple arithmetic" is misleading in this case, however, because not all programming will bear up well in repeats—some will be topical, for instance—so that perhaps five or more build-up years will be required to fill a year-long program schedule.

Children stay in an age band for four years before they "graduate" and move on to the next higher level. The second phase in the build-up process, therefore, will be to provide the children in each four-year age band with a four-year cycle of programming. This must be done to ensure that during the four-year period of time children spend in each age band, they will encounter fresh information and ideas—and not just repeats of the same programs—year after year. A realistic (efficient, affordable) third phase is then to institute a provision for perpetual renewal, by adding each year a quarter of a year's new programming—amounting to 65 hours for each of three age bands. The need for perpetual renewal results from program attrition, which can happen due to shifting educational practices and priorities, or topicality of subject matter, or because some experiments do not work or require revision.

The near-term pattern, if new productions are created at the rate of 25 percent of a four-year schedule each year, will be to accumulate a program backlog to fill first a full year's offering, then a two-year cycle, and then a three-year cycle, and so on. The eventual aim is to achieve a state of equilibrium wherein a quarter of the year's program schedule is produced anew each year, and an equal amount drops out of use. We need to program for 260 weekdays each year.

Whether one's concern may be with funding or with managing a children's schedule, the following summary suggests some desirable schedule conditions:

- *Fill the children's TV schedule through the entire calendar year.* Children of all ages watch TV and can learn from it all year round. There are no "school vacations" with at-home television. A constantly fresh program offering maintains a loyal audience, allowing the children's schedule to be its own best promotion. Television can help counteract the well-known drop-off in achievement which occurs in the summer between school years.

Table 4. Initial Yearly Costs for Proposed National Children's TV Schedule[a,b]

Age group	Scheduled hours each year	New hours each year	Cost per new hour[c] (*thousands*)	Yearly total (*millions*)	Annual cost per child
2–5	260	60	$200	$12.0	$0.86
6–9	260	65	$375	$24.4	$1.74
10–13	260	65	$400	$26.0	$1.86
Total	780	190		$62.4	$1.49 (avg)

[a]The calculations in the table are based on 14 million children per four-year age group, for a total of 42 million, as a convenient approximation.[6]

[b]A factor of 50 percent has been added to production, to cover the activities of series development, curriculum planning, pre-production research and child testing, pilot production and review, and audience building.

[c]The cost per hour is based on prevailing mid-1980s production costs in U.S. public TV in general and in children's PTV programming in particular. See Chapter notes for additional comment on program costs.[7]

During school years, those programs not actually used in the classroom can be assigned as homework.

- *Make optimum use of previously broadcast materials each year.* This practice is the key to schedule building. It is an important factor not only in creating an adequate quantity and diversity of programs but also in achieving the best possible cost-efficiency.

- *Aim to provide each four-year child age band with a full, four-year cycle of programs.*

- *Provide a sensible ratio of new to repeat programming.* Preschool children, as compared with their school-age counterparts, both enjoy repeat exposure to the same programs and derive greater educational benefit from it. Older children, like adults, have little tolerance for program repetition. The minimum renewal rate which will allow new educational needs to be met, and fresh new approaches taken, is a quarter of a year's new programming annually.

- *Slot children's programs at convenient and appropriate viewing times.*

Table 4 outlines the budget figures for a proposed national children's TV schedule. This proposal assumes that we will incorporate, and build upon, the backlog of excellent and durable programs which already exists, eventually to provide an hour each weekday for each of the three age groups. The total amount of programming required to fill this schedule is 780 hours a year.[4]

Children grow up with this amount of programming in Japan and Great Britain and thereby enjoy an opportunity to encounter new and useful information and ideas each weekday.[5] Over the important twelve-year learning period between two and thirteen, they grow up "through" programs geared to successive levels of interest and understanding, "graduating" every three to five years from one level of difficulty and interest to the next.

Sesame Street is an excellent case study to show how a sustained investment over several years can create a backlog of reusable programming. This reuse only improves the series' already highly favorable cost-efficiency, as programs and program elements are played again and again for successive "generations" of preschool children. *Sesame Street* in 1987 costs more than $11 million annually to produce. The actual expenditure for its first season was $7.2 million in 1979 dollars. Each year since, a substantially renewed series of 130 hour-long programs has been produced and broadcast. Today, however, expensively produced films, animation, and Muppet segments, reused from previous years, make up about two-thirds of each hour-long program. In times of inflated costs the savings are significant.

Only a fraction of the many hundreds of pieces of carefully crafted film and videotapes contained in this treasure store are called into use each year to assemble what is, for the children, a largely fresh 130-hour series. Most of the new program elements created consist of less costly studio-produced scenes.

Without doing a detailed cost analysis, one could estimate that the cost today to inaugurate a wholly new, 130-hour *Sesame Street* series from scratch would easily exceed $25 million. This means that the replacement value of the program segments that are now carried forward into each new *Sesame Street* season from previous years is more than $15 million.

This system of building a backlog of reusable programs and program elements is the key to creating an efficient and affordable children's schedule.

Sesame Street and its successors among CTW productions represent a massive number of program hours, outstanding in technical and artistic quality. By renewing *Sesame Street* each year as a 130-hour series, the Workshop is able to provide for an uninterrupted year-round presence in the weekday PTV schedule—and make learning an everyday pastime in preschool children's lives. This continuity is accomplished to some degree with mirrors, as it were, because each year's 130 programs exactly fill a six-month broadcast schedule, then are repeated one time in their entirety to fill out the year. This rate of repeat will not hold up in audience appeal with older children or with programs designed other than with *Sesame Street*'s largely unthemed, variety format.[8]

Sesame Street is seen by many as a model of collaborative production and research activities, but as the above illustration makes clear, it also offers some important lessons on how to develop and manage a TV schedule. This realm of concern will become especially important if and when we enter a new and expanded phase in quality children's television.

The CTW experience is instructive and may be looked upon as the model for an even larger national program package for all children. The *Sesame Street* case has shown that judicious reuse of programs and program elements can introduce major cost savings without any compromise of educational benefits.

Another key to efficiency is to require within each four-year child age group that each program serve the largest possible number of children. Programs geared to children with special needs should have a place in a comprehensive children's schedule, of course. The point to understand is that inadequate support forces a trade-off between general and specialized programming, and some balance between the two has to be struck. *Sesame Street, The Electric Company, 3-2-1 Contact*, and *Square One TV* are examples of general programs which, nevertheless, give special attention to the needs of children from minority backgrounds, the disabled, those experiencing learning difficulties, and those from lower socioeconomic circumstances.

Perspectives on Television's Cost and Efficiency

As we focus on the question of who might contribute, and how much, and, especially, on the very substantial discrepancy between the (unstable) $29 million annual amount now being spent and the $62.4 million per year needed to create and sustain our hypothetical children's schedule, it would be a great mistake to focus only on the large size of expenditure required. Every television budget must be expressed by two numbers if it is to be understood well: a usually very large number captures the total cost of a program or service, while a typically very small number represents the cost for each viewer or potential viewer. We as educators should take our lead from the television advertisers. They pay great attention to the small number— the cost per viewer reached.

The familiar ratings competition in commercial broadcasting attests that television is a nose-counting business. By the same token, the legendary high cost to run one sixty-second commercial during a ratings blockbuster such as the Superbowl—upwards of $800,000 for a single play—tells us something important about the scale we must be prepared to deal with in calculating television's cost-effectiveness ratios.[9] A single one-hour episode of a lavishly produced prime-time evening series can cost as much as $1,000,000 today. Such high expenditures to promote products and services are justified by two considerations: (1) the understanding that with audiences of many millions, the cost per viewer reached is small, and (2) the advertiser's expectation, grounded in years of industry experience, that the impact on sales will more than justify the cost.

Commercial broadcasting—radio and television combined—is a $30.6 billion-a-year industry, which thrives entirely on the cost-efficiency of advertising.[10] The equivalent of about $128 for every man, woman, and child in the population is spent each year in our country on broadcast advertising, and this amount yields annual profits of around $2.5 billion to the industry.[11]

The proposed $65 million yearly budget to support my proposed children's educational TV schedule—which, though modest, nevertheless would be the envy of the entire world—is a mere $1.49 per child per year. The per capita cost figure, calculated on our entire population, is about 26 cents a year.[12]

The 42 million children from two to thirteen years which would be served by this expenditure make up a group three-quarters the size of Great Britain's entire population. Our great population size is one of our chief national assets, and is a major factor in explaining why we are the world's largest exporter of everything from television programs to computers. It also gives us a great funding advantage over several countries which, nevertheless, surpass us in important respects in their support of quality chidren's television.

In view of the overwhelmingly favorable per-viewer cost of television just because we are a country with so large a population, our persistent failure to take advantage of television's cost-efficient educational possibilities for children is a course of economic folly.

The Limited Prospects from Within Commercial and Public Television

Now that the commercial broadcasting industry has been relieved of its legal obligations, who will schedule programs for children? Will the bright new cornucopia of cable and cassette provide the answer? Was the FCC correct in arguing that the television marketplace, through the combination of broadcast and nonbroadcast technologies, will provide abundantly and well for America's children?[13] In fact, this claim by the FCC is a distortion which tends to justify the agency's rigid adherence to supply-side ideology and underscores its insensitivity in its unwillingness to make a special exception for children.

Less than half of our child population is served today through either cable or cassette television.[14] Moreover, nobody can support a believable claim that more than three-quarters of U.S. households will be equipped to benefit from cable or cassette education within this century.[15] Showing total disregard for social equity, the FCC of the 1980s failed to take any note of the fact that cable and cassette are most widely available in high-income households with the extra disposable income to afford them, and that these technologies are least available in households where the need for supplemental education is the greatest. This inequity is partly a matter of household economics. But, also, a disproportionately large number of low-income households do not even have cable available because the industry likes to wire into more affluent neighborhoods first.[16]

Involved and concerned members of Congress reject—and refute—the FCC's argument that a solution will be forthcoming via unregulated marketplace forces. They have proposed legislation which, if passed, will override the FCC's action.[17]

One of the chief proponents of this legislation for many years was Representative Timothy Wirth, a Democrat from Colorado, who chaired the House Subcommittee on Telecommunications, Consumer Protection and Finance. Wirth stated months before the FCC's December 1983 ruling against a regulated children's offering: "We are not yet at the point where the level of competition in the video marketplace is sufficient to deregulate television broadcasting."[18]

It is proper and necessary to ask, in terms informed by the historical record, what role the marketplace realistically can be depended on to play in providing televised education and a weekday broadcast schedule for children. Having first made such an assessment, we can then take measure of our residual unmet need. To what extent can or will supply-side incentives help to sustain a significant share of even a minimally adequate children's television offering of sound educational quality?

The answer to this question, as we shall see, is that *all the very same deficiencies and disincentives which caused us as a nation to neglect the development of children's educational television in the first place also mitigate against the possibility that a solution will be forthcoming from organizations within U.S. television as the field is now structured.* This is true for commercial and public television alike. As a result, the only possible solution is for the greater part of the initiative to come from outside the existing structures of commercial and public television. This is fundamental.

Commercial TV has no business reason, not even for good public relations, to provide more than a token offering of planned educational programming comparable to the best of PTV's children's series. This observation applies equally to both the broadcast and the cable sectors. None of CTW's four children's series could have been—or would have been—produced in the U.S. by commercial broadcasters or cablecasters. The special niche of these series in American education stands distinct and apart from any vision of quality which commercial TV, even with regulation, would set out to fulfill.

Commercial broadcasters have no interest in the business of education; they are in the business of advertising. Cable does not have the audience base to support a large amount of quality educational fare, which is more expensive to plan and produce than is general programming. Currently, one major supplier of children's cable TV programs markets its program package to the cable companies as a non-producer of profits.[19] The program suppliers make money, but the cable operators do not. This pattern is not a dependable way to serve children's educational needs abundantly and well.

In any case, cablecasters provide a unique service in the children's category merely by scheduling almost anything at all, because their abundance of channel space allows them to offer children's fare at convenient times of the day not available on either the commercial or public airwaves.

But, most important of all, neither commercial broadcasters nor commercial cablecasters may be expected to (1) invest in educational innovation, (2) identify and respond to our children's and our nation's most urgent educational needs, or (3) stand accountable to the public, program by program, to produce measurable educational gains.

The FCC, in its landmark 1983 decision, reaffirmed that commercial TV broadcasters have an obligation to serve children, but left it to the industry itself to interpret that responsibility.[20] Since that time, Congress has failed in every session to pass into law proposed legislation which would override the FCC's action and impose a weekday children's scheduling requirement.[21] The 42 million children affected unfortunately cannot lobby for the passage of legislation in their own behalf. Nevertheless, they are a major and deserving constituency with an interest in it. Because they have no voice, and apparently too few surrogates to speak out for them, the bill quite possibly will not be passed.[22]

But what if it were? What if Congress did impose the much-discussed weekday children's scheduling requirement upon the industry? Might not the industry simply duplicate the existing Saturday morning forms?

We can only speculate on the question of how the industry actually would respond, but we must be prepared to do so. I personally feel that if faced with a legislated weekday requirement, the industry would pursue one—or perhaps both—of two courses of action. One is to move the traditional Saturday morning children's schedule, complete with its advertisers—of which there are only a limited number—to weekdays. The other is to create a new children's form with strong appeal to adults, as a vehicle which could continue to attract lucrative, adult-oriented advertising. This would work only for older children. The result either way would be to compromise the goal of meeting the unique information and education needs of the children. If the commercial stations were required to program each weekday for *preschoolers*, I think they would be pressured by public opinion to build in sound educational values.

Children's public service television in the U.S. should be a shared responsibility, and the commercial side should have to provide better than it now does for the (broadly defined) information and education needs of children.

The best overall solution is one which maximizes program diversity by supporting a balanced contribution from both the commercial and noncommerical sides. Commercial TV ought to retain domination over purely entertainment-oriented cartoons and live-action adventure series of the traditional Saturday morning variety. Public television has too important an educational purpose to fulfill to be squandering its resources in duplicating these entertainment formats. These light programs, when sensitively designed, fulfill a useful purpose by providing children with entertainment and a diversion. But in the past, commercial TV also has presented occasional award-winning children's variety series, news programs, and after-school specials of a caliber public television would be proud to present, and it should both continue and expand upon these efforts.

Most especially, the industry should not simply be let off the hook and allowed to shirk its responsibility to provide a solid weekday program service for children. That would be tantamount to letting them walk away with the store. The "store" in this case—the electromagnetic spectrum which carries all the commercially broadcast programs—belongs, after all, to the American public, by law. And it belongs to children no less than to adults. These children are a sixth of our population, and they are the only audience not served in any valid sense by most available varieties of adult programming. Their needs and interests can be met only by making a special provision for them.

It was this line of reasoning, in part, which caused CTW's chairman of the board, Mr. Lloyd Morrisett, to poll industry leaders in the late 1970s on their willingness to help support the PTV children's schedule. They declined at the time to do so voluntarily.

The industry has been accused, accurately, I think, of hiding behind the First Amendment. They charge that a regulated children's offering would be a form of government censorship.[23] They say that what they fear even more is the precedent that would be set for government interference in the content of their broadcast schedules.[24] Morrisett's plan gave them a chance to skirt the censorship issue, through the alternative of helping to fund the PTV children's schedule. Surely, a PTV offering, created in part to make up for commercial television's lapses in the children's area—when these lapses were caused in the first place by the industry's pursuit of the more profitable adult market—has a valid claim on a share of the industry's incremental profits.

Former Quaker Oats president Ken Mason once proposed still

another way out for the industry. He suggested that in the interests of both economy and quality, the industry should pool its resources to support a single, well-produced children's offering, to be played by all the commercial stations.[25] The industry responded by arguing that anti-trust law forbids their cooperating in this manner.[26] But a special exception to anti-trust law was granted to the insurance industry. Their exception was granted because it was seen to be in the public interest. The network response to Ken Mason's suggestion was not, therefore, dictated by unbendable law. It was, rather, a matter of will.

One might point out that the industry is in no way forbidden to act jointly to help pay for a children's PTV offering. They could even claim a tax deduction in the process—which Congress has the power to sweeten still further, should it be inclined to do so.[27]

Public TV has a unique role to play in presenting major children's educational series, tied to key nationwide educational deficiencies and designed with the participation of academic subject-matter experts. Yet, the only way children's television can grow and flourish as the instrument of planned education which it has the proven capacity to be is for national policy to let it surpass the growth rate for overall PTV funding.[28]

We cannot expect to see a systematically planned and managed, comprehensive schedule of serious educational programs emerge in public television in the absence of national policy to provide the necessary direction and support.

Public television is the one sensible location for a comprehensive out-of-school children's service with the nation's education agenda as its focus. Yet, as we turn to explore the funding prospects, we find that here is yet another system with built-in barriers. The problem is not only that the funds by which to support a $65 million-a-year children's schedule simply do not exist within public television. It is that public television itself is so chronically underfunded across the board that it cannot single out the children's area (or any other) for full development.

Children are merely one worthy and underserved PTV constituency among many, all of them competing for scarce resources. The children's area must be elevated above this competition, for how can children compete in the PTV funding tug-of-war? And what alternatives do children have? They simply do not have the options that adults have through commercial television. *The only way the chil-*

dren's area can be elevated above the leveling influence of PTV's internal competition is through some system of outside initiatives. Even so, these can be carried out only with public television's cooperation, and they must draw on as much funding support as PTV can provide, reflecting an equitable portion of the amount which the different PTV organizations spend each year, individually and collectively, on programs.

Where we have seen centers of programming excellence in the public television schedule in the past, these have arisen, by and large, through outside initiatives. Unfortunately, however, due to the strong adult bias in PTV's outside program funding, little outside underwriting is available to sustain a PTV children's schedule.

Most of the outside groups that give funds to help create new PTV programs have strong reasons to invest in shows for adults in preference to those for children. Business, in particular, will almost invariably put its capital in high-visibility evening programs with upscale adult appeal, like news and public affairs, drama, opera, science and nature, and concerts. There is nothing immoral or even illogical about this. Why should they restrict themselves to an audience too young to use their products, or even to remember their name?

A tax incentive would help, and one has been proposed in the recent past in Congress without success.[29] In today's new deregulatory environment, this remedy deserves consideration in spite of the fact that such measures tend to be unpopular in government. The Canadian and Australian film industries enjoy tax incentives which result in benefits to children, among other groups.[30]

Public television's success in raising monies through public appeals has grown rapidly since the mid-1970s, sparked by its improved program offering.[31] This promising upward spiral shows signs of slowing and, in any case, is not even close to being self-sustaining but depends on continuing large grants of program support from outside public and private sources. No one can say what fraction of PTV's revenues from voluntary individual contributions can be traced to the public's interest in a national children's schedule. There is no way for a parent to earmark a contribution to a local PTV station with assurance that it will go directly and exclusively to support the children's productions.[32]

The individual public television stations are the sole, traditional gatekeepers over voluntary public contributions as a revenue source and raised nearly $160 million in a recent year through public appeals.[33] This income goes into each station's general fund, where it is then used primarily to offset station operating expenses. Comparatively little actually goes to support the national program schedule. The combined amount, in 1987, from all PTV stations, totals about $35 million a year— which is less than half the cost of my proposed children's schedule.

Public appeals are not usually undertaken to raise dedicated support to go directly and intact to funding pools for individual programs or program areas.[34] Yet, this avenue certainly deserves to be tried in the children's category. What is needed is experimentation.

Finally, an under-utilized source of programs for the out-of-school children's schedule is the pool of public-TV programs created initially for in-school use. Although usually only 15 minutes long, these programs can be paired for broadcast in the standard, 30-minute out-of-school program slot. Selections from this source will have to be limited to those which can attract a reasonably large child audience in competition with the commercial programs available on other channels.

Current Funding Sources and Our Funding Shortfall

To pursue further the question of who will pay, no one can say with any great certainty what future funding role will actually be played by corporations, foundations, or any group which could advance children's public television. This uncertainty reflects one of our great deficiencies, the lack of year-to-year PTV funding stability, which does great harm in the children's area.

The available funding sources are the producing organizations themselves, such as the major stations in public broadcasting and CTW; philanthropic foundations; public television's program buying pool, the Station Program Cooperative (SPC) fund; the program fund of the Corporation for Public Broadcasting; and the federal government, through agencies such as the National Science Foundation, the Department of Education, and the National Endowments for the Arts and the Humanities.

The overall summary presented in Table 5 shows the combined annual contribution from all *non-government* sources to support children's PTV programming in a typical year—an amount of $24 million. After counting the government's current $4.4 million yearly contribution, there remains close to a $34 million-per-year funding need.[35]

Table 5. The Gap Between Our Expenditure and Current Yearly Need in Funding a Minimum Children's PTV Schedule—Highlighting Government's Essential Role[a]

Funder categories	Dollar amount (*millions*)	Program hours (*approximate*)
Non-government contributors:		
Children's Television Workshop	$ 7.299	
Business & industry	$ 0.350	
Foundations	$ 0.020	
PTV (Stations Program Cooperative)	$ 5.739	
PTV (CPB Program Fund)	$ 6.470	
Other	$ 4.433[b]	
Total non-government contribution	$24.3	75[c]
Current annual government contribution	4.4	13
Additional new funding needed (to be contributed mostly by government)	33.7	102
Total annual funding and hours required	62.4	190

[a]All figures are for the 1984–85 broadcast year, and reflect uncommitted amounts which may fluctuate from year to year.

[b]This figure incudes $4.276 million in funding support from *WonderWorks* co-producers and $157 thousand from Bank Street College for *The Voyage of the Mimi*.

[c]See Chapter 7, Note 36 for detail on sources of funding and program hours.

[d]Based on program costs and hours as shown in Table 4 (averaging $328,000/hour for the combined three child age groups).

Barring the unlikely appearance of some benevolent deity to simply drop the money from out of the sky, government funding is the only recourse if the otherwise unmet $33.5 million of our hypothetical yearly budget is to be realized.

Philanthropies, too, can continue as they have in the past to play a key role, should they choose to do so. But we cannot shape national policy based on assumptions about what foundations either can or actually will do. Very few of the foundations whose charters include an interest in children's education can afford to support the high initial budgets involved in television. As a result, their traditional and likely future role is to support advocacy and to participate as members of program-funding consortia.

In the past, foundations have contributed to public television—including children's public television—in a variety of important ways, beginning when the Ford Foundation spent more than a quarter of a billion dollars over the twenty-year period of the 1950s and 1960s to help create public television as a viable national institution.[36] The

Carnegie Corporation, in addition to sponsoring two broad policy studies on major directions in public broadcasting, provided the support that allowed Joan Cooney to carry out the preliminary study and write the funding proposal which led to *Sesame Street*'s creation.[37] The Carnegie Corporation and the Ford Foundation together provided most of the non-government half of *Sesame Street*'s original funding support, and both foundations later played a similar start-up funding role in launching *The Electric Company*. Among all the foundations, the John and Mary R. Markle Foundation, although comparatively small, has played a key leadership and advocacy role in U.S. children's television.[38]

Foundations are almost never sole-source funders of children's television programs. Instead, they prefer to participate through funding consortia, not only to spread the costs and the risks but also to achieve a maximum leveraging of results brought about through their contributions. Like corporations (and for largely similar reasons), foundations almost never fund a series beyond a period of two or three start-up years, no matter how well it may be achieving its intended education aims or how enthusiastically it has been received by children and their parents. This is because it is the desire of these organizations to play a unique role in supporting innovations at the outset and to help to meet unforeseen— and otherwise unmet—crises. Current foundation contributions are unstable, but to give a general indication, they run to about $1 million a year in the children's area, nearly all in the form of initial start-up support.

The most optimistic outlook is that one or more of the largest foundations will be prompted to assume a major new role. This could come about out of consideration for such factors as: (1) the recent deleterious effects of commercial TV's deregulation; (2) the current recognized crisis in education, taking into account television's unparalleled cost-efficiency and the unique role and value of carefully planned and well-produced children's at-home educational television, which by now is well established; and (3) public television's availability, but current inability, on its own, to provide an alternative to the largely wasteful and often inappropriate diet of adult-oriented television which children now consume.

Before we turn to outline the essential future role of government, we must ask what possible political consideration could prompt our elected leaders to take clear and concise action in an area so long neglected. The only answer is to plead that children be regarded as a special group, and an exception to the usual political process.

Only by a Special Exception Will a Fair Share for Children Be Forthcoming

One of the great strengths of our American political system is that, whatever inequities it may perpetuate, it is usually flexible enough to provide exceptions, to create breathing spaces in the corners of the system. For the most part, this is true of our broadcasting system as well. The adult audience could certainly be far better served than it is now. But if one is willing to look hard enough, and carefully enough, one can usually find something on television to suit almost every taste, at least some of the time. *If* one is an adult.

The child audience, however, *is ill-served in absolute terms*. Unlike most other special groups, they are heterogeneous. Their ranks encompass rich and poor, majority and minority, and include the disabled and the disturbed. The elderly, the only other large and heterogeneous audience group, benefits from the general news, and from adult cultural and entertainment-oriented programs. Children are uniquely underserved.

This situation is both tragic and thoughtless. It is tragic that urgently needed and useful educational possibilities go unrealized, and it is thoughtless to give children the impression that nobody cares enough to provide something special for them to learn from. The kids are still there in front of the set, whether the broadcasters bother to program for them or not.

As we turn now to consider the role of government, the child advocates' maxim "Children need friends in high places" serves as a fitting reminder that children cannot mount an effective lobby in their own behalf. A quality children's home-and-school education TV service can come about only by government's willingness to support half to two-thirds of the cost, through earmarked appropriations. In turn, this kind of support can come only if Congress and the Administration are willing to exercise unusual leadership and make special political exceptions to provide it.

The widely neglected condition of American children's television today is not really the fault of individuals in either commercial or public television, so much as it is the bleak harvest caused by government's prior failure to establish a forward-looking and educationally sound national policy in the matter—and to follow through on it.

Government inevitably plays, and must continue to play, a major role in deciding the overall quality of children's television in the nation. Government has an especially important contribution to make, by exercising its legislative powers in the three broad areas of regulation, tax incentives, and direct appropriation of production funds. Now is a crucial time for Congress and the Administration to make the decisions and take the initiatives that will shape the form and quality of children's television in this country.

Important events of the recent past make this an especially appropriate time for broad and decisive action. For example, government must decide how it will respond to the urgent national concern about the inability of our schools to provide all that is asked and expected of them.[39] In addition, government is the only recourse if we are to compensate for the reverses in the quality of children's commercial television brought about only recently by deregulation. The FCC's 1983 ruling against Action for Children's Television's long-neglected petition places the responsibility for taking alternative action squarely upon the shoulders of Congress.

Whatever action Congress decides to take, it must consider the heretofore ignored fact that many other similarly industrialized countries surpass us in their deliberate use of television to help children become well-adjusted and productive members of their respective societies.

Most important in all this, Congress itself or a resolved Administration will have to assume the leadership role. Educator groups will endorse the effort, but no large, well-organized professional group will emerge to speak up for children's at-home educational television as a high priority objective in its national legislative agenda. The public television community for its part will continue to look helplessly upon its children's schedule as only one large area of funding deficiency among many. Yet someone must look out for creating a sensible national response to this important education need and opportunity.

The children's television issue is one that touches everybody but belongs to nobody—to nobody, that is, with a constituency, and a lobby, and the will to advance the field as fast and as far as it needs and deserves. Independent production groups can attract and channel funding into the field, but most do not contribute funding support themselves. A rare exception is Children's Television Workshop, an independent corporation. Their successes in generating income have allowed them to become one of the nation's largest contributors of funds to support children's programs on public television. In fact, the Workshop manages consistently to spend more to support the national PTV children's schedule than about any other funder. CTW invests more than $7.5 million a year of self-generated revenues currently in the yearly renewal of *Sesame Street*, and convinces government and private organizations to contribute to the support of innovative and urgently needed children's productions monies which otherwise would be spent wholly or in large part outside the children's television field.

These efforts are wonderful as far as they go, but the Workshop by itself cannot generate nearly enough dollars to fill the total need. One problem is that no formula exists by which to duplicate *Sesame Street*'s astounding success as a revenue generator through sales of related products. Another is the proven limit to the number of funders which independent production groups can tap. Other difficulties are that production income at CTW is uncertain from year to year and derives entirely from short-term grants and its own self-generated revenues, which are important but insufficient.

Children's television has occupied a poorly articulated niche in the funding agendas of the U.S. Department of Education, and the National Endowments for the Arts and Humanities. None of these agencies sustains a regularly earmarked allocation for the field, and no clear national policy exists to channel dedicated government funds through them into the children's TV area. Only the National Science Foundation has shown a willingness to make a sustained effort for children's educational television programming in science and mathematics.

All of the governmental and quasi-governmental organizations involved in funding and managing children's educational TV programs—including the above-named agencies, plus the Corporation for Public Broadcasting and the stations of public television—bring into play a curious sort of equilibrium effect with respect to the field's overall level of funding.

They provide corrective pressure if funding for children's programs goes uncommonly low, but these agencies tend to regard with disfavor dedicated congressional appropriations which single out children, among the many groups each agency serves, for special treatment.[40] This is more of the same "leveling" effect discussed elsewhere in the case of public broadcasting, but here we see that it occurs on an even wider scale. The leveling pressures exerted through some of these organizations are often felt in a very real way. For instance, they are felt when the stations in public television, which control fund-raising through appeals for voluntary individual contributions, have an aversion to mounting dedicated appeals as a means to support productions in targeted program categories. Another important example comes from the agencies which channel government funds into education productions for children. Some oppose the creation of a separate Endowment for Children's Television, structured on the lines of the congressionally created and funded Endowments for the Arts and Humanities.[41] Yet they themselves don't meet the need.

The need for an acceptable funding mechanism is acute. Where other countries excel in providing quality in television for children, they do so through some mechanism for effectively channeling public support into the activity. They do so at a cost, and whether this cost is borne in commercial or public television, it is always, ultimately, only the public who pay.

I have no doubt that American parents would elect to pay the amount of less than a cent per day required to bring their children a year-round educational television offering of high quality, if only there were a collection-and-disbursement mechanism. The dedicated yearly TV-set tax which confers enviable benefits upon children through television in other countries is out of the question here, for historical and political reasons.[42]

But are all means for serving our children's educational needs through television simply out of the question? Have we harnessed ourselves with communications laws, systems, and traditions that bar us from realizing the highest potential of this great, ubiquitous educational device?

All the same institutional and funding barriers which initially prompted the creation of Children's Television Workshop in 1968 still exist. But today they exist in a different context: now we have demonstrated television's educational effectiveness and cost-efficiency. And we know now, unequivocally, that when programs embed sound educational content in polished and sophisticated production forms, learning becomes a voluntary, everyday child's pastime.

The more we explore the many, seemingly intractable barriers to realizing this vision in behalf of our children and our national education agenda, the more clear it becomes that government funding is an indispensable necessity. What is not so clear is the precise administrative mechanism through which a government contribution is best channeled. This is a matter which needs direction from carefully framed national policy.

Toward a National Policy on Television in Education

No person in the world has done more to advance television's productive role in children's lives than has the president of the John and Mary R. Markle Foundation, Lloyd Morrisett. In his combined capacity as leader among foundations and cofounder and chairman of the board for CTW, he has had a hand in shaping significant developments in U.S. children's television since the mid 1960s. Recently, "with the intent of reaching specific and immediate conclusions," he proposed a provocative range of objectives and actions that could give rise to a national policy for telecommunications and education.[43]

Noting the widely acknowledged need for long-term change and improvement in our nation's schools, which have been asked to do more than they can do, and further noting television's proven value as a teacher and a constructive element in children's lives, its ubiquity and remarkable cost-effectiveness, Morrisett says we must recognize that *"in this technological age there can be no effective education policy without an effective and coordinated telecommunications policy."*[44] (My emphasis.)

Morrisett proposes a policy that provides *availability* of programs at times convenient for children, *diversity* in content, style, and subject matter, *selectivity* in calling upon television when it is the best and most cost-effective solution available, *focus* in the form of different programs for different ages, and *innovation* to allow new applications and approaches to be explored.

Major action by Congress and the Administration must, of course, grow out of a wide dialogue involving the general public and soliciting the views of specialists in child development and education, television producers, and representatives of interested agencies, both from within and from outside of government. Most importantly, approaches considered and rejected in the past should be reconsidered in light of new circumstances, and ideas for new types of solutions should be invited.

How to provide adequate and stable public funding is not the only issue to be addressed in framing a national policy. We must ask also by what institutional arrangement the flow of funding should be administered. Suggesting one possible approach, Morrisett asks: "Would an Endowment for Children's Television be a responsive, cost effective and responsible manager of public funds supplementing the activities of the Department of Education, the National Science Foundation and the Corporation for Public Broadcasting?"[45] Finally, Morrisett suggests a forward-looking policy, one that will find ways now "to ensure that in future years children's programming will not be crowded out of cable television, direct broadcast satellite or other technologies because adult and other specialized programming is more economically rewarding."[46]

A still further question to be faced is how to organize this activity without interfering with local education prerogatives. While education is organized in this country as a largely state and local activity, broadcast television's extraordinary economic advantages are realized only when production is centralized, with distribution nationwide. There is an analogy in textbooks, which circumvent the problem of national curriculum setting: teachers are free to use it or not, once it is available. CTW's *The Electric Company*, for example, became for many years this country's most widely used in-school television program. A 1983 CPB survey found more than 100,000 classrooms making use of the series at that time.[47] And the series is one that children themselves have elected to view, without prompting, at home in large numbers.[48]

Well-respected subject-matter experts should play a role in creating the television programs which relate to their various specialties. The CTW model illustrates the workability of this process, as does standard practice among the several quasi-governmental agencies that fund children's PTV programming—for example, CPB and the National Endowments for the Arts and Humanities.

Another major consideration in organizing children's public service TV should be to provide maximum encouragement for non-government matching funds. Foundations and corporations manage their contributions to support public television programs in ways that produce maximum leverage. Funding managed by federal agencies has seen poor results in this regard.[49] The most successful past examples deserve to be looked upon as exemplary, and the least successful—most notably, the children's series supported in the 1970s through the Emergency School Assistance Act (ESAA) and administered through what was then the U.S. Department of Health, Education and Welfare—should be studied for their failings.[50]

The search for matching funds will not bear fruit if the programs for which this support is sought are conceived and controlled by government in ways that risk failure in competitive television terms (critical, artistic, popular). ESAA also demonstrates how government ownership of copyright shortens the effective life of programs by depriving them of non-government advocates who have a vested interest in their wide distribution, both in broadcast and in nonbroadcast forms, and in creating and making available ancillary educational materials.

Finally, government, by fulfilling its role as the only source of large and stable long-term funding available within the framework of the imperfect broadcasting system this country has evolved, could make a great contribution toward the creation of diverse production centers specializing in children's educational television, and toward the vital growth of professional talent in the field. Government's strong role is especially critical in supporting research to build a body of published experience on television's educational applications.

Proposed but never enacted were similar bills introduced by Senator John Heinz (R-PA) in 1977 and again in 1979 which would have created a National Endowment for Children's Television. The aim in both was to fund production of educational programs for children and to provide additional funds for professional training and for research on television's beneficial role in young people's lives. No action was taken on either bill. Nor did they occasion organized, wide debate. Yet wide support is essential for such a bill to pass.

Congress has the power to legislate regulatory reforms in children's television on the commercial side and to establish direct program funding, administrative structures, and tax incentives to spark contributions of program support on the noncommercial side. Bills in fact have been introduced in all these arenas in the 1980s, but as of 1988, no bill affecting program quantity has gone to a vote. Lack of wide public discussion has been a key barrier.

On two occasions during television's short history, Congress voted dedicated funds to support children's out-of-school educational programs. Both actions occurred in the early 1970s, sparked by the successes of *Sesame Street* and *The Electric Company*. One bill in fact contributed direct support to help sustain the year-to-year renewal of these two series until 1976.[51] At that time, CTW ceased renewing *The Electric Company*, and with self-generated revenues became majority funder of *Sesame Street*'s yearly renewal, with the remainder of this series' support coming from the public television stations. This funding arrangement holds true yet today as *Sesame Street* starts its twentieth consecutive season on air.

The other bill provided dedicated program funding through the aforementioned ESAA legislation between 1973 and 1980. This funding support went exclusively to produce programs aimed at reducing the isolation of ethnic minorities. This legislation in its lifetime provided an aggregate of $73 million in program support.[52] The activity was discontinued in the early Reagan years when the larger, federally administered ESAA education package of which it was a part was restructured in the form of block grants to the states. Administered by the U.S. Office of Education, ESAA funds produced such series as *Villa Alegre*, *Vegetable Soup*, *Carrascolendas*, *Rebop*, and *Infinity Factory*.

On the regulatory front, in October 1983 a House of Representatives subcommittee, under the leadership of its chairman, Timothy E. Wirth (D-CO), introduced H.R. 4097, the Children's Television Education Act. This legislative proposal was grounded in the premise that the marketplace in commercial television does not provide adequately for children. The logic of the bill was thus directly at odds with that by which the FCC only two months later dismissed the longstanding ACT petition for similar regulated reforms. The FCC's Report and Order in fact made the opposite argument, that the marketplace does provide for children adequately.[53]

The Wirth Bill died without action at the end of the 1984 session of Congress, as did a revised version which resurfaced in the form of parallel House and Senate bills introduced in 1985. The 1985 version included H.R. 3216, introduced by Wirth, and its companion in the Senate, S. 1594, sponsored by Frank Lautenberg (R-NJ). These bills, had they passed, would have required that the commercial stations carry a minimum of seven hours a week of children's age-specific educational and informational programming. The stations would have had to air at least five hours each week on weekdays.

The Wirth/Lautenberg bills also provided that each broadcaster's license renewal could be challenged by a "petition to deny," in the event of alleged noncompliance. The proposed legislation thus would have imposed a substantial evidentiary burden on the renewal applicant.

About the 1984 Wirth bill, an Action for Children's Television newsletter stated the following:

> The Wirth proposal sets a minimum for quantity in children's television, not quality. It establishes no board of censors, nor does it provide specific definitions of educational programming. Broadcasters' First Amendment rights are assured, since the bill avoids telling them *how* to do their job; it simply tells them that it must be done, that self-regulation has failed.[54]

The bills proposed no new obligations; on the contrary, they merely stated in specific terms what a station must do to meet an already existing requirement. Even the FCC's 1983 denial of ACT's petition stated: "The Commission continues to recognize the obligation of the broadcaster to serve children."[55] But the Commission's Report and Order left it to the stations to decide how this obligation is to be met. The Report and Order went on to explain, "This duty can be met with virtually any type of programming, which need not be designed to meet children's unique needs."[56]

Until such time as this view may be overriden by legislative action, it remains our government's operative direction to the commercial broadcasters. It repudiates the trusteeship principle in favor of the new "marketplace" principle which largely shaped the 1983 Report and Order.

One dissenting commissioner and the Action for Children's Television group are among those close to the case who are unwilling to concede that the FCC acted fairly, impartially, and as a well-informed body in dismissing the ACT petition. ACT successfully challenged the FCC decision, asking the U.S. Court of Appeals for the District of Columbia circuit to determine that the Commission acted arbitrarily and capriciously. ACT's appeal charged that the FCC failed to consider the benefits of educational programs, failed to provide a data base showing the availability of children's programming, and failed to consider comments concerning commercialization practices.

Former Commissioner Henry Rivera was the FCC's staunch lone champion of the children's cause during his tenure on the FCC from 1981 to 1985. Describing himself as a deregulator, Rivera argues nevertheless that the Commission's "failure to take appropriate remedial action reflects a serious error in judgment, if not also an abuse of discretion."[57] Rivera outlines his own position as follows:

> I dissent to the Commission's decision for three basic reasons. First, it changes the FCC's pre-existing children's programming policy without explaining why those changes are in the public interest, in violation of elementary principles of administrative law. Second, the majority's finding that there is sufficient programming to meet children's needs is arbitrary, because it is based on little more than conclusory assertions about the current conditions of the children's programming marketplace. In fact, record evidence strongly suggests that children's programs of the nature specified in the Children's Television Policy Statement [by the FCC in 1974] are in short supply in many markets when children are likely to be watching. Third, the legal and policy concerns advanced in opposition to a children's programming guideline are without foundation.[58]

A Teflon layer separates the true facts about the state of the children's TV "marketplace" from the assertions of fact contained in the FCC's 1983 Report and Order. It is regrettable that so crucial a ruling should have been grounded on the highly misleading information that "The Public Broadcasting System, during the 1982–83 season provided stations in the public broadcasting system, reaching over 90 percent of all television households, with some 2,050 hours of children's programming," with total disregard for the fact that scarcely more than 100 of those program hours—a scant 5 percent!—were newly produced in that or any recent season. And how disingenuous for the ruling to have highlighted that "The Corporation for Public Broadcasting has recently recognized children's programming as the number one priority in its Program Fund guidelines" at a time when the Administration was bent on slashing drastically the overall federal PTV contribution which supports this program fund. The ruling ignored the fact, further, that a "number one priority" commitment from CPB's program fund translates to a small and undependable fraction of the funding needed to support even a minimally adequate PTV children's program line-up. For example, since the time when *The Electric Company* went out of production in 1976, there have been insufficient funds to produce a major new age-specific series for the early elementary school-age "graduates" of *Sesame Street*. Solely for want of funding, they remain a nearly forgotten age group on public television.

The 1983 Report and Order faults the FCC's 1979 Task Force report "for its failure to properly consider" cable program services, yet only 17.5 percent of U.S. homes were wired to cable in 1978 when that report was prepared. The 1983 Report and Order arbitrarily focuses on the 56 percent of homes "passed" by (that is, reachable by) cable instead of on the 44 percent *not* then reachable. It leaves aside the fact that at the time the Report and Order was issued, in 1983, a 30 percent smaller number of U.S. TV households—a total of 39.3 percent—actually subscribed to cable.[59] And the ruling totally ignores the equity issue, with no consideration given to the fact that cable operators are for the most part wiring the nation's more affluent neighborhoods first.

Finally, while it is of course appropriate that the FCC consider the overall environment within which commercial broadcasters operate, it is presumptuous of the FCC to imply that cable will continue to provide programs for children. Consider, for example, that early in the history of network television it provided a wealth of regularly scheduled children's weekday programs, only to drop every one of them as business considerations began to take precedence, where at one time the considerations of system-building and public goodwill had held some sway. A recent full-page ad for the Nickelodeon children's cable TV program service features the following question in large print: "Why do 784 cable operators carry a children's channel they can't make a dime on?" Indeed—and we might ask further how long they may be expected to continue to do so. It's not that Nickelodeon isn't a fine program service. The problem is that while the FCC is letting broadcasters off the hook because cable—along with other new video forms—is arriving, the cable industry is striving to shed the obligations which communities impose upon it in return for exclusive franchise rights. They are trying to liken themselves to newspapers, in an effort to achieve the same laissez-faire status.

We can't re-invent our television institutions; we can't unscramble our egg. But we can have reforms in children's commercial television if we have the will to do so. Australia has shown us how. Australia has a commercially dominated set-up very much like our own; ten years ago, children's TV in Australia differed little from its American counterpart. Then in 1979 broadcasters were required to program for young audiences.[60] Guidelines were set, government subsidies came into play. All this was triggered by a well-publicized event—the abolishment of the Australian Broadcasting Control Board, the FCC equivalent body. The new Australian Broadcasting Tribunal, which took its place, opened an inquiry into self-regulation for broadcasters that drew more than five hundred public submissions, most of them critical of children's programming. As a result, self-regulation was denied to broadcasters. Effective in 1979, the Tribunal required that one hour of "C" classified children's programs be telecast Monday through Friday between 4:00 and 5:00 p.m. These programs must be specifically designed for the 6-to-13 age group, and while they must be primarily entertaining television, they must also by the Tribunal's mandate contribute to the social and intellectual needs of children. A further requirement provides for preschool programs. Specifically, each station is required to air a minimum of one thirty-minute preschool program Monday through Friday which may not be interrupted by commercials.

Reform worked in Australia. It worked because a public grown tired of shoddy programming and scheduling practices, and of inaction on the part of the government's appointed regulators, expressed its outrage. People were tired of what they saw and they weren't going to stand for it any more. They demanded a special deal for children.

In the U.S we have an even better platform to start from than did the Australian public. The requirement that U.S. broadcasters make a special provision for children is already their obligation under the law. Only the implementation of this requirement is at question. Congress ought to find the will to specify a weekday minimum, and it ought to pursue a course of complementarity by supporting programs for public television. The result, if our lawmakers can find the courage to do both, will be the kind of program diversity that children thrive on best.

Notes

Chapter 1. Our Crisis in Children's Television, Our Deficiencies in Children's Education

1. Source: A. C. Nielsen.

2. *Child and Teenage Television Viewing 1981* (New York: A. C. Nielsen Co.).

3. Examples: CBS's *30 Minutes*, the award-winning TV magazine show for young people that was patterned on *60 Minutes*, was canceled. NBC's *Special Treat* moved into rebroadcasts with no new shows produced. ABC dropped *Animals, Animals, Animals* on Sunday mornings, and stopped production on *Kids Are People Too*, deciding to present reruns for its major non-cartoon effort on weekends.

4. Action for Children's Television appeared before the FCC in 1970 with a proposal that required daily programming for children, and the elimination of commercials—including selling by hosts—on children's television. The FCC accepted ACT's proposal as a petition for rulemaking.

5. Source: Federal Communications Commission (1984), "Children's Television Programming and Advertising Practices: Report and Order" (*Federal Register, 49,* 1704, January 13).

6. Source: *Television Programming for Children: A Report of the Children's Television Task Force* (five volumes) (Washington, D.C.: Federal Communications Commission, 1979).

7. Source: FCC, "Report and Order."

8. Reference: Surgeon General's Scientific Advisory Committee on Television and Social Behavior (1972), *TV and Growing Up: The Impact of Televised Violence* (Report to the Surgeon General, U.S. Public Health Ser-

vice) (Washington, D.C.: U.S. Government Printing Office). See also Chapter 1, note 15.

9. Some of the key evaluation studies are reviewed in brief in Chapter 6. For access to the full technical reports on selected evaluations of CTW productions, see Bibliography entries under the following author names: for various evaluations of *Sesame Street*, G. Lesser, S. Ball, G. Bogatz, J. Minton, L. Paulson, T. Cook; for various evaluations of *The Electric Company*, S. Ball, P. Dirr, R. Herriott, R. Liebert, J. Riccobono, A. Sherdon.

10. For an excellent general description of pre-broadcast planning and formative research to guide program design, see G. Lesser (1974) *Children and Television: Lessons from Sesame Street* (New York: Random House). For examples of other writing on the subject, see the Bibliography under the following author names: M. Chen, D. Connell, S. Gibbon, G. Lesser, K. Mielke, K. O'Bryan, E. Palmer, B. Reeves, L. Rust.

11. The Bibliography mentions a few of these. Also, currently G. Lesser of the U.S. and P. Levelt of the Netherlands are collaborating in a compilation and review of published and unpublished studies and reports on *Sesame Street* and its various international adaptations, which number well in excess of 300 entries.

12. Evidence that children from low-income circumstances learn from watching *Sesame Street* and *The Electric Company* is contained in reports of major evaluations of the two series by S. Ball and G. Bogatz, and in studies by other researchers such as J. Minton and L. Paulson. Evidence of heavy *Sesame Street* viewership in low-income black and Spanish-speaking neighborhoods is reported in the Yankelovich surveys. See Bibliography under the author names indicated.

13. Examples of fully or partly CTW-owned tax-paying subsidiaries, current or previous, include Distinguished Productions, Inc., and Sesame Street Records, both subsidiaries of CTW Communications, Inc.; and Children's Computer Workshop. A Ford Foundation grant in the early 1970s helped CTW develop its capacity to produce self-generated revenues.

14. Source: *BBC Annual Report and Handbook 1986*. BBC-1 carries 746 hours of children's out-of-school programs, and BBC-2 carries 39. Their combined total is 785 hours, and the children's fraction of all schedule hours on the combined two channels is 7.2 percent. Children's out-of-school programs make up 12.6 percent of the schedule on the BBC-1 channel.

15. Sources: PBS and the several individual children's program producers who supplied PBS. The newly produced children's program hours in the 1984–85 PBS children's TV schedule were: *Sesame Street*, 39; *Mr. Rogers' Neighborhood*, 7.5; *Reading Rainbow*, 2.5; *WonderWorks*, 22; *Voyage of the Mimi*, 6.5; and *3-2-1 Contact*, 10.

16. Schools television constituted 503 hours and 10.1 percent of BBC-2's

total annual broadcast schedule in 1984–85. Source: *BBC Annual Report and Handbook 1986*.

17. Harold Howe II (1984) Introduction to Symposium on the Year of the Reports: Responses from the Educational Community. *Harvard Educational Review*, Volume 5, Number 1. Reports cited by the Symposium include:

- Boyer, Ernest (1983), *High School: A Report on Secondary Education in America* (Princeton, N.J.: Carnegie Foundation for the Advancement of Teaching);

- Goodlad, John J. (1983), *A Place Called School: Prospects for the Future* (New York: McGraw-Hill);

- Lightfoot, Sara L. (1983), *The Good High School: Portraits of Culture and Character* (New York: Basic Books).

- The National Commission on Excellence in Education (1983), *A Nation At Risk: The Imperative for Educational Reform* (Washington, D.C.: U.S. Department of Education);

- The National Science Board Commission on Precollege Education in Mathematics, Science, and Technology (1983), *Educating Americans for the 21st Century* (2 vols.) (Washington, D.C.: National Science Foundation);

- Task Force on Education for Economic Growth (1983), *Action for Excellence: A Comprehensive Plan to Improve Our Nation's Schools* (Denver: Education Commission of the States);

- The Twentieth Century Fund Task Force on Federal Elementary and Secondary Education Policy (1983), *Making the Grade* (New York: Twentieth Century Fund);

18. Harold Howe II, *Harvard Educational Review, ibid.*

19. Lack of funding caused the demise of *Zoom* and *The Electric Company*, and was responsible in part for the reduction of *Mr. Rogers' Neighborhood* to as few as ten new shows (5 hours of production) a year. *3-2-1 Contact* currently is at the end of its assured funding, with no new funding source in sight. And in spite of its highly successful premier season, *Reading Rainbow* received much less than it deserved in funding to create additional programs.

20. Source: A. C. Nielsen.

21. Source: Pifer, Alan (1978), "Perceptions of Childhood and Youth (Report of the President)," in *1978 Annual Report Carnegie Corporation of New York*.

22. Source: *The Dial* (June 1983).

23. *Ibid*.

24. Source: Quoted in CTW newsletters and press reports. The author himself heard Marland make this observation in public on many occasions.

25. From A. C. Nielsen data, we know that each week, *Sesame Street* attracts six million preschoolers for an average of 3.1 viewings each, giving a total of 18.6 million viewings. In 52 weeks, that comes to 967 million preschooler viewings. At a series production cost in Fiscal Year 1985 of $9,719,000, the cost per child per viewing comes to just one cent.

26. Source: CTW Newsletter. Note, however, that *The Electric Company* continued to play weekdays on PBS in repeat for eight years after its last renewed season in 1976–77. As a result, the cost-per-viewer ratio continued to improve over the course of those eight years.

27. Source: The annual back-to-school forecast from the National Center for Education Statistics projects a $4,263 annual expenditure rate per pupil for the 1986–87 school year. Assuming a 190-day school year, this translates to $22.42 per pupil per school day.

28. Population source: U.S. Bureau of the Census, Current Population Reports Series, P–25, No. 952.

29. For details on current expenditure, see Table 5 in Chapter 7. The 1984–85 expenditure for children's programs aired on public television, new plus repeat programs, was $28.7 million.

30. Based on the total national population of 239 million men, women, and children.

31. From the annual back-to-school forecast issued by the National Center for Education Statistics. The U.S. population figure used in arriving at my per capita calculation is 239 million.

32. In 1985 dollars.

33. The right of cable companies to wire into the wealthier neighborhoods of a community first has been upheld by the courts.

34. My own projection. Nobody has argued a convincing case that more than three-quarters of U.S. homes will have access to cable by the year 2000. The National Cable Television Association reported that in the ten largest television markets, 65 percent of homes were still without access to cable in 1985. And the 1985 Field Guide from *Channels* reports that high installation costs have frightened the biggest multiple-system operators away from major markets, leaving some cities looking hard for qualified bidders. Also, in the largest cities cable faces the greatest amount of broadcaster competition for TV advertising. According to *TV and Cable Factbook* (Washington: Television Digest, annual) cable had 37.5 million subscribers in 1986, not all of which are households. There are about 88 million TV households nationwide.

35. In Chapter 7, I propose a rate of funding support for children's out-of-school public TV programs of $62.4 million per year, to provide 260 days per year of weekday programming. Given that there are 42 million 2- to 13-year-olds in the U.S., the cost per year per child is $1.49.

36. The cost for the television in the example above is less than six-tenths

of a cent per child per day ($0.0057). The cost for the book is $1.49 divided by five, or 30 cents a day. Television's cost-advantage is 53 to one.

Chapter 2. Commercial Television: How and Why It Fails Children

1. Source: Television Bureau of Advertising, and Radio Advertising Bureau.

2. Quoted from *Broadcasting Cablecasting Yearbook 1988*.

3. Television Bureau of Advertising.

4. *Variety* on October 8, 1986, reported that in fiscal 1985 NHK realized $1.42 billion in total revenues, $1.375 billion from TV-set license fees paid by Japanese households and the remainder from profits of subsidiaries. The *World Bank Atlas 1985* put Japan's 1985 population figure at 120 million.

5. The *BBC Annual Report and Handbook 1986* reports that license income of 723.1 million British pounds (which converts to $904 million U.S.) was collected for the year ending March 1985. The World Bank Atlas puts Britain's 1985 population at 56 million, giving a per capita BBC expenditure of $16.14.

6. Source: Corporation for Public Broadcasting (May 1988), *Public Broadcasting Income Fiscal Year 1987 (Preliminary)*. This report gives the total fiscal 1987 income for public broadcasting from all sources as $1.294 billion. A U.S. population figure of 239 million was used to calculate the per capita rate.

7. Reform efforts triggered by the failure of commercial TV broadcasters to provide an adequate weekday children's offering are the 1970 ACT petition to the FCC, the FCC's 1974 Policy Statement and its 1979 Task Force Report, and the House and Senate reform bills proposed beginning in 1983. See Chapters 3 and 7.

8. See the 1979 report titled *Programming for Children: A Report of the Children's Television Task Force* (five volumes) (Washington, D.C.: Federal Communications Commission).

9. Source: Television Advertising Bureau.

10. Comment made by Mrs. Marion Wright Edelman, president of Children's Defense Fund of Washington, D.C., at a conference held to discuss the subject and rationale of this book.

11. See Chapter 1 Notes on other children's programs dropped or put into repeats with the arrival of Mark Fowler as FCC Chairman and chief deregulator, also in the early 1980s.

12. The First Amendment to the U.S. Constitution protects the right of free speech.

13. The Broadcasting Act of 1934 holds the commercial broadcasters re-

sponsible to program in a manner that serves the public "interest, convenience, and necessity." See Chapter 3 for a review of the manner in which this mandate has been interpreted in the case of children's TV programming. See especially the reviews of the 1974 FCC Report and Order and the 1983 FCC Report and Order on children's programming.

14. 1974 FCC Report and Order.

15. An excellent thorough review of broadcasting history and law as they affect children is contained in William Melody (1973), *Children's Television: The Economics of Exploitation* (New Haven, Conn.: Yale Univ. Press).

16. See my extensive quotes of the 1974 FCC Report and Order in Chapter 3.

17. Melody, *Children's Television, op. cit.*

18. Several recent bills in Congress have proposed legislated reforms in children's commercial TV. See late sections of Chapter 7 for a detailed overview.

19. For the definitive history of U.S. broadcasting and the events described here, see Erik Barnouw's critically acclaimed trilogy *A History of Broadcasting in the United States* and the overview and sequel, also by Barnouw, titled *Tube of Plenty: The Evolution of American Television.*

20. Source: A. C. Nielsen.

21. See the 1977 book by Nippon Hoso Kyokai (Japanese Broadcasting Corporation–NHK) titled *50 Years of Japanese Broadcasting.* (Tokyo: NHK).

22. Based on 1984–85 budget year, in which NHK's license income was the equivalent of $1.42 billion (as reported in the October 8, 1985, issue of *Variety*), and U.S. public broadcasting income was $1.1 billion (as reported by CPB).

23. The logic of this frequently heard assertion is riddled with holes. As regards children, we Americans don't believe in giving them always what they want, but prescribe that they go to school, and eat a balanced diet in the school cafeteria. The commercial broadcasters fought for and won relief in recent years from performing community ascertainment studies to determine what their viewers want. Britain and Japan proved long ago that where public broadcasting is dominant, people "want" (i.e., watch in majority numbers) a high-quality public service program line-up.

24. Each year the BBC issues a Handbook which contains its full charter and describes its programs, operations, budgets and departments.

25. The Independent Broadcasting Authority (IBA) issues an annual Handbook which describes its charter and policies, the program service, and issues in the relationships the among the IBA, the regional broadcasting licensees, and the British public.

26. The Exchequer levy is 66.7 percent of all profits above and beyond 2.8% of revenues or $812,000 whichever is the greater.

27. This pessimistic view follows the FCC's thirteen years of inaction

(1970–83), whereupon it ruled against a regulated weekday children's offering. Since then, federal bills have failed for three consecutive years to become law, in proposals aimed at overturning the FCC's ruling.

28. This argument is made by the FCC in its 1983 Report and Order denying the ACT petition calling for a regulated weekday children's offering. My main comments on the FCC's argument appear in Chapters 3 and 7.

29. The mid- to late 1970s was an era of much touted cultural cable channels that all died aborning, with substantial financial losses incurred in some cases.

30. Among the business realities are the failure of cable to become the lucrative advertiser's medium which many cable investors had thought it would become upon achieving 30 percent penetration of U.S. households; the high cost of wiring in large cities; unexpectedly high rates of "churn" (i.e., of subscriber turn-over); rapid growth (or expectations of growth) in competing technologies, such as videocassettes and direct broadcast satellite systems; and the failed market (so far) for ancillary, non-TV data services.

31. Further discussion in support of this point appears in Chapter 7.

32. The FCC's 1983 Report and Order, in support of its "marketplace" logic, relied *not* on marketplace alternatives which already exist, but called for more programs for children on public TV, and counted in the benefits of yet-to-be-developed technologies such as DBS and videodiscs.

Chapter 3. The FCC: The View from Beneath the Sand

1. As reported in the February 14, 1983, issue of *Broadcasting* magazine, in a speech the prior week at Arizona State University, Fowler said: "I have no enthusiasm for mandated minimums when it comes to children's programming.... The reality is that no broadcaster has ever had his license imperiled on a children's programming issue, and I do not foresee starting up a new obstacle course."

2. Source: A. C. Nielsen.

3. From: Les Brown (1977), *The New York Times Encyclopedia of Television* (New York: Times Books).

4. Source: A. C. Nielsen.

5. Juvenile courts function under laws which recognize children as a special category. Minors cannot be held liable for breach of contract. Child labor laws protect children from exploitation in the workplace.

6. The FCC since 1980, under the chairmanship of Mark S. Fowler, has set great store by the principle of marketplace solutions as an alternative to regulation. Later in this chapter and in Chapter 7, I discuss the inappropriateness of this principle in the area of children's programming. The FCC's 1983 ruling which denied Action for Children's Television's petition for reg-

ulated reforms leaned heavily on the marketplace principle in rationalizing its decision.

7. See Table 1 in Chapter 2, which shows that in television's early years, commercial broadcasters presented great amounts of children's fare.

8. For an excellent overview of research on the issue of violence and stereotyping on television, see: *Television and Behavior: Ten Years of Scientific Progress and Implications for the Eighties* (Washington, D.C.: Government Printing Office, 1982).

9. *Ibid.*

10. But at the same time, stereotypes of a subtle variety continue. For example, see Chester M. Pierce, "Social Trace Contaminants: Subtle Indicators of Racism in TV," in S. B. Witget and R. P. Abeles, eds. (1980), *Television and Social Behavior: Beyond Violence and Children* (Hillside, N.J.: Lawrence Erlbaum Associates). See also F. Earle Barcus (1983), *Images of Life on Children's Television: Sex Roles, Minorities, and Families* (New York: Praeger).

11. See 28 FCC 2nd 368 (1971), 36 Fed. Reg. 1429 (published January 29, 1971).

12. See: *Report and Policy Statement*, 50 FCC 2nd 1 (1974), 39 Fed. Reg. 39396 (published November 6, 1974). The proceeding came to be known as Docket 19142.

13. From Peggy Charren.

14. I am indebted for portions of my summary on the FCC's 1974 Policy Statement to Nicholas P. Miller, former communications counsel to the State Communications Subcommittee and to the President's Office of Telecommunications Policy. See his article in the journal *Television and Children*, Spring 1981.

15. Please note that I have represented here a selection of excerpts whose order and juxtapostion may depart from those of the original. My presentation, I believe, properly underscores the positive tone and intensity of the 1974 Policy Statement, in contradistinction to the arbitrary language and conclusions of the eventual 1983 FCC Report and Order.

16. See Chapter 1, note 3 on the complete discontinuation or drastic reduction of renewal rates in network children's productions. For example: CBS's *Captain Kangaroo* and *30 Minutes*, NBC's *Special Treat*, ABC's *Animals, Animals, Animals* and *Kids Are People Too*.

17. See FCC's 1983 Report and Order.

18. I concur. ACT succeeded in its demand of an explanation for the FCC's 1983 decision to soften its children's television policy, asking the U.S. Court of Appeals for the District of Columbia Circuit to determine that the Commission acted arbitrarily and capriciously. ACT charged that the FCC failed to consider scientific testimony on the programming needs of children, failed to consider the benefits of educational programs, failed to provide a

data base showing the availability of children's programming, and failed to consider comments concerning commercialization practices. In Chapter 7, I cite dissenting FCC Commissioner Henry Rivera's similar objections to the decision.

19. For detailed data on the current and recent PTV children's offering, see Chapters 4 and 7. Note that although *Sesame Street* offers a 130-program series each year, only about 30 percent—or roughly 39 hours—consist of newly produced elements. The FCC's data may also have included some children's instructional programs, which properly fall in quite a different category.

20. See chapter note 19, *ibid*.

21. See Chapter 7 for more detail, including a discussion of additional provisions in the recent legislation, and comment on the fate of the proposed bills to date.

22. Total FY 1986 income for the Japan Broadcasting Corporation (NHK), the public broadcasting organization in Japan, was the approximate equivalent of $2.2 billion, or roughly twice the funding level that year for U.S. public broadcasting.

23. See: Japan Broadcasting Corporation (1977), *50 Years of Japanese Broadcasting* (Tokyo: NHK).

24. On the BBC's annual income, refer to the *BBC Annual Report and Handbook 1986*, and to *Variety*, October 8, 1985, regarding the NHK's annual income.

25. Both the BBC and the NHK are keenly sensitive to their need as centralized entities to serve regional needs well. For the interested reader, the BBC now publishes its regional expenditure.

26. David Glencross (March 1986), "Thirty Years of Independent Television in the U.K.," *EBU Review*, Volume XXXVII, Number 2, pp. 34–39.

27. As reported in *Variety*, January 16, 1985.

28. This requirement is widely reported in journalistic accounts of the IBA's operating procedure, and is published along with the rest of the IBA charter in the IBA annual report.

29. The history of IBA actions on licensing may be found in the successive IBA annual reports.

30. The *BBC Annual Report and Handbook 1986* reports that the BBC carried 785 hours of children's programs (not counting 483 hours of schools programs) in the year 1985. By tradition, one-quarter of that total is repeat programming, and three-quarters new.

31. Source: *Channels of Communication* (March 1985), Volume 5, Number 5, p. 70.

32. As reported in Action for Children's Television's news magazine, *Re: ACT*, by ACT's director of public relations, Cynthia Alperowicz (1984, Volume 13, Number 1, p. 6).

33. Prior to the FCC's 1983 ruling against a weekday children's requirement, Lloyd Morrisett polled executives in commercial television to test their willingness voluntarily to set up and sustain a funding mechanism to support PTV children's programs. They declined. The general idea surfaces frequently in the writings of journalists and some advocates.

34. For a more complete account of the Australian reforms, see Chapter 7.

35. On current and needed expenditure levels to support the PTV children's offering, see Chapters 4 and 7.

Chapter 4. Public Television: A Tug-of-War for Scarce Funds

1. These three were a grant of $2 million from United Technologies to *3-2-1 Contact* in 1980, one of $2.5 million from IBM to *Square One TV* in 1987, and a succession of grants given over several years to support *Mr. Rogers' Neighborhood* by the Sears Roebuck Foundation.

2. See Table 5 in Chapter 7, which lists the amounts of funding for public TV's out-of-school children's programs, from all sources, in a typical recent year.

3. See Chapter 1 for reference to the much-written-about problems of U.S. schools.

4. For a succinct overview of this historical period in broadcasting's development, see Erik Barnouw (1975), *Tube of Plenty: The Evolution of American Television*. See also his excellent trilogy on U.S. broadcast history, listed in the Bibliography section.

5. Barnouw, *Tube of Plenty*.

6. *Ibid*.

7. *Ibid*.

8. See: *A Public Trust: The Report of the Carnegie Commission on the Future of Public Broadcasting* (1979) (New York: Bantam Books).

9. Source: A. C. Nielsen.

10. From personal conversations with successive heads of BBC's children's television department. The point is that instead of being led by the ratings when programming for children, as is most often done on the U.S. commercial TV stations, the BBC seeks to lead and "uplift" children's tastes in television.

11. Source: *Public Broadcasting Income Fiscal Year 1987 (Preliminary)* (Washington, D.C.: Corporation for Public Broadcasting).

12. Source: *Washington Post*, May 31, 1988 (p. C6), article by John Carmody.

13. Source: *Standard and Poor's Industry Surveys* (June 29, 1986), Vol. 154, No. 25, Sec. 1.

14. Source: Obserservation made by Mr. Yoshizumi Asano during 1981

symposium of "Public Role and Systems of Broadcasting," held in Tokyo in September 1981 under sponsorship of the Hoso-Bunka Foundation.

15. As noted elsewhere, the number of hours of new production for the 1984–85 broadcast season was 87.5 hours. (See Chapter 1 notes.)

16. Source: Corporation for Public Broadcasting.

17. See Chapter 1 notes for list of programs and new program costs for the 1984–85 PTV out-of-school children's schedule.

18. Detail on the Ford Foundation's contributions to U.S. public broadcasting may be found in the foundation's annual reports. This contribution was made over a period of approximately twenty years, ending about 1971.

19. The Annenberg/CPB Project, the result of this generous grant, is administered by Corporation for Public Broadcasting in Washington, D.C.

20. Agency for Instructional Television is headquartered in Bloomington, Indiana.

21. Source: *Annual Report Fiscal Year 1985* (Washington, D.C.: Corporation for Public Broadcasting).

22. Yearly amounts spent on children's PTV series fluctuate, but the point that *Sesame Street*'s funding accounts for about a third of that for all PTV children's programming is valid for most recent years.

23. For more discussion on foundations and their funding philosophy as it affects children's television productions, see Chapter 7. Only one foundation grant, of $20,000, went to support children's public television in the 1984–85 broadcast season. Without performing the calculation, one might suppose that the average foundation contribution for recent years has been around $1 million to $2 million a year.

24. United Technologies Corporation gave $2 million to help support the initial season of *3–2–1 Contact*, in 1981, and IBM gave $2.5 million in 1987 for the initial season of *Square One TV*. Much smaller amounts are typical. Only the Sears Roebuck Foundation has given long-term support to help sustain production of a successful children's series (*Mr. Rogers' Neighborhood*) over a period of many years.

25. See further discussion late in Chapter 7. This mention was in the Cooperative Research Act. Direct federal funding was made to the field during the decade of the 1970s through the Emergency School Aid Act. For a splendid critical assessment of both of these Congressional appropriations, see Keith Mielke, *et al.* (April 1975), *The Federal Role in Funding Children's Television Programming*, Vol. 1: Final Report (Bloomington, Ind.: Institute of Communication Research).

Chapter 5. *The Prix Jeunesse and a Worldwide Vision of Quality*

1. For an excellent historical overview of the activities of the Japan Prize International Educational Programme Contest from its inception in 1964

through 1979, see: Koji Minouri (Fall 1979), *The Japan Prize Contest: The Past, Present and Future—A Brief Review of the Past Eleven Contests in Light of Certain Unforgettable Entries* (Tokyo: NHK—Nippon Hoso Kyokai (Japan Broadcasting Corporation)). For further information, write to Secretariat, The Japan Prize Contest, c/o NHK, Ninnan, Shibuya-ku, Tokyo 150, Japan.

2. The observation that countries with the strongest public service tradition in TV are most prominently represented among Prix Jeunesse winners is entirely impressionistic. I haven't done tallys to verify the point, but certainly the U.S. is under-represented in light of its size and its massive national expenditure on television.

3. See Chapter 1 notes for references to the current research literature on TV stereotyping.

4. See George Gerbner and Larry Gross (April 1976), "The Scary World of TV's Heavy Viewer," *Psychology Today*, pp. 41–46.

5. For an excellent comprehensive bibliography on the subject, see: John Murray (1980), *Television and Youth: 25 Years of Research and Controversy* (Boys Town, Nebr.: Boys Town Press).

6. The positive side of television, and especially its potential for informing and educating the public, is a prominent theme in a major recent overview of research on television. See: D. Pearl *et al.*, eds. (1982), *Television and Behavior: Ten Years of Scientific Progress and Implications for the Eighties. Vol. 2: Technical Reviews* (Washington, D.C.: U.S. Department of Health and Human Services).

Chapter 6. Sesame Street *and the CTW Vision of Quality*

1. See: D. Yankelovich (April 1973), "A Report on the Role and Penetration of *Sesame Street* in Ghetto Communities (Bedford-Stuyvesant, East Harlem, Chicago, and Washington, D.C.)" (New York: Children's Television Workshop).

2. For a history of the founding activities leading to *Sesame Street*'s initial broadcast season in 1969–70, see: Richard Polsky (1974), *Getting to Sesame Street: Origins of the Children's Television Workshop* (New York: Praeger).

3. Source: The funding proposal for the initial 130-hour *Sesame Street* series, titled "Television for Preschool Children," dated February 1968.

4. The 1968 proposal cited immediately above references University of Chicago educator Benjamin Bloom on the rate of intellectual development during the child's early years.

5. "Television For Preschool Children," *op. cit.*

6. For the technical reports on the original round of the Surgeon General's studies on television and social behavior, see: John P. Murray, Eli A. Rubinstein, and George A. Comstock, eds. (1972), *Television and Social Behavior* (Five volumes) (Washington, D.C.: Government Printing Office).

7. Source: A. C. Nielsen.

8. See in the Bibliography references to the television histories written by Erik Barnouw, which include the history of TV as a potent instrument in politicking.

9. Source: A. C. Nielsen reports to CTW on PBS' and *Sesame Street*'s household penetration, nationwide, in 1969 and 1970.

10. In 1979, CTW commissioned a nationwide survey of *Sesame Street* viewership carried out by the Newspaper Advertising Bureau. The study found that an estimated 88.3 percent of 2- to 5-year-olds in the country were reported to be viewers, with 58.4 percent described by parental report to be "regular" viewers. Among the over 10 percent reported not to be viewers, the study found that three-quarters of these households said they were out of range of the public television signal, while two-thirds reported that they receive a "poor" signal. Source: *CTW News*, February 1980, Number 46.

11. Source: A. C. Nielsen, in yearly reports to Children's Television Workshop.

12. For reference to the two ETS studies, see separate entries in the Bibliography under Samuel Ball and Gerry Ann Bogatz.

13. See Bibliography for references to two studies by R. Diaz-Guerrero *et al.*, a study by Hans-Bredo-Institut, and one by Gavriel Salomon.

14. See: Tom Cook *et al.*, (1975), *Sesame Street Revisited* (New York: Russell Sage).

15. The CTW-sponsored nationwide survey of *Sesame Street* viewership carried out by the Newspaper Advertising Bureau in October 1979 reports estimated viewing levels of 88.3 percent among 2- to 5-year-olds, 66 percent among 6- to 8-year-olds, and 36 percent among 9- to 11-year-olds. Source: *CTW News*, February 1980, Number 46.

16. Source: CTW-commissioned audience surveys carried out by the A. C. Nielsen television rating service. Two separate surveys by the Corporation for Public Broadcasting show the same pattern.

17. See Diaz-Guerrero *et al.*, *op. cit.*

18. *Sesame Street* advisors as listed in the series' 1972–73 funding proposal are: Dr. Gerald S. Lesser, Harvard University Graduate School of Education, Chairman; Miss Maria J. Canino, Puerto Rican Association for Community Affairs; Diego Castellanos, New Jersey Public Broadcasting Authority; Dr. Courtney B. Cazden, Harvard University Graduate School of Education; Mrs. Maria B. Cerda, ASPIRA, Inc., of Illinois; Dr. Jeanne Chall, Harvard University Graduate School of Education; James P. Comer, M.D., Yale Child Study Center; Mrs. Ahwanetta Cutler, Board of Education, New York; Leon Eisenberg, M.D., Massachusetts General Hospital; Dr. Shirly Feldman, City College of New York; Mrs. Allonia Gadsden, The Emerson School Inc.; Dr. Edythe J. Gaines, School Dist. 12, Bronx; Miss Mildred Gladney, University of Nebraska; Mrs. Dorothy Hollingsworth, Planning Model Cities,

Seattle, Washington; Nathan I. Huggins, Columbia University; Dr. J. McVicker Hunt, University of Illinois; Hernan La Fontaine, The Bilingual School—P.S. 25, Bronx, N.Y.; Dr. Enrique Hank Lopez, New York, N.Y.; Dr. Francis Mechner, Universal Education Corporation, N.Y.; Chester M. Pierce, M.D., Harvard University Graduate School of Education; Lee Polk, Educational Broadcasting Corp.; Armando B. Rendon, Washington, D.C.; Dr. Lauren B. Resnick, University of Pittsburgh; Professor Florence G. Roswell, City College of New York; Maurice Sendak, author and illustrator of children's books; Paul K. Taff, Connecticut ETV Corporation; Dr. Daniel Valdez, Metro State College, Denver; Dr. Doxey A. Wilkerson, Yeshiva University; Dr. Jack Yuen, San Francisco State College.

A special group of consultants worked with the CTW Research department in formulating and reviewing summative evaluation plans. This group, the CTW Research Advisory Committee, included at one time the following: Dr. Gerald S. Lesser, Chairman; Professor Richard C. Atkinson, Stanford University; Professor William W. Cooley, University of Pittsburgh; Dr. Luis Rivera, Escuela Infantil del Barrio, East Harlem, New York; Dr. Richard Santos, San Antonio, Texas; Dr. Doxey A. Wilkerson, Yeshiva University.

19. For a report on how we established an effective researcher-producer partnership in creating *Sesame Street*, see David D. Connell and Edward L. Palmer, *Sesame Street: A Case Study*, in J. D. Halloran and M. Gurevitch, eds. (1971), *Broadcaster/Researcher Cooperation in Mass Communication Research* (Leeds: J. A. Kavanagh and Sons, Ltd.).

20. For an account of the instructional goals of *Sesame Street*—how they were arrived at and how implemented by the television producers—see: Gerald S. Lesser (1974), *Children and Television: Lessons from Sesame Street* (New York: Random House).

21. Chapters 1 and 7 both contain presentations on the extraordinary cost-efficiency of television as an educational medium.

22. Following is a very brief sampling of published CTW formative research studies: Edward L. Palmer (1974), "Formative Research in the Production of Television for Children," in David R. Olsen, ed., *Media and Symbols: The Forms of Expression, Communication, and Education* (Chicago: University of Chicago Press, 1974). Also: Samuel Y. Gibbon, Edward L. Palmer, and Barbara R. Fowles, (1975), "*Sesame Street, The Electric Company* and Reading," in John B. Carroll and Jeanne S. Chall, eds., *Toward a Literate Society* (New York: McGraw-Hill). Also: Keith M. Mielke and Milton Chen, (1983), "Formative Research for *3-2-1 Contact*: Methods and Insights," in Michael J. Howe, ed., *Learning from Television: Psychological and Educational Research* (London: Academic Press).

23. Source: A. C. Nielsen report on the home-viewing audience for the 1971–72 broadcast season of the *The Electric Company*.

24. *Ibid*. See also the several survey documents authored by Robert Herriott and Roland J. Liebert, as mentioned in the Bibliography.

25. See: Robert E. Herriott and Roland J. Liebert (1972), *The Electric Company In-School Utilization Study: The 1971–72 School and Teacher Surveys* (New York: Children's Television Workshop). See also subsequent surveys by these two authors, as mentioned in the Bibliography .

26. *The Electric Company*'s status as the most-used TV program in U.S. schools is documented in two nationwide studies, in 1977 and 1983, carried out jointly by Corporation for Public Broadcasting and the National Center for Education Statistics. See Bibliography entries under Dirr, Peter, and Riccobono, J. A.

27. Commissioner Marland's characterization of *Sesame Street* and *The Electric Company* as the two best educational investments ever made in this country appears frequently in CTW newsletters and press releases for the early 1970s. This author heard Marland repeat the statement on several occasions at first hand.

28. See Bibliography for separate entries under the names of Samuel Ball and Ann Bogatz for references to the two evaluation studies on *The Electric Company* carried out by Educational Testing Service.

29. The Lincoln Heights, Ohio, study is reviewed in more detail in the following: "Special Report: *The Electric Company* Helps Boost School's Reading Scores," in: *Children's Television Workshop Newsletter*, No. 32, March 8, 1974. See also: Gibbon, Palmer, and Fowles, "*Sesame Street, The Electric Company*, and Reading," in Carroll and Chall, *Toward a Literate Society*.

30. See: Kenneth G. O'Bryan and Harold Silverman (1973), *Research Report: Experimental Eye-Movement Study* (New York: Children's Television Workshop). (Also in: ERIC Document Reproduction Service No. ED 126 870.)

31. See Chapter 1 notes for references to formative research about Children's Television Workshop and Gerald S. Lesser, *Children and Television: Lessons from Sesame Street*.

32. See chapter note 31, *ibid*.

33. See: Milton Chen (1972), *Verbal Response to The Electric Company: Qualities of Program Material and the Viewing Condition Which Affect Verbalization* (New York: Children's Television Workshop). (See also: ERIC Document Reproduction Service No. ED 126 862).

34. In this way, CTW secured the status of *The Electric Company* as a legitimate extension of the nation's education agenda in reading. The advisors included not only prominent academics but also classroom teachers of reading.

35. See: National Assessment of Educational Progress (1979), *Attitudes*

Toward Science: A Summary of Results from the 1976–77 National Assessment of Science (Report No. 08-5-02) (Denver, CO: National Assessment of Educational Progress). See also: Gerald S. Lesser (1980), "The Rationale for a TV Series on Science and Technology," in *CTW International Research Notes*, Number 3.

36. See: M. Mead and R. Metraux (1957), "Image of the Scientist Among High School Students," in *Science*, Volume 126.

37. Several national educational organizations joined around 1983 to make a special national issue of the need for improved science preparedness in schools, among them the National Academy of Education, the American Association for the Advancement of Science, and the National Science Foundation.

38. See Chapter 6 notes for reference to survey data on school use of *The Electric Company*. The A. C. Nielsen television survey organization also surveyed children's home viewing during each of the series' 14 seasons on air, commissioned by Children's Television Workshop. As a general statement, *The Electric Company* during most of these 14 years on air attracted roughly equal numbers of home and school viewers of elementary school age, with the combined total ranging from about 5.5 to 6.5 million children who viewed on a regular (weekly or more frequent) basis.

39. The expert reading advisors who helped the Children's Television Workshop create *The Electric Company* generally agreed that roughly 50 percent of all children experienced difficulty in the early 1970s learning the reading/decoding skills taught by the series (personal communications).

40. This argument is heard so frequently it needs no documentation. The key point is that widely published research over several decades demonstrates that broadcast TV can teach children. But see Gavriel Salomon's interesting work on amount of invested mental effort required by different media of presentation.

41. Information on the distribution of CTW productions abroad is from the CTW International department, 1 Lincoln Plaza, New York, N.Y. 10023.

42. For an excellent case study of the effect of *Sesame Street* coproduction process on a country's production style and capacity, see separate articles by Lewis Bernstein and Ruth Ben-Shaul, in CTW International Research Notes (Fall 1983), Number 4.

43. For illustrative case study descriptions of the CTW model of researcher-producer cooperation, see Bibliography, under Gibbon; Lesser; Mielke; and Palmer.

44. Organizations which, having learned the CTW model, then reapplied it (but always with modifications to fit their own specific situations) include: Televisa, in Mexico, producer of *Plaza Sesamo*; Radio Television Española, in Spain, producer of *Barrio Sesamo*; the Arabian Gulf States Joint Program Production Institution, in Kuwait, producer of

Iftah Ya Simsim; and the Instructional Television Centre, in Israel, producer of *Rechov Sumsum*.

45. See the Cook and Curtin article in the Bibliography.

46. For selected writings on formative research, see Bibliography, under Chen; Connell; Gibbon; Lesser; Mielke; O'Bryan; and Palmer.

47. *Ibid*. In addition, see: Jennings Bryant and Daniel Anderson, eds. (1983), *Children's Understanding of Television: Research on Attention and Comprehension* (New York: Academic Press).

48. For reference to these methods and the studies which have made use of them, consult the Bibliography under Bryant; Chen; and Mielke.

49. See note 27 regarding statements by former Commissioner of the U.S. Office of Education, Dr. Sidney Marland, claiming that *Sesame Street* and *The Electric Company* were the two best educational investments our government ever made. Government was one contributor among many to the funding of these series.

50. As of the 1988–89 broadcast season, *Sesame Street* starts its twentieth consecutive, renewed season on air; *The Electric Company* is no longer being broadcast, having completed 14 uninterrupted years on air; and *3-2-1 Contact* will air for its ninth consecutive season.

Chapter 7. Conclusions

1. See Chapter 1 for calculations showing that we could support a $62.4 million-a-year children's TV program offering for just six-tenths of a cent a year for each of the 42 million 2- to 13-year-olds in the country, based on a 260-day year.

2. For detailed calculations showing the ratio of new to repeat children's programming on U.S. public television, see Chapter 1.

3. See Chapters 1 and 3 for detail of the 1985 expenditure on U.S. children's PTV programs (the most recent year for which complete expenditure amounts are available). The total 1985 expenditure from all sources was about $28 million.

4. The 780-hour figure represents 260 hours per year (one hour per weekday) for each four-year child age group in the range of ages from two through thirteen.

5. See Chapters 1 and 3 for more detail on the Japanese and British children's offerings.

6. Population source: U.S. Bureau of the Census, Current Population Reports Series, P-25, No. 952. For convenience, I have assumed equal numbers of children in each four-year age group.

7. Key considerations in costing children's PTV programs include the following: (a) program costs can (and should) vary considerably depending on format; (b) longer series as a rule are more cost-efficient to pro-

duce than shorter ones; (c) series created with extensive educational planning and research, ancillary learning activities, and audience building are more expensive than those which do not include these elements; and (d) series which seek to maximize viewership by incorporating excellence in artistry and technical effects, in order to compete with the most popular of commercial TV's entertainment forms, cost more than those which do not. A fact of life in the funding of children's programs is that children are a demanding and voluntary audience, so that, as a consequence, small-budget series attract a significantly smaller viewership than do series produced with larger budgets. Also, longer series not only are more efficient in terms of per-program production cost but also tend to attract larger numbers of child viewers per program, because children tend to find and return again and again to view program series that are available at the same time and place in the TV schedule over a long period of time. The cost-efficient ideal in this regard is to provide each age group (2- to 5-year-olds, 6- to 9-year-olds, and 10- to 13-year-olds) with a dependable and uninterrupted year-round offering in a set time period. Finally, the cost per schedule hour tends to be smaller over the long term for preschoolers, who not only tolerate but enjoy and benefit educationally from a considerable amount of program repetition, than for school-age children who (more like adults) have little tolerance for repeats for most program forms. (This is not to say, however, that entirely original programming for preschoolers will *as a general rule* cost less than will entirely original programming for older children. It generally will cost the same.)

8. I cannot cite a source on this point, but based on my own extensive experience of commissioning and reviewing audience survey data, I feel confident that a detailed analysis of past survey data will prove the accuracy of my point.

9. See: *Broadcasting Cablecasting Yearbook 1986* (New York: Associated Press Broadcasting Services).

10. Source: Television Bureau of Advertising, and Radio Advertising Bureau.

11. *Ibid*.

12. The 26-cent-per-year figure is based on the yearly budget of $62.4 million proposed earlier in the chapter, and a total U.S. population figure of 239 million. The source of this population figure is cited in other chapters.

13. See Chapter 3 and associated Chapter 3 notes for my review of and references to the 1983 FCC ruling against a regulated weekday commercial TV children's offering.

14. See Chapter 3 notes for my presentation of facts and assumptions concerning factors which will tend to limit cable TV's growth between now and the end of the century.

15. *Ibid*.

16. In fact, the right of cable companies to wire first more profitable areas of communities was challenged and has been upheld in the courts.

17. For a detailed review of proposed legislation, see later sections in this chapter.

18. As quoted in *The New York Times*, February 22, 1983.

19. From a mid-1980s advertisement attempting to sell the Nickelodeon children's cable TV service to cable operators.

20. See Chapter 3 notes for reference to the FCC's 1983 Report and Order in this matter.

21. A detailed review of the proposed legislation appears in a later section of this chapter.

22. My pessimism is based on the failure of a congressional bill to go to vote in any of three successive legislative sessions in the period from 1984 through 1986; the active opposition to its passage by broadcasters and—as I document later in the chapter—by some legislators; and the absence of a lobby with strength proportionate to the size of the nation's 2- to 13-year-old child population. Yet another factor, subtle but potentially significant, is that the commercial TV networks leave a large portion of the time period between the end of the school day and the start of early evening network news programming as a vehicle by which these stations carry local advertising. And since the after-school time period is a natural one in which to carry a regulated children's weekday offering, the threat of such regulation is a direct and special threat to significant source of established local-station income. Many legislators are sensitive to this threat, as evidenced by the fact that far fewer of them became co-sponsors of a bill proposing a regulated weekday commercial TV children's offering in 1985, an off-election year, than had done so in 1986 (as revealed to this writer by an informed Washington source closely involved in the attempt to push the bill through in both of the two legislative sessions in question).

23. This charge is prominent in the FCC's published summary of outside comment invited by the FCC. See, for example, the 1983 FCC Report and Order referenced in Chapter 3 and in the Bibliography.

24. *Ibid.*

25. Personal communication between Ken Mason and this writer.

26. *Ibid.*

27. Canada and Australia are two countries with histories of considerable success in supporting specialized television programming through tax incentives.

28. Chapter 4 reviews some of the problems in PTV in singling out particular categories of programming for special funding emphasis, particularly as a permanent policy. PTV also eschews government allocations of funds to dedicated program categories in appropriations which go directly to PTV agencies.

29. See later reference to a tax-incentive bill proposed by Senator John

Heinz in 1979, whose intent was to improve children's television. The bill did not go to a vote; nor was it re-introduced in subsequent sessions of Congress.

30. Tax incentives are for many reasons difficult to pass through Congress. Among the reasons are the current spirit of tax reform with its emphasis upon closing, not opening, tax breaks, and the fact that the Office of Management and Budgets, which routinely evaluates all legislative proposals which have tax consequences, reviewed and advised Congress against passing the Senator Heinz bill referred to in the previous Chapter note.

31. The amount raised by the PTV stations in Fiscal Year 1984 through appeals for voluntary public contributions was $158 million, according to the publication, *Facts About PBS* (January 1986) (Washington, D.C.: Public Broadcasting Service).

32. The point is that the stations channel the money into their general funds, and do not disburse it to their production suppliers, as a general rule. The money thus helps stations to transmit giver-specified programs, but does not directly fund the programs themselves.

33. Members of the public are, of course, free to contribute directly to the independent or station-producing organizations which supply children's programs to PTV. However, this is not so far an actively or well-developed channel for individual contributions.

34. At the time of this writing, Children's Television Workshop is conducting an experiment in fundraising through a direct public appeal. No results are yet available to report.

35. Funding for children's TV programs which appeared in PTV's 1984–85 national schedule came from the following sources, in the amounts shown:

- Corporation for Public Broadcasting gave funding support to *3-2-1 Contact* ($1 million), *Reading Rainbow* ($470,270), and *WonderWorks* ($5 million). Total: $6,470,270.

- The Station Program Cooperative (partly from SPC_{10} and partly from SPC_{11}) gave funding support to *Reading Rainbow* (340,370), *Mr. Rogers' Neighborhood* ($948,185), *Sesame Street* ($3,106,000), *3-2-1 Contact* ($93,300), *WonderWorks* ($1 million), and *The Electric Company* ($251,000). Total: $5,738,855.

- Foundations gave funding support to *Reading Rainbow* ($20,000). Total: $20,000.

- Businesses gave funding support to *Mr. Rogers' Neighborhood* ($200,000), and *Reading Rainbow* ($150,000). Total: $350,000.

- Children's Television Workshop gave funding support to *Sesame Street* ($6.613 million) and *3-2-1 Contact* ($686,000). Total: $7.729 million.

- Coproducers of *WonderWorks* gave valued contributions ($4.276 million). Total: $4.276 million.

- An independent producer, Bank Street College, gave funding support for *Voyage of the Mimi* ($157,000).
- Government gave $1 million through U.S.D.E. and $1.5 million through NSF to help fund *3-2-1 Contact*, $1.143 through U.S.D.E. for *Voyage of the Mimi*, and through NEH and NEA a combined total of $724,000 for *WonderWorks*. Total: $4.367 million.

  Source: All of the information above is from the individual producing organizations directly.

36. The specifics of the Ford Foundation's involvement appear in the organization's annual reports covering the period of years in question.

37. For the two major Carnegie Foundation policy studies of U.S. public broadcasting, see Bibliography under "Carnegie Commission . . . " and under Mahoney *et al.*

38. The Markle Foundation's leadership has been provided by Mr. Lloyd Morrisett.

39. See Chapter 1 and related chapter notes for reference to the raft of recent reports lamenting the inability of our schools to meet adequately the nation's need in children's education.

40. The agencies seek maximum autonomy and discretion, even though their funding comes from government. This is proper, since it would be inappropriate under our system for government agencies to be in a censorship role, to exert pressure for funding quotas in various program categories, or to intrude overly much on the prerogatives of the agency boards in setting broad directions and priorities.

41. Personal communications. More discussion on the idea of a National Endowment for Children's Television appears later in Chapter 7.

42. A yearly radio or TV receiver tax no doubt would be opposed by the commercial broadcasters through their powerful lobby, the National Association of Broadcasters. That the idea has no currency is obvious from the fact that it has never been on the agenda of public broadcasters, even though they languish for adequate funding support.

43. See: Lloyd N. Morrisett, (1984), "Television: America's Neglected Teacher," in *The John and Mary R. Markle Foundation Annual Report 1982/1983* (New York: The Markle Foundation).

44. *Ibid.*

45. *Ibid.*

46. *Ibid.*

47. See: J. A. Riccobono (1985), *School Utilization Study: Availability, Use, and Support of Instructional Media, 1982–83. Final Report.* (Washington, D.C.: Corporation for Public Broadcasting and National Center for Education Statistics).

48. Source: A. C. Nielsen. In the series' early years on the air, around three million 6- to 11-year-olds viewed regularly in their homes.

49. The most thorough and insightful critical review of the ESAA-funded children's television initiative, a report funded by government, is: Keith Mielke and Barry Cole (April 1975), *The Federal Role in Funding Children's Television Programming. Vol. 1: Final Report.* (Bloomington, Ind.: Institute for Communication Research) (U.S.O.E. OEC-0-74-8674).

50. *Ibid.*

51. The legislation in question is the Cooperative Research Act. The federal portion of support for *Sesame Street* and *The Electric Company* in 1976 shifted to come under the new Special Projects Act (created under Title IV of the Education Amendments of 1974, P.L. 93-380), which replaced the Cooperative Research Act. The conference committee which finalized this new act specified its intention that the act "will be used to provide adequate financial support for *Sesame Street* and *The Electric Company*" (Education Amendments of 1974, 93rd Congress, 2nd Session, Report 93-1026 Conference Report). However U.S.O.E. Commissioner Bell made Fiscal 1976 the terminal funding season for the two series, and effectively subverted the possibility of further congressional line support in recommending that the two series be funded through a line item in the federal appropriation for public broadcasting. His stated rationale was that the development and demonstration nature of the two series had been concluded, making them inappropriate activities under the new Special Projects Act.

52. The ESAA legislation resulted in a $73 million TV expenditure by the time it ran its course in the early 1980s. The source of this information is an untitled document supplied to this author by Dr. Frank Withrow, former administrator of the ESAA-funded productions in the Office of Libraries and Learning Resources, U.S. Office of Education, listing ESAA expenditures program by program.

53. See Chapter 4 and associated chapter notes for reference to the FCC's activities in the area of children's television.

54. Source: Article by Cynthia Alperowicz (1984), "All Eyes on Congress: For or Against Children?," in *Re: ACT*, Volume 13, Number 1.

55. See Bibliography under "Federal Communication Commission" for reference to the FCC's 1983 Report and Order.

56. *Ibid.*

57. Comment by former FCC Commissioner Henry Rivera (1981–85) in *Re: ACT*, Volume 13, Number 1.

58. *Ibid.*

59. Source: *Broadcasting Cablecasting Yearbook 1984* (New York: Broadcasting Publications, Inc.).

60. For an authoritative review of this situation in Australia, see: Patricia Edgar (1984), "How Australia Fought for Mandatory Children's Programming... and Won," in *Re: ACT*, Volume 13, Number 1.

Bibliography

The Electric Company: *Formative Research and Summative Evaluation*

Ball, Samuel, and Gerry Ann Bogatz (1973). *Reading with Television: An Evaluation of The Electric Company.* Vol. 1. Princeton, N.J.: Educational Testing Service (Arlington, Va.: ERIC ED 073 178.)

Ball, Samuel, and Gerry Ann Bogatz (1973). *A Summary of the Major Findings from "Reading with Television: An Evaluation of The Electric Company."* Princeton, N.J.: Educational Testing Service. 14 pp.

Ball, Samuel, Gerry Bogatz, Kathryn M. Kazarow, and Donald B. Rubin (1974). *Reading with Television: A Follow-up Evaluation of The Electric Company.* Princeton, N.J.: Educational Testing Service. 122 pp. (Arlington, Va.: ERIC ED 122 798.)

Bogatz, Gerry Ann, and Samuel Ball (1973). *Reading with Television: An Evaluation of The Electric Company.* Vol. 2. Princeton, N.J.: Educational Testing Service (Arlington, Va.: ERIC ED 073 178.)

Cazden, Courtney B. (1974). *Watching Children Watch The Electric Company: An Observational Study in Ten Classrooms.* New York: Children's Television Workshop. 90 pp. (Arlington, Va.: ERIC ED 126 861.)

Chen, Milton (1972). *Verbal Response to The Electric Company: Qualities of Program Material and the Viewing Conditions which Affect Ver-*

balization. New York: Children's Television Workshop. 48 pp. (Arlington, Va.: ERIC ED 126 862.)

Cooney, Joan Ganz (1975). *Five Years of The Electric Company: Television and Reading, 1971–1976*. New York: Children's Television Workshop. 28 pp. (Arlington, Va.: ERIC ED 122 805.)

Gibbon, Samuel Y., Edward L. Palmer, and Barbara R. Fowles (1975). *Sesame Street, The Electric Company*, and reading. In John B. Carroll and Jeanne S. Chall, eds., *Toward a Literate Society: A Report from the National Academy of Education*. New York: McGraw-Hill.

Herriott, Robert E., and Roland J. Liebert (1972). *The Electric Company In-School Utilization Study: The 1971–72 School and Teacher Surveys*. New York: Children's Television Workshop. 164 pp. (Arlington, Va.: ERIC ED 073 709.)

Liebert, Roland J. (1973). *The Electric Company In-School Utilization Study: Vol. 2: The 1972–1973 School and Teacher Surveys and Trends Since 1971*. New York: Children's Television Workshop (Arlington, Va.: ERIC ED 094 775.)

O'Bryan, Kenneth, and Harry Silverman (1972). *Report on Children's Television Viewing Strategies*. New York: Children's Television Workshop. 17 pp. (Arlington, Va.: ERIC ED 126 871.)

——— (1973). *Research Report, Experimental Program Eye Movement Study*. New York: Children's Television Workshop. 10 pp. (Arlington, Va.: ERIC ED 126 870.)

Palmer, Edward L. (1978). *The Electric Company* and the school marketplace. In Robert Carlisle, ed., *Patterns of Performance: Public Broadcasting and Education 1974–1976*. Washington, D.C.: Corporation for Public Broadcasting.

Rust, Langbourne W. (1971). *Attributes of The Electric Company Pilot Shows That Produced High and Low Visual Attention in 2nd and 3rd Graders*. New York: Children's Television Workshop. 48 pp. (Arlington, Va.: ERIC ED 126 872.)

——— (1971). *The Electric Company Distractor Data: The Influence of Context*. New York: Children's Television Workshop. 9 pp. (Arlington, Va.: ERIC ED 122 812.)

——— (1974). *Visual Attention to Material in The Electric Company: Summary of Attribute Research*. New York: Children's Television Workshop. 7 pp. (Arlington, Va.: ERIC ED 122 813.)

Sproull, Natalie L., Eric F. Ward, and Marilyn D. Ward (1976). *Reading Behaviors of Young Children Who Viewed The Electric Company*. A final report. New York: Children's Television Workshop. 174 pp. (Arlington, Va.: ERIC ED 122 815.)

Sesame Street: *Formative Research and*
Summative Evaluation

Anderson, Daniel R., and Stephen R. Levin (1976). Young children's attention to *Sesame Street. Child Development*, Vol. 47, No. 3, pp. 806–811.

Anderson, Daniel R., Stephen R. Levin, and Elizabeth P. Lorch (1977). The
effects of TV program pacing on the behavior of preschool children.
A-V Communication Review, Vol. 25, No. 2, pp. 159–166.

Amey, Lorne J. (1976). *Visual Literacy: Implications for the Production of
Children's Television Programs*. Nova Scotia: Halifax.

Ball, Samuel, and Gerry Ann Bogatz (1970). *The First Year of Sesame Street.
Final Report. Vol. 1: An Evaluation*. Princeton, N.J.: Educational
Testing Service. (Arlington, Va.: ERIC ED 047 823.)

—— (1970). *A Summary of the Major Findings in "The First Year of Sesame
Street: An Evaluation."* Princeton, N.J.: Educational Testing Service.
30 pp. (Arlington, Va.: ERIC ED 122 799.)

—— (1971). *The Second Year of Sesame Street: A Continuing Evaluation.
Vol. I.* Princeton, N.J.: Educational Testing Service. (Arlington, Va.:
ERIC ED 122 800, 801.)

—— (1972). Summative research of *Sesame Street*. Implications for the
study of preschool children. In A. D. Pick, ed., *Minnesota Symposium
on Child Psychology, Vol. 6*. Minneapolis, Minn.: University of Minnesota Press, pp. 3–17.

Blackwell, Frank, ed. (1971). *Reactions to Sesame Street in Britain in 1971.
Part 1.* London: Independent Television Authority. 53 pp.

—— (1972). *Reactions to Sesame Street in Britain 1971. Part 2.* London:
Independent Television Authority. 140 pp.

Berghaus, Margot, Janpeter Kob, Helga Marencic, and Gerhard Vowinckel
(1978). *Vorschule im Fernsehen: Ergebnisse der Wissenschaftlichen
Begleituntersuchung zur Vorschulserie "Sesamstrasse."* (*Preschool on
Television: Findings of Research Accompanying the Preschool Series
"Sesamstrasse."*) Weinheim v.a.: Beltz. 204 pp.

Bogatz, Gerry Ann, and Samuel Ball (1971). *The Second Year of Sesame
Street: A Continuing Evaluation.* Vol. 2. Princeton, N.J.: Educational
Testing Service. (Arlington, Va.: ERIC ED 122 801.)

—— (1971). *A Summary of the Major Findings in "The Second Year of
Sesame Street: A Continuing Evaluation."* Princeton, N.J.: Educational Testing Service. (Arlington, Va.: ERIC ED 122 802.)

Burdach, Konrad J. (1976). *Wirkungsforschung zu Sesame Street: Uberlick
und Methodenkritische Evaluierung.* (*Effect Research on Sesame
Street: A Survey and Critical Evaluation of the Methods Used.*) *Fernsehen und Bildung*, Vol. 10, Nos. 1–2, pp. 55–85.

Charlton, Michael, et al. (1975). *Die Auswirkung von Szenen zum Sozialen Lernen aus der Fernseh-Serie "Sesamstrasse" auf Borstellungsinhalte und Spielverhalten von Kindern. (The Effects of Social Learning Episodes from the TV Series "Seamstrasse" on Contents of Imagination and Playing Behavior of Children.)* Zeitschrift fur Sozialpsychologie, Vol. 6, No. 4, pp. 348–59.

Coates, Brian, H. Ellison Pusser, and Irene Goodman (1976). The influence of "Sesame Street" and "Mister Rogers' Neighborhood" on children's social behavior in the preschool. *Child Development*, Vol. 47, No. 1, pp. 138–44.

Connell, David D., and Edward L. Palmer (1971). *Sesame Street:* a case study. In James D. Halloran, ed., *Broadcaster-Researcher Co-operation in Mass Communication Research*, pp. 66–88. Leeds: Kavanagh.

Cook, Thomas D., et al. (1975). *"Sesame Street" Revisited: A Study in Evaluation Research.* New York: Russell Sage Foundation.

Cook, Thomas D., and Ross F. Conner (1976). The Educational Impact: *Sesame Street* around the World. *Journal of Communication*, Vol. 26, No. 2, pp. 155–64.

Cooney, Joan Ganz (1970). *The First Year of Sesame Street. Final Report. Vol. I. A History and Overview.* New York: Children's Television Workshop. (Arlington, Va.: ERIC ED 047 821.)

——— (1974). *Sesame Street at Five: The Changing Look of a Perpetual Experiment.* New York: Children's Television Workshop. 25 pp. (Arlington, Va.: ERIC ED 122 804.)

Daniel Yankelovich, Inc. (1971). *A Report of Three Studies on the Role and Penetration of Sesame Street in Ghetto Communities (Bedford-Stuyvesant, East Harlem, Chicago, and Washington, D.C.).* New York: Children's Television Workshop. 100 pp. (Arlington, Va.: ERIC ED 122 820.)

——— (1973). *A Report on the Role and Penetration of Sesame Street in Ghetto Communities (Bedford-Stuyvesant, East Harlem, Chicago, and Washington, D.C.).* New York: Children's Television Workshop. 97 pp. (Arlington, Va.: ERIC ED 122 821.)

——— (1973). *Results of the Study on the Role and Penetration of Sesame Street and The Electric Company in Ghetto Communities.* New York: Children's Television Workshop. 10 pp. (Arlington, Va.: ERIC ED 122 822.)

Diamond, Naomi (1974). *The Reception of the Canadian Segments of Sesame Street.* Toronto: Canadian Council on Children and Youth.

Diaz-Guerrero, Rogelio, and Wayne H. Holtzman (1974). Learning by televised "Plaza Sesamo" in Mexico. *Journal of Educational Psychology*, Vol. 66, No. 5, pp. 632–43.

Diaz-Guerrero, Rogelio, Isabel Reyes-Lagunes, Donald B. Witzke, and Wayne H. Holtzman (1976). *Plaza Sesamo* in Mexico: an evaluation. *Journal of Communication*, Vol. 26, No. 2, pp. 145–54.

Dericum, Christa (1976). *Zur Geshichte der Sesame Street. (On the History of Sesame Street.) Fernsehen und Bildung*, Vol. 10, Nos. 1–2, pp. 12–24.

Filep, Robert, and Gary Millar, eds. (1970). *Sesame Street: Viewing Patterns in Inner City Los Angeles and Chicago. A Survey of Two Cities*. New York: Institute for Educational Development. 123 pp. (Arlington, Va.: ERIC ED 047 788.)

Filep, Robert T., Gary R. Millar, and Pearl T. Gillette (1971). *The Sesame Street Mother Project. Final Report*. El Segundo, Calif.: Institute for Educational Development. (Arlington, Va.: ERIC ED 055 676.)

Filipson, Leni (1971). *Sesame Street in Sweden: A Study of the Pilot Programme Sesam*. Stockholm: Swedish Broadcasting Corp.

Gibbon, Samuel Y., and Edward L. Palmer (1970). *The First Year of Sesame Street. Final Report. Vol. 5. Pre-reading on Sesame Street*. New York: Children's Television Workshop. (Arlington, Va.: ERIC ED 047 825.)

Gorn, Gerald J., Marvin E. Goldberg, and Rabindra N. Kanungo (1976). The role of educational television in changing the intergroup attitudes of children. *Child Development*, Vol. 7, No. 1, pp. 227–80.

Hans-Bredow-Institut, Hamburg, ed. (1975). *Begleituntersuchung zur Fernsehserie "Sesamstrasse": Augewahlte Ergebnisse des Gesamtprojekts. (Summative Research on the TV series "Sesamstrasse": Some Selected Results from the Overall Project.)* Hamburg: Hans-Bredow-Institut.

Internationales Zentralinstitut fur das Jugend- und Bildungsfernsehen, Munchen (1976). *Sesame Street—International*. Munchen: Internationales Zentralinstitut fur das Jugend- und Bildungsfernsehen.

Lasker, Harry M. (1973). *The Jamaican Project. Final Report*. New York: Children's Television Workshop. (Arlington, Va.: ERIC ED 125 865.)

Lasker, Harry, and Naomi Bernath (1974). *Status of Comprehension Study of Sesame Street Affect Bits*. New York: Children's Television Workshop. (Arlington, Va.: ERIC ED 126 866.)

Lemercier, K. I., and G. R. Teasdale (1973). *Sesame Street*: Some effects of a television programme on the cognitive skills of young children from lower SES backgrounds. *Australian Psychologist*, Vol. 8, No. 1, pp. 47–51.

Lesser, Gerald S. (1972). Learning, teaching, and television production for children: The experience of *Sesame Street. Harvard Educational Review*, Vol. 42, pp. 232–72.

——— (1974). *Children and Television: Lessons from Sesame Street*. New York: Random House.

Levin, Stephen A., and Daniel R. Anderson (1976). The development of attention: *Sesame Street* around the world. *Journal of Communication*, Vol. 26, No. 2, pp. 126–35.

Liebert, Robert M. (1976). Evaluating the evaluators: *Sesame Street* around the world. *Journal of Communication*, Vol. 26, No. 2, pp. 165–71.

——— (1976). Amerikanische forschungsergebnisse zu *Sesame Street*: Folgerungen fur die gestaltung von vorschulprogrammen. *Fernsehen und Bildung*, Vol. 10, Nos. 1–2, pp. 42–54.

London Weekend Television (1972). *Sesame Street: London ITV Area, Audience Observational Tables*. London: London Weekend Television.

Meichenbaum, Donald H., and Lorraine Truk (1972). Implications of research on disadvantaged children and cognitive-training programs for educational television: Ways of improving "Sesame Street." *Journal of Special Education*, Vol. 6, No. 1, pp. 27–50.

Miller, Jack, and Rom Skavarcius (1970). *Does Sesame Street Teach? Performance Gains of Preschool Viewers and Non-viewers*. New York: Children's Television Workshop. 167 pp. (Arlington, Va.: ERIC ED 122 809.)

Minton, Judith Haber (1975). The Impact of *Sesame Street* on readiness. *Sociology of Education*, Vol. 48, pp. 141–51.

Palmer, Edward L. (1970). Begleituntersuchungen zu der sendereike "Sesame Street." (Formative research on the series "Sesame Street.") *Fernsehen und Bildung* Vol. 4, Nos. 1–2, pp. 258–62.

——— (1972). Formative research in educational television production: The experience of the Children's Television Workshop. In Wilbur Schramm, ed., *Quality in Instructional Television*, pp. 165–87. Honolulu: University Press of Hawaii.

——— (1974). Formative research in the production of television for children. In David R. Olsen, ed., *Media and Symbols: The Forms of Expression, Communication, and Education*, pp. 303–28. Chicago, Ill.: National Society for the Study of Education.

Palmer, Edward L., Milton Chen, and Gerald S. Lesser (1976). Sesame Street: Patterns of international adaptation. *Journal of Communication*, Vol. 26, Nos. 1–2, pp. 109–23.

——— (1976). Internationale Auswerkungen von *Sesame Street* und ausblick auf kunftige forschungen. (Broader international effects of *Sesame Street* and perspectives of future research.) *Fernsehen und Bildung*, Vol. 10, Nos. 1–2, pp. 101–7.

Paulson, F. Leon (1974). Teaching cooperation on television: An evaluation of *Sesame Street* social goals programs. *A-V Communication Review*, Vol. 22, No. 3, pp. 229–46.

Polsky, Richard M. (1974). *Getting to Sesame Street: Origins of the Children's Television Workshop*. New York: Praeger.

Reeves, Barbara Frengel (1970). *The First Year of Sesame Street: Final Re-*

port. Vol. 2: The Formative Research. New York: Children's Television Workshop. 200 pp. (Arlington, Va.: ERIC ED 047 822.)

Reeves, Barbara Frengel (1971). The reactions of children in six small viewing groups to *Sesame Street* shows nos. 261–74. New York: Children's Television Workshop. 35 pp. (Arlington, Va.: ERIC ED 122 823.)

Renckstorf, Karsten (1973). Begleituntersuchungen zur "Sesamstrasse"— Beispiel massenmedialer wirkungs-forschung. (Formative studies on "Sesamstrasse"—an example of research on mass media effects.) *Fernseh und Audiovisuelle Medienalyse,* pp. 31–71. Koln: Pedagogisches Institut der Stadt Koln.

Rogers, Janet M. (1972). A summary of the literature on "Sesame Street." *Journal of Special Education,* Vol. 6, No. 1, pp. 43–50.

Salomon, Gavriel (1974). *Sesame Street in Israel: Its Instructional and Psychological Effects on Children.* Jerusalem: Hebrew University. 105 pp. (Arlington, Va.: ERIC ED 122 814.)

—— (1976). Cognitive skill learning across cultures. *Journal of Communication,* Vol. 26, Nos. 1–2, pp. 138–44.

—— (1977). Effects of encouraging Israeli mothers to co-observe *Sesame Street* with their five year olds. *Child Development,* Vol. 48, No. 3, pp. 1146–51.

Salomon, Gavriel, et al. (1972). *Educational Effects of Sesame Street on Israeli Children.* Jerusalem: Hebrew University. (Arlington, Va.: ERIC ED 070 317.)

Samuels, Bruce (1970). *The First Year of Sesame Street. Final Report. Vol. 4: A Summary of Audience Surveys.* New York: Children's Television Workshop. 31 pp. (Arlington, Va.: ERIC ED 047 824.)

Schliecher, Klaus (1972). Sesame Street *fur Deutschland? Die Notwendigkeit einer vergleichenden mediendidactik.* (*Sesame Street* for Germany? The need for comparative media didactics.) Dusseldorf: Schwann. 99 pp.

Shapiro, Bernadette Nelson (1975). *Comprehension of Television Programming Designed to Encourage Socially Valued Behavior in Children: Formative Research on Sesame Street Programming with Social and Affective Goals.* New York: Children's Television Workshop. 228 pp. (Arlington, Va.: ERIC ED 122 863.)

Sprigle, Herbert A. (1971). Can poverty children live on *Sesame Street? Young Children,* Vol. 26, pp. 202–17.

—— (1972). Who wants to live on *Sesame Street? Childhood Education,* Vol. 49, No. 3, pp. 159–65.

Sproull, Natalie (1973). Visual attention, modeling behaviors, and other verbal and nonverbal meta-communication of pre-kindergarten viewing *Sesame Street. American Educational Research Journal,* Vol. 10, No. 2, pp. 101–14.

Ulrich, David (1970). A behavioral view of *Sesame Street. Educational Broadcasting Review*, Vol. 4, No. 5, pp. 17–22.

Vowinckel, Gerhard (1976). Fernsehen und soziales lernen: Autonomie bei vorschalkindern durch "Sesamstrasse"? (Television and social learning: Autonomous behavior of preschool children through "Sesamstrasse"?) *Rundfunk und Fernsehen*, Vol. 24, Nos. 1–2, pp. 39–48.

Yamamoto, Toru (1976). The Japanese experiment: *Sesame Street* around the world. *Journal of Communication*, Vol. 26, No. 2, pp. 136–137.

———— (1976). "Sesame Street" in Japan. In H. Eguchi *et al.*, eds., *Studies in Broadcasting*. Tokyo: Nippon Hoso Kyokai, pp. 63–86.

Yin, Robert K. (1973). *The Workshop and the World: Toward an Assessment of the Children's Television Workshop*. Santa Monica, Calif.: Rand. 51 pp.

Zehrfeld, Klaus (1976). Die Zusammenarbeit von wissenschaftlern und fernsehproduzenten im Children's Television Workshop. (The cooperation between researchers and TV producers in Children's Television Workshop.) *Fernsehen und Bildung*, Vol. 10, Nos. 1–2, pp. 24–33.

Other Sources

Akamatsu, T. John , and Mark H. Thelen (1971). The acquisition and performance of a socially neutral response as a function of vicarious reward. *Developmental Psychology*, Vol. 5, No. 3, pp. 440–45.

Akiyama, Takashiro (1982). TV use in kindergartens and nursery school. *The NHK Report on Broadcast Research*, Vol. 32, No. 7.

———— (1983). Experiments with and development of TV programs for infants. *The NHK Monthly Report on Broadcast Research*, Vol. 33, No. 7.

Akiyama, Takashiro, and Sachiko Imaizumi Kodaira (1986). *The Role of Educational Broadcasts in Japanese Schools* (2nd edition). Tokyo: NHK Broadcasting Culture Research Institute.

Akiyama, Takashiro, et al. (1981). The reaction of 2-year-old children to television (1)—Research project on television programming for 2-year olds, report No. 1. In *Japan Journal of Educational Technology*, Vol. 5.

Allouche-Benayoun, B. J. (1975). The influence of moving pictures on children and young people: French research activities from 1970–1975. *Fernsehen und Bildung* (special English issue), Vol. 9, No. 2–3, pp. 137–57.

Alperowicz, Cynthia (1984). All eyes on Congress: For or against children? *Re: ACT*, Vol. 13, No. 1.

Annis, Phyllis M. (1974). Research into TV and the preschool child. *Educational Media International*, No. 4, pp. 13–19.

Arnove, Robert F., ed., (1976). *Educational Television: A Policy Critique and Guide for Developing Countries*. New York: Praeger.

Baran, Stanley J. (1974). Television as teacher of prosocial behavior: What the research says. *Public Telecommunications Review*, Vol. 2, No. 3, pp. 46–51.

———(1977). Television programs as socializing agents for mentally retarded children. *A-V Communication Review*, Vol. 25, No. 3, pp. 281–89.

Baran, Stanley J., and Timothy P. Meyer (1974). Imitation and identification: Two compatible approaches to social learning from the electronic media. *A-V Communication Review*, Vol. 22, No. 2, pp. 167–79.

——— (1975). Retarded children's perceptions of favorite television characters as behavioral models. *Mental Retardation*, Vol. 13 pp. 28–31.

Barcus, F. Earle (1983). *Images of life on children's television: Sex roles, minorities, and families*. New York: Praeger.

Barnouw, Erik (1966). *A Tower in Babel: A History of Broadcasting in the United States to 1933*. New York: Oxford University Press.

——— (1968). *The Golden Web: A History of Broadcasting in the United States, 1933–1953*. New York: Oxford University Press.

——— (1970). *The Image Empire: A History of Broadcasting in the United States from 1953*. New York: Oxford University Press.

——— (1975). *Tube of Plenty: The Evolution of American Television*. New York: Oxford University Press.

———(1978). *The Sponsor: Notes on a Modern Potentate*. New York: Oxford University Press.

Bettelheim, Bruno (1977). *The Uses of Enchantment: The Meaning and Importance of Fairy Tales*. New York: Alfred a. Knopf.

Bibliography of Works on Mass Communication Published by Scandinavian Scholars in English and List of Scandinavian Communication Researchers (1975). Tampere, Nordicom, ed. Tampere: Nordicom. 64 pp.

Blakely, Robert J. (1979). *To Serve the Public Interest: Educational Broadcasting in the United States*. Syracuse, N.Y.: Syracuse University Press.

Blum, Eleanor (1980). *Basic Books in the Mass Media*. Urbana: University of Illinois Press.

Burns, Tom (1978). *The BBC: Public Institution and Private World*. London: Macmillan.

British Broadcasting Corporation (1980). *BBC Handbook 1980: Incorporating the Annual Report and Accounts 1978–79*. London: British Broadcasting Corporation.

British Broadcasting Corporation, ed. (1974). *Children as Viewers and Listeners: A Study by the BBC for Its General Advisory Council*. London: British Broadcasting Corp.

Brown, J. Ray (1977). Sozial wunschbare Wirkungen des Fernsehens-gibt es die? Ergebnisse sozialwissenschaftlicher Forschung zu prosozialen Effecten des Fernsehens. *Media Perspektiven*, Vol. 11, pp. 625–35.

Brown, James W. and Shirley N. Brown, eds. (1985). *Educational Media Yearbook 1985*. Littleton, Colo.: Libraries Unlimited.

Brown, Les (1971). *Television: The Business Behind the Box*. New York: Harcourt Brace Jovanovich.

——— (1977). *The New York Times Encyclopedia of Television*. New York: Times Books.

Brown, Ray, ed. (1976). *Children and Television*. Toronto: Cassell and Collier Macmillan Publishers.

———, ed. (1976). *Children and Television*. London: Cassell and Collier Macmillan.

Bryan, James H., and Nancy H. Walbeck (1970). The impact of words and deeds concerning altruism upon children. *Child Development*, Vol. 41, pp. 747–57.

Cantor, Muriel G. (1980). *Prime-time Television: Content and Control*. Beverly Hills, Calif.: Sage Publication.

Carlsson, Ulla (1978). *Mass Communication Researchers in Sweden: Swedish Mass Communication Research* (Publications in English, French and German). Tampere Nordicom, ed. Tampere: Nordicom. 29 pp.

Carnegie Commission on the Future of Public Broadcasting (1979). *A Public Trust*. New York: Bantam Books.

Cater, D., and S. Strickland (1975). *TV Violence and the Child: The Evolution and Fate of the Surgeon General's Report*. New York: Russell Sage Foundation.

Children and Television. An Abstract Bibliography. (1975). Urbana, Ill.: ERIC Clearinghouse on Early Childhood Education. 61 pp.

Chu, Godwin C., and Wilbur Schramm (1979). *Learning from Television: What the Research Says*. Washington, D.C.: National Association of Educational Broadcasters.

Cole, Barry, and Mal Oettinger (1978). *Reluctant Regulators: The FCC and the Broadcast Audience*. Reading, Mass.: Addison-Wesley.

Collins, Andrew (1975). The developing child as a viewer: The effects of television on children and adolescents. *Journal of Communication*, Vol. 25, No. 4, pp. 35–44.

Comstock, George, and Marilyn Fisher (1975). *Television and Human Behavior: A Guide to the Pertinent Scientific Literature*. Santa Monica, Calif.: Rand. 344 pp.

Comstock, George, and George Lindsey (1975). *Television and Human Behavior: The Research Horizon, Future and Present*. Santa Monica, Calif.: Rand. 120 pp.

Comstock, George, et al. (1975). *Television and Human Behavior: The Key Studies*. Santa Monica, Calif.: Rand. 251 pp.

———— (1978). *Television and Human Behavior*. New York: Columbia University Press.

Cook, T. D., et al. (1975). *Sesame Street Revisited*. New York: Russell Sage Foundation.

Cook, Thomas D., and Thomas R. Curtin (1986). An evaluation of the models used to evaluate television series. *Public Communication and Behavior*, Vol. 1, pp. 1–64.

Corset, Pierre (1972). Les jeunes enfants et la télévision. *Télévision et Éducation*, No. 28, pp. 7–71.

Cowan, Geoffrey (1979). *See No Evil: The Backstage Battle Over Sex and Violence in Television*. New York: Simon and Schuster.

CTW Research Bibliography (1968–76). Research Papers Relating to the Children's Television Workshop and Its Experimental Educational Series: *Sesame Street* and *The Electric Company*. New York: Children's Television Workshop. 20 pp.

Denney, Douglas R. (1972). Modeling and eliciting effects upon conceptual strategies. *Child Development*, Vol. 42, pp. 810–23.

———— (1972). Modeling effects upon conceptual style and cognitive tempo. *Child Development*, Vol. 43, pp. 105–19.

Diaz-Guerrero, R., and W. H. Holtzman (1974). Learning by televised *Plaza Sesamo* in Mexico. *Journal of Educational Psychology*, Vol. 64, No. 5.

Diaz-Guerrero, R., I. Reyes-Lagunes, D. B. Witzge, and W. H. Holtzman (1976). *Plaza Sesamo* in Mexico: an evaluation. *Journal of Communication*, Vol. 26, No. 2.

Dirr, P. J., and R. J. Pedone (1979). *Uses of Television for Instruction 1976–77: Final Report of the School TV Utilization Study*. Washington, D.C.: Corporation for Public Broadcasting and National Center for Education Statistics.

Dorr, Aimee (1986). *Television and Children: A Special Medium for a Special Audience*. Beverly Hills, Calif.: Sage Publications.

Dunn, Gwen (1974). *Television and the Preschool Child*. London: Independent Television Authority.

———— (1977). *The Box in the Corner: Television and the Under-Fives: A Study*. New York: Macmillan.

Edgar, Patricia (1984). How Australia fought for mandatory children's programming... and won. *Re: ACT*, Vol. 13, No. 1.

Ellis, Connie (1976). *Current British Research on Mass Media and Mass Communication: Register of Ongoing and Recently Completed Research*. Leicester: Leicester Documentation Centre for Mass Communication Research, Centre for Mass Communication Research, University of Leicester. 74 pp.

———— (1977). *Current British Research on Mass Media and Mass Commu-*

nication: Register of Ongoing and Recently Completed Research. Leicester: Leicester Documentation Centre for Mass Communication Research, Centre for Mass Communication Research, University of Leicester. 77 pp.

Faith-Ell, Peggy, Cecilia von Feilitzen, Leni Filipson, et al. (1976). *Children's Research at Sveriges Radio*. Stockholm: Sveriges Radio Audience and Programme Research Department. 10 pp.

Federal Communications Commission (1960). Network programming inquiry: Report and statement of policy. *Federal Register*, 25, 7291–7296, August 3.

——— (1974). Children's television programs: Report and policy statement. *Federal Register*, 39, 39396–39409, November 6.

——— (1979). *Television Programming for Children: A Report of the Children's Television Task Force*. 5 Volumes. Washington, D.C.

——— (1984). Children's television programming and advertising practices: Report and Order. *Federal Register*, 49, 17–4, January 13.

Feilitzen, Cecilia von (1975). Findings of Scandinavian research on child and television in the process of socialization. *Fernsehen und Bildung* (special English issue), Vol. 9, No. 2–3, pp. 54–84.

Feilitzen, Cecilia von, and Olga Linne (1974). *Children and Identification in the Mass Communication Process: A Summary of Scandinavian Research and Theoretical Discussion*. Stockholm: Sveriges Radio, Audience and Programme Research Department. 39 pp.

——— (1975). Identifying with television characters. The effects of television on children and adolescents. *Journal of Communication*, Vol. 25, No. 4, pp. 51–55.

Filipson, Leni (1976). *The Role of Radio and TV in the Lives of Preschool Children: Summary*. Stockholm: Swedish Broadcasting Corp.

Friedman, Arnold J. (1983). Is children's programming growing up in America? *TV World*, Vol. 6, No. 6.

Friedrich, Lynette K., and Aletha H. Stein (1975). Prosocial television and young children: The effects of verbal labeling and role playing on learning and behavior. *Child Development*, Vol. 46, No. 1, pp. 27–38.

Fujitake, Akira (1973). Some comments on the studies of the effects of mass media of communication. In H. Eguchi *et al.*, eds., *Studies in Broadcasting*, pp. 113–20. Tokyo: Nippon Hoso Kyokai.

Furu, Takeo (1971). *The Function of Television for Children and Adolescents*. Tokyo: Sophia University.

Gerbner, G., L. Gross, M. Eleey, M. Jackson-Beeck, S. Jeffries-Fox, and N. Signorielli (1977). Violence profile #8: Trends in network television drama and viewer conceptions of social reality, 1967–1976. Philadelphia: Annenberg School of Communications, University of Pennsylvania.

Gibson, George H. (1977). *Public Broadcasting: The Role of the Federal Government, 1912–76.* New York: Praeger Special Studies.

Greenberg, Bradley S., ed. (1970). *Television Behavior Among Disadvantaged Children.* New York: Praeger.

Greenfield, Patricia Marks (1984). *Mind and Media: The Effects of Television, Video Games, and Computers.* Cambridge, Mass.: Harvard University Press.

Grusec, Joan E. (1973). Effects of co-observer evaluations on imitation: A developmental study. *Developmental Psychology,* Vol. 8, No. 1, p. 141.

Hatano, Giyoo (1971). Recent Japanese studies on "TV and the child." In H. Eguchi et al., eds., *International Studies of Broadcasting,* pp. 157–79. Tokyo: Nippon Hoso Kyokai.

Head, Sydney W., with Christopher H. Sterling (1982). *Broadcasting in America: A Survey of Television, Radio, and New Technologies.* (4th ed.) Boston: Houghton Mifflin.

Henderson, Ronald W., Rosemary Swanson, and Barry J. Zimmerman (1975). Training seriation responses in young children through televised modeling of hierarchically sequenced rule components. *American Educational Research Journal,* Vol. 12, No. 4, pp. 479–89.

―――― (1975) Inquiry response induction in preschool children through televised modeling. *Developmental Psychology,* Vol. 11, No. 4, pp. 523–24.

Herriott, R. E. and R. J. Liebert (1972). *The Electric Company In-School Utilization Study: The 1971–72 School and Teacher Surveys.* Research Triangle Park, N.C.: Research Triangle Institute. (ERIC Document Reproduction Service No. ED 973 709.)

Himmelweit, H. T., A. N. Oppenheim, and P. Vince (1958). *Television and the Child.* London: Oxford University Press.

Homberg, Erentraud (1978). *Preschool Children and Television: Two Studies Carried out in Three Countries.* New York: K.G. Saur Publishing Company.

Howe, Michael J. A. (1977). *Television and Children.* London: New University Education.

――――, ed. (1983). *Learning from Television: Psychological and Educational Research.* New York: Academic Press.

Johnston, J., and J. Ettema (1982). *Positive Images: Breaking Stereotypes with Children's Television.* Beverly Hills, Calif.: Sage.

Katz, Elihu, Michael Gurevitch, and Hadassah Haas (1973). On the use of the mass media for important things. *American Sociological Review,*

Bibliography

Vol. 38, No. 2, pp. 164–81. Also in H. Eguchi et al., eds. (1973)
Studies of Broadcasting, pp. 31–65. Tokyo: Nippon Hoso Kyokai.

Katz, Elihu, and George Wedell (1978). *Broadcasting in the Third World: Promise and Performance*. London: Macmillan.

Kikuchi, T., et al. (1981). *TV in the Lives of Children 0 to 6 Years Old*. Tokyo: NHK Public Opinion Research Institute.

Kline, Gerald F., and Peter Clarke, eds. (1971). *Mass Communications and Youth: Some Current Perspectives*. Beverly Hills, Calif.: Sage.

Kob, J. (1975). *Sesamstrasse*. Hamburg, Germany: Hans-Bredow Institute.

Kodaira, Sachiko Imaizumi (1985). Symposium: Tomorrow's children and television—Comparisons between Japan and other countries. *The NHK Monthly Report on Broadcast Research*, Vol. 35, No. 6.

———— (1986). *Television for Children in Japan: Trends and Studies*. Tokyo: NHK Broadcasting Culture Research Institute.

Kondo, H. (August 1980). What is TV for children? *Radio TV Education*.

Krugmann, Herbert E., and Eugene L. Hartley (1970). Passive learning from television. *Public Opinion Quarterly*, Vol. 34, No. 1, pp. 184–90.

Leiffer, Aimee Dorr (1973). *Encouraging Social Competence with Television*. New York: Children's Television Workshop. 35 pp. (Arlington, Va.: ERIC ED 122 807.)

Leiffer, Aimee Dorr, Andrew W. Collins, Barbara M. Gross, and Peter H. Taylor (1971). Developmental aspects of variables relevant to observational learning. *Child Development*, Vol. 42, pp. 1509–16.

Leiffer, Aimee Dorr, Neal J. Gordon, and Sherryl Browne Graves (1974). Children's television: More than mere entertainment. *Harvard Educational Review*, Vol. 44, No. 2, pp. 213–45.

Leiffer, Aimee Dorr, and Gerald S. Lesser (1976). *The Development of Career Awareness in Young Children*. Cambridge, Mass.: Harvard University Center for Research in Children's Television. 72 pp. (Arlington, Va.: ERIC ED 121 299.)

Lesser, Gerald S. (1974). *Children and Television: Lessons from Sesame Street*. New York: Random House.

Lesser, Harvey (1977). *Television and the Preschool Child: A Psychological Theory of Instruction and Curriculum Development*. New York: Academic Press.

Levin, Harvey J. (1980). *Fact and Fancy in Television Regulation: An Economic Study of Policy Alternatives*. New York: Russell Sage Foundation.

Liebert, Robert M. (1975). Creating effective television for children: Recent steps toward a theory of production. *Fernsehen und Bildung* (special English issue), Vol. 9, Nos. 2–3, pp. 163–74.

Liebert, Robert M., John M. Neale, and Emily S. Davidson (1973). *The

Early Window: Effects of Television on Children and Youth. New York: Pergamon Press.

Liebert, Robert M., and Rita W. Poulos (1976). Television as a moral teacher. In Thomas Lickona, ed., *Moral Development and Behavior: Theory, Research and Social Issues*, pp. 284–98. New York: Holt, Rinehardt and Winston.

Liebert, Roland J. (1973). *The Electric Company In-School Utilization Study: The 1972–73 School and Teacher Survey and Trends Since Fall 1971.* Research Triangle Park, N.C.: Research Triangle Institute. (ERIC Document Reproduction Service No. ED 094 775.)

Mahony, Sheila, Nick DeMartino, and Robert Stengel (1980). *Keeping PACE with the New Television.* Washington, D.C.: National Association of Educational Broadcasters.

Meline, Caroline W. (1976). Does the medium matter? Fostering creativity in children. *Journal of Communication*, Vol. 26, No. 3, pp. 81–89.

Melody, William (1973). *Children's Television: The Economics of Exploitation.* New Haven, Conn.: Yale University Press.

Meyer, Manfred, and Ursula Nissen (1976). Bibliographie zu *Sesame Street. Fernsehen und Bildung.* Vol. 10, Nos. 1–2, pp. 134–46.

Meyer, Timothy (1973). Children's perceptions of favorite television characters as behavioral models. *Educational Broadcasting Review*, Vol. 7, No. 1, pp. 25–33.

Mielke, Keith, Roland C. Johnson and Berry Cole (April 1975). *The Federal Role in Funding Children's Television Programming. Vol. 1: Final Report.* Bloomington, Ind.: Institute of Communication Research.

Minton, Judith H. (1973). The impact of *Sesame Street* on reading readiness of kindergarten children. *Dissertation Abstracts International*, 33, 3396A.

Monaghan, Robert R., et al. (1974). *Mr. Rogers' Neighborhood and the Handicapped Child Interface: Exploring and Assessing Integration of Educational Media and Professional Services to the Handicapped Child. Final Report.* Washington, D.C.: U.S. Department of Health, Education and Welfare, Office of Education, Bureau of Education for the Handicapped. (Arlington, Va.: ERIC ED 108 424).

Morris, Bridget (1975–76). *Children's Response to Preschool Television: A Method of Assessing the Response of Preschool Children to Programmes Made for Them.* London: Independent Television Authority. 103 pp.

Morris, William N., Halina M. Marshall, and Robert S. Miller (1973) The effect of vicarious punishment on prosocial behavior in children. *Journal of Experimental Child Psychology*, Vol. 15, pp. 222–36.

Morrisett, Lloyd N. (1983). Television: America's neglected teacher. *The*

John and Mary R. Markle Foundation Annual Report 1982/83. New York: The Markle Foundation.

Murray, John (1980). *Television and Youth: 25 Years of Research and Controversy.* Boys Town, Nebr.: Boys Town Center.

Murray, John, and Gavriel Salomon, eds. (1984). *The Future of Children's Television: Results of the Markle Foundation/Boys Town Conference.* Boys Town, Nebr.: Boys Town Center.

National Institute of Mental Health (1982). *Television and Behavior: Ten Years of Scientific Progress and Implications for the Eighties, Vol. 1.* Washington, D.C.: Government Printing Office. (For Vol. II, see Pearl, D., et al.)

Noble, Grant (1975). *Children in Front of the Small Screen.* Beverly Hills, Calif.: Sage Publications.

Nyhan, Michael J., ed. (1976). *The Future of Public Broadcasting.* New York: Praeger Special Studies.

Palmer, Edward L., and Aimee Dorr (1980). *Children and the Faces of Television: Teaching, Violence, and Selling.* New York: Academic Press.

Paulson, F. L. (1974). Teaching cooperation on television: An evaluation of *Sesame Street* social goals programs. *A-V Communication Review*, Vol. 22, No. 3.

Pearl, D., L. Bouthilet, and J. Lazar (1982). *Television and Behavior: Ten Years of Scientific Progress and Implications for the Eighties, Vol. 2.* Washington, D.C.: National Institute of Mental Health. (For Vol. 1 see bibliographic entry under National Institute of Mental Health).

Pifer, Alan (1978). Perception of childhood and youth. *Annual Report—Carnegie Corporation of New York.* New York: Carnegie Corporation of New York.

Pisarek, Walery (1976). Mass media and socialization: A selected international bibliography. In James D. Halloran, ed., *Mass Media and Socialization*, pp. 57–116. Leicester: International Association for Mass Communication Research.

Plost, Myrna, and Marvin J. Rosen (1974) Effect of sex of career models on occupational preferences of adolescents. *A-V Communication Review*, Vol. 22, No. 1, pp. 41–50.

Poulos, Rita W., Eli A. Rubinstein, and Robert M. Liebert (1975). Positive social learning: The effects of television on children and adolescents. *Journal of Communication*, Vol. 25, No. 4, pp. 90–97.

Reeves, Byron, and Bradley S. Greenberg (1973). Children's perception of television characters. *Human Communication Research*, Vol. 3, No. 2, pp. 113–27.

Reeves, Byron, and M. Mark Miller (1978). A multidimensional measure of children's identification with television characters. *Journal of Broadcasting*, Vol. 22, No. 1, pp. 71–86.

Riccobono, J. A. (1985). *School Utilization Study: Availability, Use, and Support of Instructional Media, 1982–83. Final Report*. Washington, D.C.: Corporation for Public Broadcasting and National Center for Education Statistics.

Ridberg, Eugene H., Ross D. Parke, and E. Mavis Hetherington (1971). Modification of impulsive and reflective cognitive styles through observation of film-mediated models, *Developmental Psychology*, Vol. 5, No. 3, pp. 369–77.

Roberts, Donald F. (1973). Communication and children: A developmental approach. In Ithiel de Sola Pool et al., eds., *Handbook of Communication*, pp. 174–215. Chicago: Rand McNally.

Roberts, Donald F., and Wilbur Schramm (1971). Children's learning from the media. In Wilbur Schramm, ed., *The Process and Effects of Mass Communication*, pp. 596–611. Urbana: University of Illinois Press.

Ronnenberger, Franz, ed. (1971). *Sozialisation Durch Massenkommunikation, Bd. V*. Stuttgart: Enke.

Rowland, W. (1983). *The Politics of TV Violence*. Beverly Hills, Calif.: Sage.

Rubinstein, Eli, et al. (1974). *Assessing Television's Influence on Children's Prosocial Behavior*. Stony Brook, N.Y.: Brookdale International Institute.

Rydin, Ingegard (1976). *Children's Understanding of Television: Preschool Children's Perception of an Information Programme*. Stockholm: Swedish Broadcasting Corp.

——— (1976). *Information Processes in Preschool Children*. Stockholm: Swedish Broadcasting Corporation.

Salomon, G. (1974) *Sesame Street in Israel: Its Instructional and Psychological Effects on Children*. Jerusalem: Hebrew University.

Salomon, Gavriel (1976). Cognitive effects of visual media. In Klaus F. Riegel, ed., *The Developing Individual in a Changing World. Vol. II: Social and Environmental Issues*, pp. 487–94. The Hague: Mouton.

Salomon, Gavriel, and Akiba A. Cohen (1977). Television formats, mastery of mental skills, and the acquisition of knowledge. *Journal of Educational Psychology*, Vol. 69, No. 5, pp. 612–19.

Scherer, Klaus R. (1971). Stereotype change following exposure to counterstereotypical media heroes. *Journal of Broadcasting*, Vol. 15, No. 4, pp. 99–100.

Schramm, Wilbur (1977). *Big Media, Little Media: Tools and Technologies for Instruction*. Beverly Hills, Calif.: Sage.

Schramm, Wilbur, Jack Lyle, and Edwin B. Parker (1961). *Television in the Lives of Our Children*. Stanford, Calif.: Stanford University Press.

Sherdon, A. W., and J. C. Greenblatt (August 31, 1977). *A Survey of the Use of The Electric Company for Classroom Instruction, 1976–1977.* Research Triangle Park, N.C.: Research Triangle Institute.

Shirai, T., T. Sakamoto, et al. (1982). *What Television Could Do for Preschoolers.* Tokyo: Japan Radio-TV Education Association.

Singer, Jerome L., and Dorothy G. Singer (1976). Can TV stimulate imaginative play? Fostering creativity in children. *Journal of Communication*, Vol. 26, No. 3, pp. 74–80.

Smith, F. Leslie (1979). *Perspectives on Radio and Television: An Introduction to Broadcasting in the United States.* New York: Harper and Row.

Sprafkin, Joyce N., Robert M. Liebert, and Rita W. Poulos (1975). Effects of a prosocial televised example on children's helping. *Journal of Experimental Child Psychology*, Vol. 20, pp. 119–26.

Stein, Aletha H. (1972). Mass media and young children's development. In Ira Gordon ed., *Early Childhood Education. The Seventy-first Yearbook of the National Society for the Study of Education, Part II*, pp. 181–202. Chicago, Ill.: University of Chicago Press.

Stein, Gerald M., and James H. Bryan (1972). The effect of a television model upon rule adoption behavior of children. *Child Development*, Vol. 43, pp. 268–73.

Sterling, Christopher H., and John M. Kittross (1978). *Stay Tuned: A Concise History of American Broadcasting.* Belmont, Calif.: Wadsworth Publishing.

Stevenson, Harold W., Ann G. Friedrichs, and William E. Simpson (1970). Learning and problem solving by the mentally retarded under three testing conditions. *Developmental Psychology*, Vol. 3, No. 3, pp. 307–12.

Surgeon General's Scientific Advisory Committee on Television and Social Behavior (1972). *TV and Growing Up: The Impact of Televised Violence.* Report to the Surgeon General, U.S. Public Health Service. Washington, D.C.: Government Printing Office.

Television and Behavior: Ten Years of Scientific Progress and Implications for the Eighties (1982). Washington, D.C.: Government Printing Office.

Temporary Commission on Alternative Financing for Public Telecommunications (1982). *Alternative Financing Options for Public Broadcasting: Report to the Congress.* Washington, D.C.: Federal Communications Commission.

Thelen, Mark H. (1970). Long-term retention of verbal imitation. *Developmental Psychology*, Vol. 3, No. 1, pp. 29–31.

—— (1971). The effect of subject race, model race, and vicarious praise on vicarious learning. *Child Development*, Vol. 42, pp. 972–77.

Thelen, Mark H., and Jerry L. Fryrear (1971). Effect of observer and model race on the imitation of standards of self-reward. *Developmental Psychology*, Vol. 5, No. 1, pp. 133–35.

Turow, Joseph (1981). *Entertainment, Education and the Hard Sell: Three Decades of Network Children's Television*. New York: Praeger.

Tydeman, J., et al. (1982). *Teletext and Videotext in the United States: Market Potential, Technology, Public Policy Issues*. New York: McGraw-Hill.

U.S. Office of Technology Assessment (1982). *Information Technology and Its Impact on American Education*. Washington, D.C.: Congress of the United States.

Unwin, Derick and Ray McAleese, eds. (1979). *Encyclopedia of Educational Media Communications and Technology*. Westport, Conn.: Greenwood Press.

Wackman, Daniel B., and Ellen Wartella (1977). A review of cognitive development theory and research and the implication for research on children's responses to television. *Communication Research*, Vol. 4, No. 2, pp. 203–24.

Werner, Anita (1971). Children's television in Norway. *Gazette*, Vol. 17, No. 3, pp. 133–51.

Werner, Peter, ed. (1977). *Information Programmes for Children 7 to 12 Years Old*. Geneva: European Broadcasting Union.

Williams, Frederick (1982). *The Communications Revolution*. Beverly Hills, Calif.: Sage.

Wood, Donald and Donald G. Wylie (1977). *Educational Telecommunications*. Belmont, Calif.: Wadsworth Publishing.

Yates, Gregory C. R. (1974). Influence of televised modeling and verbalization on children's delay of gratification. *Journal of Experimental Child Psychology*, Vol. 18, No. 2, pp. 333–39.

Zeigler, Sherilyn K. (1970). Attention factors in televised messages: Effects on looking behavior and recall. *Journal of Broadcasting*, Vol. 14, No. 3, pp. 307–15.

Index

0649